Democracy in Latin America

Democracy in Latin America

Surviving Conflict and Crisis?

GEORGE PHILIP

polity

First published in 2003 by Polity Press in association with Blackwell Publishing Ltd

Editorial office:
Polity Press
65 Bridge Street
Cambridge CB2 1UR, UK

Marketing and production:
Blackwell Publishing Ltd
108 Cowley Road
Oxford OX4 1JF, UK

Distributed in the USA by
Blackwell Publishing Inc.
350 Main Street
Malden, MA 02148, USA

A catalogue record for this book is available from the British Library.

Library of Congress Cataloging-in-Publication Data
Philip, George D. E.
Democracy in Latin America: surviving conflict and crisis? / George Philip.
p. cm.
Includes bibliographical references (p.) and index.
ISBN 0-7456-2759-5 – ISBN 0-7456-2760-9
1. Democracy – Latin America.   2. Democracy – Latin America – Case studies.   I. Title.
JL966 .P49 2003
321.8'098 – dc21
2002013557

Typeset in 10 on 12 pt Palatino
by SNP Best-set Typesetter Ltd., Hong Kong
Printed and bound in Great Britain by MPG Books Ltd, Bodmin, Cornwall

For further information on Polity, visit our website: http://www.polity.co.uk

Contents

Contents

Acknowledgements

I would like to express my thanks to a number of people who read earlier drafts of individual chapters, or, in the case of two anonymous readers from Polity Press, the whole work. Those who can be named include Francisco Panizza, Nicola Phillips, Julia Buxton and Susana Berruecos. I would also like to thank Carmina Borja, who acted as my research assistant while the work was being prepared for publication. Polity's own co-operation and help has been invaluable. I remain responsible for any errors that persist in the work.

Much of the research for chapters 3 and 5 was funded by the ESRC as part of a project on comparative civil service reform and the role of ideas on policy transfer. The co-researchers were Francisco Panizza and Klaus Goetz. Earlier visits to Peru and Venezuela were financed by the LSE's STICERD. My thanks to them as well.

I am grateful to the *Financial Times* and IDEA, who are the publishers of *Emerging Markets Today*, for permission to reproduce tabular material that appears in chapter 6.

Abbreviations

AD	Acción Democrática
APRA	Alianza Popular Revolucionaria Americana
COPEI	Comité de Organización Política Electoral Independiente
FARC	Fuerzas Armadas Revolucionarias de Colombia
IDB	Inter-American Development Bank
IFI	International financial institution (e.g., the IMF, the World Bank, etc.)
IMF	International Monetary Fund
ISI	Import substituting industrialization
IU	Izquierda Unida
MAS	Movimento al Socialismo
MNR	Movimiento Nacionalista Revolucionario
MRTA	Movimiento Revolucionario Túpac Amaru
NAFTA	North American Free Trade Agreement
OAS	Organization of American States
PAN	Partido Acción Nacional
PRI	Partido Revolucionario Institucional
PRD	Partido de la Revolución Democrática
PPT	Patria Para Todos
USAID	US Agency for International Development

Introduction: Democracy and its Discontents in Latin America

Since 1980 there has been an enormous extension of democratic governance both internationally and in Latin America. Democracy has spread to some countries with little or no democratic history, and in Latin America it has endured conditions that would almost certainly have brought down democracies in the past. Yet, this time round, democracy has survived so far – albeit narrowly in some cases. For anybody who prefers democracy as a form of government, this must be encouraging.

However, what has happened is worrying in a different way. Latin America has remained democratic so far, but democracy does not seem to have solved many policy problems. There is more poverty in the region today than there was twenty years ago (ECLAC 2001). What little per capita economic growth has taken place has been more than offset by rising inequality. Partly because of poor policy performance, there is evidence of considerable popular disenchantment with the working of democratic institutions in Latin America (Lagos 1997; Linz and Stepan 1996; Diamond 1999). More recently there have been some signs of disillusion with democracy itself.[1]

It is also clear that democratization has not invariably been accompanied by constitutional stability. There have been many political shocks. These have not so far had the effect, as they might have done in the past, of leading to full-scale democratic breakdown, but they do seem to show a weakness in the operation of democratic institutions. Institutional problems cannot be blamed for everything that has gone wrong in the region since democratization, but they do matter.

[1] See the Latinobarómetro report in *The Economist*, 26 July 2001.

The essential argument of this work can be described quite simply. In general, and allowing for considerable variation between different countries, pre-democratic patterns of political behaviour – institutional, organizational and cultural – have all too often survived democratization. Democracy has indeed brought free and competitive elections to the region. However, broader institutional changes that, in many first-world countries, preceded democratization and were believed necessary for democracy to work have not in general taken place. In some countries democratization has indeed brought about other kinds of positive institutional change. Nevertheless in much of the region authoritarian legacies have survived the democratic transition. The bureaucracy remains patrimonialist, law enforcement is weak and public opinion will often support open law-breaking by political leaders.

As a result, there is a marked partisan quality about the workings of the state and the political process itself. This has sometimes led to the over-empowerment of the state, though at other times it has made the executive weak and helpless. There are complex reasons for this, but one factor is that – in the absence of popular respect for formal rules – public opinion has at times become the immediate arbiter of political conflict. Unpopular governments find it hard to do anything at all because their legitimacy is not respected More generally, where the state is biased towards incumbents, it becomes very difficult to separate government from politics at almost any level of decision-making. As a result those partisan aspects of democracy that are a necessary part of the democratic process tend to dominate the entire state. The result is to create high levels of political conflict and uncertainty. Excessive partisanship also tends to destroy any impartial basis for holding governments accountable.

One way of looking at the problem of state bias is to reconsider theories of democracy itself. There is a theory of democracy associated with Joseph Schumpeter. In Schumpeter's words, 'the democratic method is that institutional arrangement for arriving at political decisions in which individuals acquire the power to decide by means of competitive struggle for the people's vote' (Schumpeter 1943, p. 269). In fact Schumpeter is much more careful to set out necessary preconditions for the success of the process than has sometimes been allowed by his critics. However, whatever subsequent critics have asserted, Schumpeter's analysis has merit. Schumpeter is right to point out that democratic politics is a rough business in which – even in the most sophisticated and civilized political societies – principles of right and wrong are often submerged in the struggle for power. What he does not sufficiently point out is that successful democracies check and control their core executive institutions as well as merely electing them. Elections alone will not be able to do the necessary job of limiting political partisanship.

Latin American democracy during the 1980s and 1990s showed many Schumpeterian characteristics. It produced some lavishly (and illegally) financed elections, the partisan use of the state for political purposes, state illegality of various kinds (as well as anti-government illegality), corruption to the point of organized racketeering, and a considerable number of political shocks. Very occasionally (as in Mexico in 1988) we see something that looks like outright frustration of the popular will. More often we see elective democracy developing into a ruthless battle for wealth and power in which the constitution has at times been subverted, laws routinely broken and public opinion shamelessly manipulated. The consequences have often been economic crisis, poor policy performance generally and a disillusioned public opinion.

Democratic theorists since Schumpeter have generally been dissatisfied with definitions of democracy that require little more than voting. There is much more awareness that poor quality democracy can exist. There is, as a result, more concern for and understanding of the workings of democratic institutions. However, while the literature on Latin American politics has paid a great deal of attention to the rule of elective institutions – such as congress, electoral systems and parties – there have been fewer attempts to relate the working of state institutions to the democratic process (as distinct from the policy process). Important works on democratic consolidation (notably Linz and Stepan 1996) do highlight the importance of impartial bureaucratic practices and effective law enforcement to the quality of democracy. Yet on the whole these issues have received less attention than some others.

On the face of it the combination of democratization, market-oriented reform, development failure and democratic non-consolidation is a disturbing one. It challenges the notion that democracy can in principle work almost anywhere where the democratic rules are applied, and should eventually produce good governance. It also challenges the notion that free-market reforms are a sufficient means of pursuing economic progress. Latin American experience does indeed show that there is more to successful democracy than the holding of regular elections. Well-run democracies need institutions that the process of democratic contestation does not necessarily create.

It is entirely possible that institutional problems can be the result, in part, of faulty institutional design. However, cultural orientations matter as well, partly because they help determine the degree of public

respect for the formal rules and partly because they are likely to indicate a preference for some kinds of governance over some others (for
example, presidentialism over parliamentarianism or the other way
around). In practice, one cannot build a democracy by setting out a set
of formal rules and expecting them to be respected and obeyed. The
rules need to be popularly regarded and therefore somehow embed-
ded in a political culture.

This work therefore claims that we need a historical-institutional as
well as a rational-choice institutional dimension if we are to understand politics in Latin America. It argues that the most important single
reason why the rules of constitutional democracy have not always been
able to get a grip on the political process throughout Latin America has
to do with the adaptiveness of pre-democratic patterns of political
behaviour. The first part of this work outlines some of these patterns.
It claims that, in many countries in the region, there has not been
enough change from pre-democratic days to make democratic consolidation possible.

It would be mistaken to suggest that every Latin American country
is identical, even though the existence of biased states and the widespread popular distrust of institutions are common to a number of
countries. Later chapters in this work therefore consider three cases –
Venezuela, Peru and Mexico – in which the political process has developed in different ways. Venezuela's democratic system was briefly the
pride of Latin America – and also of some academic Latin American-
ists. However, Venezuelan democracy was characterized by weak law
enforcement and a heavily patrimonial state bureaucracy. These characteristics were inherited from earlier authoritarian systems, and
would have been hard to change in the context of a democratic transition constrained by the political realities of the Cold War. Economic
issues to do with oil dependency mattered as well. However, executive
power had become so corrupted by 1992 that the government failed to
notice a large-scale military conspiracy, evidence for which was staring
them in the face. After this failed coup attempt, the country's democratic leaders could not re-establish respect for the existing constitutional process. It is instructive to see why this was and why the system
was in the end overthrown by Hugo Chávez Frías.

Chávez has not so far succeeded in building a new institutional
system in Venezuela, but his rise certainly exposed some of the weaknesses of the old system. However, Chávez, unlike his predecessors,
does not seem to be a believer in the virtues of consolidated democratic systems, even in principle. He espouses a simple idea of democratic leadership that we might usefully call Bolivarian, while many of his
political opponents have been equally partisan in their political behav-

iour. It is evident that institutional problems remain, and may in fact have deepened since 1998.

Peru's democratic system, less highly regarded in the past than that of Venezuela, and facing some genuinely severe problems, was almost overthrown in April 1992 when President Fujimori sent in troops to close the national congress. However, while many observers regarded this move as patently anti-democratic, it proved very popular in Peru itself. Peru's pre-1992 political institutions, notably the political parties, congress and the judiciary, were regarded with public contempt rather than respect. More 'authoritarian' institutions, such as the military and a non-accountable presidency, were in 1992 more trusted by the Peruvian people than formally democratic ones.

It is understandable why Fujimori remained as popular as he did for as long as he did. The Peruvian state, in the hands of a capable if corrupt autocrat, did achieve policy successes that eluded some of his predecessors. While there were unquestionably abuses of power under Fujimori, the decisive weakening of Peru's formal representative institutions after 1992 did not stand in the way of some real policy achievements. The Fujimori government's defeat of Sendero Luminoso was one of the very few major policy successes achieved anywhere in the region during the 1990s. Another was Peru's peace settlement of 1998 with Ecuador. The purpose of this observation is not to advocate authoritarian government, but to point out some of the policy limitations of institutionally flawed forms of democracy.

Finally Mexico after 1982 underwent a slow process of democratization but without a parallel strengthening of institutional systems. Mexican authoritarianism was quite different in character to its South American counterpart, but the process of democratization via elections but without much institutional reform was similar – at any rate up to 1994. The nature and perhaps working of Mexico's democratic institutions have since then had far more in common with those of South America than was ever the case with its authoritarian institutions. To the extent that these have permitted the development of a non-partisan concept of accountability in Mexico, this has been more the result of international pressures – including economic ones – than anything else. The result of weak domestic accountability was that the Mexican presidency remained unconstrained by laws, and this fact had a good deal to do with the way in which the 1994–5 'tequila crisis' developed.

From a comparative viewpoint, Latin America provides an excellent political laboratory of the working of political systems in which there are regular and contested elections and a cultural preference for democracy, but in which there are serious institutional difficulties. Any such comparative approach may appear to produce pessimistic conclusions, but there are optimistic implications as well. One of them is that democracy has survived and, on occasion, even prospered in Latin America despite some evident problems. Much of this work is taken up with a discussion of why democracy did not break down under crises of governance, as many of the region's democracies did before 1980. The other is that institution-building, while difficult to achieve, is not impossible. There is a growing intellectual consensus that the reform of poorly working state institutions is necessary for the achievement of sustained economic progress (World Bank 2002). The same is true of democracy. Not every reform effort has succeeded – the author's impression is that most of them to date have failed – but the emphasis on institutional reform is surely correct. If the reform agenda is to be taken seriously, it is important to get a better understanding of the consequences of problems in executive institutions, both for democracy and development – especially in today's globalized capitalist world.

Democratic Non-Consolidation in Latin America

This work looks at some of the ways in which path dependency and the logic of democratic consolidation have interacted in Latin America since 1982. On the whole, they have been in conflict. Evidently there are different national contexts, and the same story does not apply uniformly across the whole of the region. However, where there have been problems with democratic consolidation (a term defined in more detail below), it is generally possible to link them to pre-democratic institutional practices. Democratization has indeed made a difference to the region, but not so great a difference as most committed democrats once hoped and expected.

There has been a good deal of discussion among political scientists about how to differentiate what we might regard as institutionally effective democracies and less effective democracies. The concept of democratic consolidation, while not without problems, helps us here. Przeworski has famously stated that 'democracy is consolidated when under given political and economic conditions a particular system of institutions becomes the only game in town' (1991, p. 26). Furthermore, 'democracy is consolidated when it becomes self-reinforcing' (ibid.). Other writers such as Linz and Stepan (1996) and Diamond et al. (1997) have broadly accepted this definition. Diamond defines democratic consolidation as 'a discernible process by which the rules, institutions and constraints of democracy come to constitute "the only game in town"' (Diamond 1997, p. xvi). There is a theory underlying these definitions, which is that, as Montesquieu puts it, 'the people . . . are in certain respects the monarchy' (quoted in Przeworski 1991, p. 26). It is they who ultimately have the responsibility of upholding the constitutional process. In much of Latin America, though not all of it, these conditions are evidently unfulfilled. Democracy may be the only game in town, but the formal institutions of the democratic process are not the only rules, and public opinion may not always uphold them.

Przeworski's definition of democratic consolidation has been the subject of much discussion, and not everybody accepts it. The concept is discussed in more detail below. What is, though, clear is that there is less disagreement about the empirical facts that have to be explained. Despite their other differences, almost all scholars accept that there is a problem with democratic institutionalization in much of Latin America. There are many countries in which elections are routinely held, but which are hard to describe as fully democratic. Whatever the precise words used, there is something recognizable in the behaviour of political systems, in Latin America and no doubt elsewhere, that hold regular elections but tend to stagger on from crisis to crisis, neither stabilizing nor breaking down.

There is also likely to be a relationship between precariously institutionalized political systems and relatively poor economic performance. It is reasonable to suppose that wealth holders are likely to see politically unstable or unmanageable countries as potentially risky. They will therefore tend to avoid them. This reluctance to invest will slow down growth rates and worsen economic inequality due to the fact that rates of return on capital will have to be high in order to attract any investment at all. Globalization, understood as (among other things) a set of processes that make it easier to shift money across the world, is likely to make it even harder for countries whose political institutions are problematic to attract capital at a reasonable cost, since it facilitates the 'exit' option. In fact capital flight has been a major problem in Latin America since the 1970s. It is also entirely likely that there is a relationship between development failure and the non-consolidation of institutions, in that poor policy performance may increase popular discontent, and this may tend to de-institutionalize the political process.

Freedom House indicators

Empirically, enough time has now passed for us to have a reasonably clear picture of how Latin America's democracies have been transformed since the present wave of democratization began at the turn of the 1980s. In fact the record shows that there has not been much transformation at all. No Latin American country has so far moved openly from democracy to dictatorship since 1980. Neither, though, has there been much progress since 1990 in making the majority of Latin

American countries more securely free, law abiding or polyarchic. If we take Freedom House figures as a basis for discussion, then the lack of relationship between democratic longevity and political freedom is clear. ('Free' is not the same thing as 'consolidated', but there is a relationship between the two.)

At first sight Freedom House figures for 2000 seem to indicate a relatively optimistic picture. If we take the data for South America, then six countries (Argentina, Uruguay, Ecuador, Chile, Paraguay and Bolivia) are described as 'free' and only four (Brazil, Colombia, Peru and Venezuela) as 'partially free'. This might seem reasonably encouraging. However, one ominous factor is that all four 'partly free' countries score less highly on Freedom House indicators than they did in 1990. This regression has occurred despite the holding of regular, contested elections in all four. Colombia and Venezuela have held regular elections since 1958 (contested ones since 1974 in the case of Colombia) but this relative longevity does not seem to have helped matters. Peru, whose recent political evolution is considered again in a later chapter, is an even clearer example of a country that moved the 'wrong' way in the 1990s.

Moreover the Freedom House description of Ecuador, Paraguay and Bolivia as 'free' seems unduly generous in view of recent political events in those countries. There was popular support for a coup attempt in Ecuador in January 2000 and considerable backing in Paraguay for the lawless career of General Lino Oviedo. In 1999 the Paraguayan president was impeached by congress and removed from office on charges that included the murder of the vice-president. In 2000 there was still some unrest within the military over this decision.

Meanwhile in 1997 the electorate in Bolivia chose a former military dictator to be the president. Since then there have been several outbreaks of civil commotion and the imposition of states of siege. An earlier president of Bolivia was heavily involved in the organization of illegal narcotic exports, though he was never brought to justice. Bolivia has so far mainly avoided real political upheaval at the top. However, as Whitehead points out (Whitehead 2001), elected governments have needed to rely on emergency powers quite regularly, the rule of law is very incomplete and the public administration remains significantly patrimonial. These three countries, therefore, do not give the impression of being entirely free societies or consolidated democracies.

One of the remaining countries counted as 'free' is Argentina, but it is unlikely that Argentina will retain this classification in 2002. The history of democratic Argentina has been one of recurring crisis. At the end of the 1980s there was both hyperinflation and military unrest, though the military activists were unpopular and did not prosper. President Alfonsín (1983–9) voluntarily ended his term early in order to forestall complete democratic breakdown. Carlos Menem's presidential term did see a considerable improvement in Argentina's economic performance and in the general quality of its economic management. However, there was strong evidence of executive tampering with the supreme court and the judiciary, and evident public suspicion that some of this was done to prevent insiders from facing corruption allegations. Subsequent to leaving office Menem was arrested and charged with corrupt involvement in the selling of weapons to Ecuador, although charges were later dropped.

Fernando de la Rúa, who was elected president of Argentina in 1999, was a more constitutionally minded politician than Menem, but his government's economic performance was poor. When debt default became unavoidable at the end of 2001 it was clear that there was among the Argentine public a high degree of frustration because of economic failure. This led to rioting, the decision of the Argentine congress to withdraw support from an elected president, and two presidential resignations in close succession in December 2001. (This does not include the resignation of designated interim figures, of which there were two others.) Overall Argentina cannot be regarded as consolidated. It is much too prone to development problems and political crisis.

Most observers would, however, accept that the final two countries in South America, Chile and Uruguay, are indeed free – and relatively consolidated by comparison with the others. The ending of General Pinochet's untouchability after his arrest in London in October 1998 seems to have demonstrated a self-reinforcing attitude to Chilean democracy. Even so, as Linz and Stepan (1996) and Latinobarómetro have both pointed out, the Chilean public is by no means totally committed to democracy as a preferred system of government. In the Latinobarómetro poll published by *The Economist* on 26 July 2001, only 45 per cent of the Chilean sample answered yes to the statement 'Democracy is preferable to any other kind of government' (79 per cent did so in Uruguay); 19 per cent agreed that 'In certain circumstances an authoritarian government can be preferable to a democratic one' (as against 10 per cent in Uruguay). Yet Chile was one of the few countries of the region whose economic performance during the previous decade was strongly positive. Would a less favourable economic record have led to more popular support for non-democracy?

To sum up for South America, therefore, there seems to be little evidence to refute Uruguay's claim to have made an unproblematic transition to democracy. Slightly more scepticism is in order in the case of Chile, where there is a definite undercurrent of popular discontent with the system. However, Chile scores much better than a clear majority of democracies of the region – Brazil, Venezuela, Colombia, Ecuador, Peru, Paraguay, Bolivia and Argentina. In some of these countries (not all) the trend seems to be away from democratic stability. Taking the region as a whole, the most striking evidence is of an absence of trend.

In Mexico and Central America, the picture is again mixed. According to Freedom House indicators, Mexico, Guatemala, Honduras, Nicaragua and El Salvador are partly free. Costa Rica, the Dominican Republic and Panama are seen as free. Costa Rica would be judged by most observers to be one of Latin America's three genuine polyarchies (the others being Chile and Uruguay). However, the Dominican Republic and Panama both democratized in the aftermath of US invasion. In virtually all of the small countries of the region, international influences are of key importance. Changing directions in US foreign policy may have been more important in these cases than domestic factors (Rueschemeyer et al., 1992).

The case of Mexico will be considered in detail in a later chapter. At the end of the 1980s Mexico was not fully democratic at all. It did democratize during the 1990s, but Mexican democracy is still a fairly young plant. What is notable about Mexico, however, is that the period of democratization and market reform produced some severe financial crises. Mexico nearly defaulted on its debts in 1982, 1986, 1989 and 1995. In each case, the United States proved reasonably supportive – though not unconditionally so. Without significant US intervention and support – much more than that offered to Argentina or the Andean countries – Mexico could, on more than one occasion, have faced economic catastrophe. If it had done so, would the process of democratization have been threatened? One must assume the possibility.

While there are a range of national experiences, to which national path dependencies are no doubt relevant, we also have a reasonably general picture of the political evolution of the region as a whole – or, rather, the lack of political evolution. The political systems of most South American democracies and some Central American ones have neither become freer (in Freedom House terms) nor broken down. What is significant is the absence of trend.

We therefore seem to be faced in Latin America with systems that are not institutionally self-reinforcing but nevertheless somehow self-sustaining. We will therefore be asking two questions. One is how these systems have worked in practice in some Latin American countries. There are many differences between non-consolidated systems, but there are some common regional factors as well – at any rate within Latin America. The other question is why non-consolidated democracies have not either consolidated or broken down into non-democracy.

Academics have so far paid more attention to the non-deepening of democracy than to its non-breakdown (Haynes 2001). Yet, in respect of Latin America at least, non-breakdown may be the more surprising feature of the two. After all there have been many democratic break-downs in South and Central America in the past. Furthermore many of the institutional characteristics blamed for democratic breakdown in the past remain in place, and Latin America's economic performance is generally worse today than it was in the 1960s and early 1970s when military intervention was common. Despite this, democracy, of a kind, has survived.

Defining and characterizing
non-consolidated democracy

As noted, this work derives the term 'democratic consolidation' from Przeworski's central criterion – self-reinforcement. However, there is a significant literature on democratic consolidation, which contains some disagreements, and there are incompatible definitions of (and ideas about) consolidation. Some authors have even detected the develop-ment of 'consolidology' as a subject of study (Schedler 1998; Haynes 2001, p. 1). As noted, others are sceptical about the entire approach (Whitehead 2001). The sceptics are right about some things at least. Above all, we need to be careful about postulating a 'natural' transi-tion from democratization to consolidated democracy. Latin American experience shows that non-consolidated democracies can survive over quite long periods of time.

The standpoint adopted here is that the concept of democratic consolidation is useful because it gives us something to measure. The notion of self-reinforcement also makes the concept less obviously judgemental than some other ways of evaluating democracy – such as the notion of 'freedom' already discussed. What matters is how people regard their own political institutions and how they behave towards them in practice.

This work is less concerned with consolidation than with its antithe-sis, non-consolidation. The discussion focuses empirically on cases of overt and successful political illegality, because this offers tangible evidence of a failure of institutional self-reinforcement. It regards democracy as being non-consolidated if an ambitious but otherwise reasonable person (or group of people) can expect to achieve or main-tain majority public support either in spite of or because of the open flouting of the formal rules of the political process. Where this condition is met, overt rule-breaking can make sense as a political strategy, and (actual or potential) open illegality therefore becomes an inherent part of the political process. All that is definitionally necessary is this one specific aspect. Democracy, at its most basic level, has to do with the rule of the people as expressed through elections. Yet, in non-consolidated democracies, the people have the right to vote but are nevertheless sufficiently alienated from the process of government either not to care whether the formal rules are broken or not, or else positively to welcome law-breaking. The people participate in the system, but do not guard it by defending its rules. It is not suggested that there is no regard for rules at all – a non-consolidated democracy need not be an anarchy – but that there is no predictable or coherent regard for them. Because of this seeming incoherence, non-consolidated democracies are systems that cannot be analysed satisfactorily either in terms of the formal rules alone or on the basis of complete disregard of the formal rules. We therefore need both institutional and extra-institutional forms of political analysis.

This definition, on its own, does not tell us much about the specifics of how any particular non-consolidated democracy might work. There is no reason to suppose that non-consolidated democracies need behave in any very similar way to each other – any more than consolidated ones do. Non-consolidation only makes sense as a concept when taken in conjunction with the specific features of any particular system. However, the concept of non-consolidation does add an extra dimension to our understanding of politics when we use it in conjunction with other forms of political analysis.

The working of consolidated democracies can be understood in terms of respect for laws, rules and procedures because consolidation involves the stabilization of shared expectations. Linz and Stepan (1996) point out that, as they define the term, democratic consolidation must be behavioural, attitudinal and constitutional. The rules not only exist, but they are internalized, accepted and valued. Under such circumstances, overt rule-breaking alienates people and is therefore impossibly costly – so much so that, for most practical purposes, its likelihood can safely be discounted. We can therefore plan our own actions in the light of stable expectations about the reaction of others.

This kind of planning needs to be different in non-consolidated systems because one's expectations of the behaviour of one's allies and adversaries will necessarily be less secure. If non-consolidated democracies are not based mainly on formal rules, then on what are they based? It would be tempting to answer 'informal rules', but such an answer would be too simple. There certainly are informal rules that shape political behaviour in non-consolidated democracies – more so than in consolidated democracies, though informal rules exist to some extent in all systems. However, the notion of 'informal' or 'unwritten' rules involves an idea of structured behaviour that may be hard to apply across the range of non-consolidated democratic systems. An event such as a military coup attempt or a conspiracy to rig a popular vote is likely to be based on a mixture of formal rules, informal rules, and pure political calculation at a time of high uncertainty. One cannot just say 'the rules are what people do' because, due to these uncertainties, there may be no common understanding at all. The question of what sustains non-consolidated democracy therefore needs specific, empirical answers.

A part of the answer may come from a country's political culture. If public opinion does not generally care whether rules or laws are enforced or not – sometimes even preferring non-enforcement – then this could help explain why democratic institutions need not be the only game in town. There is survey evidence of the appropriate kind and quality dealing with Latin America (Lagos 1997; Diamond 1999; Linz and Stepan 1996), and this supposition is, to an extent, borne out. There are very significant variations between countries, but on the whole it is clear that the Latin American democratic state and the region's key democratic political institutions do not enjoy a high level of public trust. The concept of democracy is widely accepted, but specific organizations and institutions – the presidency, the congress, political parties, the courts, etc. – are regarded with suspicion or worse (Lagos 1997). This survey evidence suggests that many Latin Americans regard law-breaking as an ever-present feature of their system and are prepared to offer political support to law-breaking political leaders under what they consider to be appropriate circumstances. They do not consider this viewpoint incompatible with a preference for democracy as a form of government.

Within Latin America there also seems to be a reasonably significant relationship between institutional stability and popular attachment to institutional systems. Countries such as Uruguay that score high on one indicator also score high on the other. It is important to remember that there are a small number of Latin American democracies that can be considered consolidated. However, this work is concerned mainly with those countries that score low in public trust and low in institutional stability and yet remain democracies.

For these countries, the evidence of cultural distrust is illuminating, but it is not the whole story. A country's political culture is determined by its institutions, its history, its economy, its position in the international order and a range of other factors as well. Political culture changes over time; it varies from place to place and it is usually influenced by realities. Cultural distrust is an interesting finding, but we need to look further. Why are so many Latin Americans as cynical about their democratic institutions as seems to be the case? A plausible answer might be that their institutions operate in such a way as to generate mistrust among reasonable people.

A major attempt to link cultural findings with institutional analysis is provided in the work of Linz and Stepan (1996). These authors seek to provide a list of objective criteria according to which the degree of consolidation can be assessed in any particular case. Linz and Stepan refer to five arenas of democratic consolidation (1996, p. 7). One is civil society, which has to be 'free and lively'. Another is political society, which has to be 'relatively autonomous and valued'. A third is the rule of law, and there needs to be a spirit of constitutionalism. Then there is the state apparatus, which has to be run according to 'Weberian' bureaucratic norms so as to be usable by democratic governments of widely differing persuasions. Finally there is economic society, where there has to be institutionalization of a number of processes that protect property rights, allow markets to work well and achieve economic growth. Democracies in which these conditions are met are likely to consolidate. Deconsolidation is still possible, though Linz and Stepan claim that this is unlikely to happen unless fresh problems emerge that the existing set of institutions cannot resolve. This, though, is an empirical and not a definitional argument.

As some critics have pointed out, this approach can be both very complex and very demanding (for example, Whitehead 2001). This need not be a problem as long as we avoid the supposition that all non-consolidated democracies, or indeed all consolidated democracies, are essentially the same. In fact the evolution of democracy in different parts of the world highlights some diverse experiences and intriguing contrasts (Haynes 2001). However, the whole point of defining consolidation as we have is that consolidated democracy can then be treated as a distinctive form of government where formal rules and procedures dominate informal ones.

It is also reasonable to suppose that successful democratic consolidation must involve some element of rupture with the past. Pre-democratic rules of the game come to be replaced by democratic ones. Empirically, in fact, we can distinguish between some processes of democratization that seem to have marked a genuine rupture with the past, and others (including those in many Latin American countries) where there has been no more than a partial break. Democratization may change political behaviour decisively but need not always do so. Where it does not do so, then we are likely to have non-consolidated democracy and some marked continuity with pre-democratic patterns of politics. In several Latin American countries, this is actually what we do find. In such cases, historical-institutional and cultural factors evidently do matter, and they may work against democratic consolidation.

This book has a specific regional focus, based as it is on Latin America, and a particular interpretative slant, since it gives particular weight to those historical-institutional factors that have impeded consolidation. Its empirical scope is therefore more limited than Linz and Stepan's, and it should therefore be possible to proceed with a slightly less complex and comprehensive set of 'arenas' than those authors found necessary to introduce in a broader context. The main hypotheses presented in this work in fact draw on Linz and Stepan's five arenas of contestation but also somewhat modify them to cover specific Latin American conditions.

A key explanatory factor suggested here is the existence of conflicting philosophies behind Latin American presidentialism. Full reasoning is given in the next chapter, but the essential point is that presidentialism in many Latin American countries has become a contested hybrid system of government prone to generate conflict and mistrust. It is not inevitable that presidentialism will have this effect, and not every presidential system is alike – not even within Latin America. However, the fact that there are conflicting concepts of presidentialism within particular countries in the region does, as we shall see, make it more likely that high profile political law-breaking will occur, win popular acceptance and succeed. Linz and Stepan (1996, p. 4) do regard what they call 'institutional indeterminacy' as a problem, but later subsume this point under the broader arena of political society. The claim here is that problems of presidentialism are sufficiently important in Latin America to warrant separate treatment.

Public opinion can best defend democratic institutions if the majority of people accept and understand the philosophy underlying them. Nobody supposes that a perfectly coherent institutional philosophy is necessary or even possible. Britain is still a democracy despite its House of Lords and monarchy, and the USA is also a democracy despite its electoral college system. Both of these seem historical oddities rather than essential parts of a democratic process. However, presidentialism is absolutely central to the workings of the political process throughout Latin America and it is a focus of intense conflict. We cannot understand why figures such as Venezuela's Chávez, Peru's Fujimori and Mexico's Salinas have proved so intensely controversial without taking into account real divisions within Latin American public opinion as to what the role of the presidency should be.

This discussion is also very much concerned with the non-impartial – let us call it biased – character of the state. Two of the Linz and Stepan arenas are apposite here. One of them is that respect for the rule of law is relatively weak, both at ordinary societal level and at the level of high politics. There is lacking, at both elite and popular level, any spirit of constitutionalism, in the sense of over-riding respect for impartial law enforcement. The other is that Latin American bureaucracies are typically (not exclusively) based on patronage to an extent that is comparatively unusual within the democratic world. While the USA is sometimes held out as an example of a patronage bureaucracy (Peters 1989), there is relatively speaking far more patronage in Latin America. Moreover the USA does have a strong culture of law enforcement, which somewhat reduces the importance of patronage to bureaucratic behaviour. The US bureaucracy, moreover, is responsible to congress as well as the presidency in a way that is not commonly the case in Latin America. The typical Latin American bureaucracy has literally thousands of presidential appointees at the top, is not usually responsible to congress and is constrained by law only if there are political reasons for this.

To sum up this part of the argument, this work accepts that there is such a thing as democratic consolidation and claims that most Latin American countries have not achieved it. It also accepts the Linz and Stepan argument that we can put forward sensible criteria measuring consolidation and broadly accepts their five arenas – albeit with minor modifications aimed to fit the Latin American context better. Democratic consolidation is more likely to occur if there is a coherent concept of governance that is domestically legitimate and given tangible (not necessarily perfect) expression in the way that political institutions actually work. It is also more likely to occur if there is an effective system of law enforcement – run with impartiality, competence and genuine teeth – to protect political institutions from corruption and the excesses of partisan contestation. It should also be facilitated by a principle of bureaucratic impartiality – called Weberian here for reasons of conciseness – because it is important that the general public, including those who voted for losing candidates in previous elections, broadly trust the state. It probably also requires a reasonable economic performance because severe economic setback can be politically destabilizing (on which see Przeworski et al., 1997).

Bounding non-consolidated democracy

Empirically it is fairly clear that these criteria for democratic consolidation have not generally been met in Latin America. A more difficult question has to do with the way in which the region's non-consolidated systems might be expected to evolve. We cannot be sure what their future political dynamic is likely to be, but we do now have considerable experience of democratic non-consolidation and some widely expected outcomes have not occurred. As we have seen, an evolutionary 'stages of democracy' theory does not fit the Latin American facts. Perhaps less easy to explain is why these apparently precarious systems of democracy have not completely broken down. The question of why some flagrant violations of institutional rules have not so far led to the total breakdown of democracy is certainly worth asking. On the face of it, one might suppose that non-consolidated systems might produce increasing returns to power or unsustainable levels of political polarization and therefore undermine democracy altogether. As a preliminary conclusion that will receive more elaboration in the text, there seem to be several factors that have so far prevented this from happening.

Public opinion is one of them. As we have seen, public opinion is not always pro-constitution in Latin America, but it genuinely is pro-democracy – or has been up to now. The point at which the majority of the people may come to feel that a constitution-breaking president has gone 'too far' may be unpredictable, but there may be such a point nevertheless. 'The people as monarch' seem, in Latin America at least, to be more tolerant of rule-breaking in a popular cause than of outright rejection of democracy. This popular attitude is probably not a sufficient explanation for the boundedness of non-consolidated democracy but it is surely part of the explanation.

Another factor is international. At the very beginning of the 1980s, neither the US government nor the European Community much cared whether a Latin American republic was a democracy or not. By the mid-1980s Washington had made clear its preference for democratic government. Even so the Mexican authorities received no serious rebuke from Washington for violating the principle of electoral transparency in 1988, and Fujimori faced no more than minor problems after closing the Peruvian congress in 1992. More recently, neither the USA nor Britain objected at all to the short-lived Carmona coup in Venezuela in April 2002. Overall, the international community was – and possibly remains – more tolerant of non-consolidated democracy than it is of outright non-democracy. International approval or disapproval has implications for the economic prospects of the country in question, and therefore for the preferences of business interests and, indeed, the citizenry as a whole.

Thirdly there is the nature of presidential governance. While this has its problems, it does allow a political flexibility that parliamentary systems might lack. The complex coalition-building that is necessary in a parliamentary setting is much less necessary to a presidential system. A presidential system can continue in place even when the party system has virtually broken down altogether – as happened in Peru in the 1990s. The role of presidentialism in bounding non-consolidated democracy is therefore quite complex. It may make it harder for systems to consolidate, while at the same time making it less likely that non-consolidated systems will break down altogether.

Finally, there seems to be a particular kind of political learning that has taken place in some countries. Because the rules themselves offer no guarantee of political security, there will always be a tendency for some political organizations and actors to export the risks of uncertainty to others – to seek, as it were, to get their retaliation in first. Authoritarian presidentialism is feared by potential losers, who seem to have become increasingly adept at resisting it. The intense quality of political partisanship in the region has often tended to weaken executive power rather than to strengthen it. This is not at all what some earlier scholars of hyper-presidentialism (notably O'Donnell 1994) once expected.

We therefore need to beware simple 'slippery slope' arguments suggesting that non-consolidated democracy will necessarily evolve in the direction either of renewed authoritarianism or of anarchy. Politics in non-consolidated systems can involve quite complex relationships between rule observance and rule-breaking, and these may, in turn, lead to some potentially stable if informal balances. For example, much of the popularly accepted rule-breaking that occurs is likely to require some rule observance for it to happen at all. Thus, a successful military coup will require military discipline among the participants. It may also be the case that some informalities (i.e., predictable breaches of the rules) are based on the observance of 'unwritten rules' that are not so very difficult to detect. There is of course an extent to which non-consolidated democracy cannot be understood in terms of any single set of rules. However, it can sometimes be understood, in part, as the outcome of clashing ideas about institutions within a given political system. Organizations can cohere around their own rules, even when the overall rules of the system are lacking in both teeth and popular support. This means that ambitious political leaders who live by rule-breaking may still have to observe some rules and be able to break others only under some rather specific circumstances.

Another reason why non-consolidation can involve complex balances is that the formal rules may not have been designed to be obeyed in the first place. There are areas of public administration in Latin America in which attempts to follow procedures to the letter may lead to hopeless 'red tape' kinds of problem (on Mexico, see Moctezuma

Barragán and Roemer 2001). Alternatively (or additionally) there may be a collective action problem at the centre of the political system. An actor who obeys formal rules may end up losing a prisoner's dilemma game if he or she makes the false assumption that others will obey the formal rules as well. In fact, nobody really trusts anybody else to obey all of the formal rules, which is why some rule-breaking may come to be seen as inevitable.

At one extreme, non-consolidated democracy can define a situation in which the formal rules are largely fictitious in the sense that they are not enforced while informal rules are. An army officer from the Dominican Republic provided a concise definition of this when answering a question about the constitution from the American political scientist Abraham Lowenthal. 'The Constitution is one thing. In the military we are something different' (quoted in Lowenthal 1976). However, at other times the formal rules may be widely observed and appear binding on all parties until there is a crisis. This is then resolved on the basis of some kind of partisan ascendancy without much relationship to the spirit of the law or the formalities of the constitutional process. Good examples of the way in which periods of what seemed to be reasonably stable government gave way to sudden crises occurred in Venezuela after 1989 and in Argentina after 1999.

Non-consolidation and path dependency

As noted, this work claims that problems with democratic consolidation in Latin America have a historical-institutional dimension. They are, in part, the result of inheritances from previous authoritarianism. Pre-democratic modes of political behaviour can survive democratization, and have done in practice. The fact that regular and contested elections have changed the formal rules of the game has not always prevented pre-democratic means of organizing power from putting on 'alternative shows in town'. Authors from an earlier generation have produced observations about Latin American politics that remain illuminating to this day. For example, in a work on Latin America published in 1967, Anderson claimed that 'Latin American government is based on a flexible coalition of diverse power contenders which is subject to revision at any time if the terms under which the original government was formed are deemed violated' (Anderson 1967). This account almost perfectly describes post-1992 Venezuela.

What is more interesting still, some pre-democratic practices have chameleon characteristics so that they are capable of penetrating systems that may look as though they are fully consolidated democratic polyarchies (i.e., legitimate pluralist systems bounded by law) but which turn out not to have been genuinely consolidated at all. Venezuela's Punto Fijo system is a case in point here, and a similar point has been made about Brazilian patrimonialism, which somehow re-emerged at a relatively late stage of the democratization process (Hagopian 1996; Weyland 1997).

One means of transmitting political practices from pre-democratic to democratic systems exists within the internal working of organizations. This kind of transmission is particularly likely in systems with strong organizations and relatively weak over-arching institutions. Another means of transmission lies in cultural preference, which in Latin America sometimes translates into popular support for powerful political personalities. One of the characteristics of some Latin American politics is that it is governed by men (sometimes women) rather than laws. Mexico between 1982 and (at least) 1994 would be an example here, as would the last few years of the Fujimori administration in Peru.

However, efforts to provide a coherent account of how non-consolidated democracy works in practice are inevitably difficult and not only because of different national circumstances. The whole point about democratic non-consolidation is that it actually is difficult to theorize beyond a certain point because of the uncertainties that are inherent to the way it works. This is a point to which we shall return in the concluding chapter.

2

Unbalanced Presidentialism, Weak Law Enforcement and Political Contestation

This chapter further develops the discussion on how Latin America's non-consolidated democracies work. It starts by considering core executives because, as explained in the last chapter, it would be hard to imagine institutional consolidation without some kind of coherence at the centre of the political system. This is significantly lacking in some parts of the region. The chapter then goes on to consider problems of law enforcement, which are seen as being due – essentially – to a path-dependent tradition of executive arbitrariness. The final part of the chapter considers the role of public opinion and organizational power.

Presidentialism in theory and practice

Latin American executive systems are all presidential or semi-presidential – in most cases fully presidential. Before discussing the political consequences of presidentialism in Latin America, we need first to define it. This is not entirely a straightforward matter because there are significant variants of presidentialism. Linz (1994, p. 6) defines it as a system dominated by two features. The president receives a popular mandate directly from the people, either through direct election or (as in the US case) via some form of electoral college system. A legislature (whether unicameral or bicameral) is directly elected also. Both are elected for fixed terms, and in principle the tenure of office of each is independent of the other.

This definition is simple enough to be taken as a point of departure. It should, though, be noted at the outset that there are significant variations between presidential systems as thus defined, as well as changes over time. Some forms of presidentialism have worked better than others. To anticipate the discussion a little, Latin American presidentialism has tended to work well when ways have been found of linking the president with broader political forces within a society (Lanzaro 2001). It has tended to work badly when pro- and anti-presidential alliances have evolved into warring factions and polarized the system.

Although there are many factors determining whether or not there is a tendency towards partisan polarization, institutional rules and political choices both matter. In some countries specific mechanisms have been set up to link the presidency with congress or the party system. For example, in Bolivia the electorate selects the president directly only if the front runner wins 50 per cent of the popular vote. This has not happened since 1982. Alternatively the congress chooses the president, though only from among the two candidates with the most popular votes. (Until 1994 the third-placed candidate could also be chosen and, on one occasion, actually was.) In other cases, arrangements have been essentially voluntary, such as the negotiation of effective coalition agreements. Chile has been governed by an alliance of parties since 1989. While neither of these arrangements can be said to amount to the transformation of presidentialism into what Linz calls 'semi-presidentialism' (1994, pp. 48–56), they do make a difference.

Lijphart (1993) and Linz (1994) famously criticized pure presidentialism in the Latin American context and thereby generated an enormous literature. However, their initial thesis, that presidentialism is an inherently flawed political system, has not generally been accepted (see Lanzaro 2001; Mainwaring and Shugart 1997; Haggard and McCubbins 2001). Apart from the point that there are many different variants of presidentialism there is also the empirical fact that, when given the choice – as the Brazilian electorate was in 1993 – Latin American voters tend to prefer presidentialism to parliamentarianism. In the end, one of the things that determines whether a system works well or badly is its cultural legitimacy. Systems that might seem eccentric in principle (such as the British monarchy) work well enough in practice if they are sufficiently accepted by the people.

We now have a reasonable amount of evidence about how Latin American political systems have worked during the most recent wave of democratization. There is a sense in which critics of presidentialism have (thus far) been proved wrong. There has been no case of democratic breakdown, and there have been enough constitutional changes in enough Latin American countries to dispel any idea that presidentialism is a fixed system that cannot cope with changing political reality. Like all viable political systems, presidentialism in Latin America can evolve. The problem is that, in some countries though by no means all, it has evolved in ways that have heightened partisanship and political conflict rather than reducing or institutionalizing it. In other words, although presidentialism is not an insuperable barrier to democratic consolidation, it has sometimes worked in ways that have made this harder to achieve.

For this reason, criticisms of presidentialism are worth revisiting. The problem is not so much that there are unavoidable operational flaws in the workings of presidential systems. The experience of vote-counting in the US elections of 2000 should remind us that this can happen anywhere and may not matter as much as one might expect. A more difficult situation occurs when there is a basic clash of concept about how presidentialism should work. One can see this clash of concept in some Latin American countries in a way that does not happen with US presidentialism or, indeed, across the whole of Latin America.

Presidentialism as a system of government can be understood by different people in quite different ways. Originally, those individuals who drew up the US constitution designed its presidential system so as to reflect and shape a particular philosophy of human behaviour that was inherently distrustful of central government. Latin American presidentialism was, however, created and has since been supported by people who, even if they sometimes described themselves as liberals, were by no means liberals in the classical Anglo-American sense – i.e., people instinctively suspicious of government. On the contrary, they wanted a strong system of political leadership. Although Shugart and Haggard claim that 'in presidential regimes, policy making is by definition characterised by a separation of power' (2001, p. 64), this has not invariably been the case in Latin America. US presidentialism has been historically based on ideas of checks and balances, while Latin American presidentialism was often based on a search for leadership. We might call it Bolivarian rather than Madisonian.

Allowing for some inevitable exceptions, Latin American presidents were until 1982 widely regarded as leaders whose role it was to use the powers of the state either to protect the social order or to direct social or economic transformation. Many of them were imposed, or imposed themselves, by force. While by no means all were simple authoritarians, it is not at all clear that there was much popular or indeed intellectual support for checks-and-balances systems. Some of the most spectacularly successful politicians in Latin American history – Argentina's Perón, Brazil's Vargas, Mexico's Calles and later Cárdenas, Chile's Ibáñez, Peru's Velasco and Cuba's Castro – were authoritarian centralists. While it is not surprising that authoritarianism as such should be a centralizing form of government, it is noteworthy that some authoritarian or semi-authoritarian figures in the region were for a time very popular.

Presidentialism in Latin America survived democratization. It is evidently the case that a democratic presidential system should work differently from an authoritarian one. The problem is that a democracy that keeps on a similar set of formal institutions from pre-democratic days runs the risk of retaining traditional patterns of behaviour and traditional popular expectations about politics alongside them. Even if there is an initial break from authoritarian presidentialism, the old-style system may retain some allure for those disappointed with the new democratic order. The continuing success of populist or neo-populist politics in some parts of Latin America is evidence of this.[1]

Empirically, the Latin American pattern as a whole has been rather varied. In some countries, there has been a self-conscious and effective search for institutional and conceptual means of adapting to a new democratic reality (Lanzaro 2001). In others constitutional innovations essentially failed, as ultimately happened with the Punto Fijo system in Venezuela. In some countries, elected presidents attempted to bring back old-style personalism despite operating constitutions that provided for checks and balances. This often proved to be a recipe for partisan conflict. As we shall see in later chapters, post-1982 presidents such as Chávez in Venezuela, Fujimori in Peru, Collor in Brazil, and Menem in Argentina all fell into this category.

The problem, then, is not so much with the formal properties of presidentialism but the conflicting ways in which it has been conceptualized and the historical baggage that it has sometimes carried. If the formal political institutions of a country embody conflicting concepts, then they cannot act as satisfactory focal points around which disagreements can be resolved. Instead the tendency will be for political conflict to weaken such institutionalization as there is. A tradition of weak law enforcement makes the problem worse, because it has the effect of reducing confidence in what might otherwise be an effective mechanism for settling disputes. One could fill many pages of any work on Latin American politics with quotations from law-breaking but essentially popular figures. One of the most memorable was from the Brazilian Adhemar de Barros, who won the mayoralty of São Paulo in 1948 on the slogan 'I steal but I get things done'.

One might see the inherited institutional pattern as involving several problems. For one thing, inherited institutional factors such as patrimonialism and weak law enforcement may offer some short-term

---

[1] See the special issue on populism and neo-populism in the *Bulletin of Latin American Research* (2000).

advantages to aspirant Bolivarian presidents. They may hold out the prospect of increasing returns to power. Moreover if neither the bureaucracy nor the courts can provide political leadership, then it falls to the president to make things happen. Popular frustration with partisan and patrimonial state behaviour under weak presidential figures may encourage voters to choose a Bolivarian figure in order, as they hope, to shake things up and reform poorly functioning institutions. Additionally, the checks-and-balances institutions that constitutionally exist (notably the actual or potential role of impeachment) have generated dangerously high levels of political partisanship in cases where presidents are suspected (correctly or otherwise) of Bolivarian tendencies. Opponents of the government fear Bolivarian presidentialism and will do everything they can to weaken executive power in order to stop it. In some countries, as noted, mediating processes have been specifically created to deal with this problem. However, in their absence, the overall result is a lack of focal points that might facilitate conflict resolution.

Anticipated reactions based on fear of hyper-presidentialism can therefore be a problem even in the absence of a successful Bolivarian presidential figure. O'Donnell's famous and much discussed argument (O'Donnell 1994), to the effect that Latin America was likely to develop a form of hyper-presidentialism (which he called 'delegative democracy'), has not, in general, been borne out (Panizza 2000c). There have indeed been cases of hyper-presidentialism, but also periods of intense executive weakness. However, O'Donnell's account has continuing value provided that one treats delegative democracy as something that popular Latin American politicians may attempt to impose and that opponents of the government of the day are likely to fear. Attempts to create hyper-presidentialism can and do lead to intense conflicts within Latin American democracies. For as long as there are aspirant authoritarian centralists for whom Latin American electorates are sometimes prepared to vote, then these conflicts will recur.

This work defines the resulting situation as being one of unbalanced presidentialism. Presidents can sometimes seem to be very strong, semi-dictatorial, figures. However, their sources of strength tend to be partisan and plebiscitary rather than institutional. When times are difficult, presidents can become weak and almost powerless figures who can be removed from office altogether. The empirical record of some countries of the region is set out in Box 1 below.

Having made these observations about the region's historical background, we can now return to some of the formal institutional aspects of Latin American presidentialism in order to consider how they interrelate. One of Linz's main objections to presidentialism (Linz 1994) is what he calls the 'dual legitimation' issue. The point here is that pure presidentialism involves the separate election and functioning of president and congress. However, the executive and legislative branches of government, while separate, need to be able to work together. If they cannot do so, then political crisis is likely to develop because the

Box 1   Major constitutional changes and departures, selected countries

Argentina
1989 Alfonsín ends his term early in favour of president-elect Menem.
1993–5 Menem, originally elected for a single term, negotiates a constitutional change to permit re-election.
1995 Menem is re-elected.
1998 Menem considers asking for a further constitutional change to permit second re-election. Lacking in support, he withdraws.
1999 De la Rúa is elected according to the constitution.
2001 De la Rúa is forced to resign by congress. Rodríguez Saa takes over as interim president but resigns after a week, again due to problems with the majority party in congress.
2001 Duhalde takes office, with new elections initially scheduled for October 2003.
2002 Duhalde agrees to bring forward the 2003 elections by six months.

Peru
1990 Fujimori elected to the presidency as an independent candidate.
1992 Fujimori closes congress with military support. A constituent assembly is elected to draw up a new constitution.
1993 The new constitution is approved by plebiscite allowing Fujimori's re-election as president and reducing the powers of congress.
1995 Fujimori is re-elected president with a congressional majority.
1996–7 Fujimori manoeuvres to get congressional support to stand for president yet again. Congress forces the issue by impeaching judges opposed to a further presidential re-election.
2000 Fujimori is re-elected for a third term but the integrity of the election is impugned.
2000 Fujimori is formally impeached by congress after taking refuge in Japan when on a state visit to Asia.
2001 Fresh elections are held in Peru.

Venezuela
1989 Carlos Andrés Pérez is elected president.
1992 There are two coup attempts.
1993 Pérez is impeached and removed from office. Ramón J. Velásquez takes the presidency for six months. Caldera is then elected president. He serves just one full term, as the constitution intended.
1994 In July there is a brief crisis in relations with congress in which the suspension of congress is seriously discussed.
1998 Congress changes the date of congressional elections, bringing them forward by a month.
1998 Chávez is elected president in December, after an anti-Chávez majority had already been elected to congress in November.
1999 Chávez organizes the closure of congress and its replacement by a constituent assembly.
2000 Chávez gains approval in a plebiscite for a new constitution that increases the length of his presidential term and reorganizes and limits the power of congress.
2002 Chávez survives a coup attempt.

Box 1 *Continued*

Ecuador

1996 Abdalá Bucaram is elected to the presidency for a four-year term.

1997 Bucaram is removed from office for mental instability. Congress chooses the new president, against the view of the vice-president who believes that she should succeed. The decision is made after a meeting in the office of the commander of the joint staff (Fitch 2001). Elections are brought forward to 1998 and a new constitution is promulgated.

1998 New presidential elections are held. Jamil Mahuad is elected.

2000 (January) President Mahuad is briefly overthrown by the military and forced to resign. His vice-president, Neboa, succeeds to the remainder of the presidential term.

Brazil

1990 Francisco Collor is elected to the presidency.

1992 Collor is impeached for corruption and removed. He is replaced by Itmar Franco.

1994 Cardoso is elected president for a single term.

1996–7 Brazil's constitution is changed to permit re-election.

1998 Cardoso is elected for a further term.

leaders of each are likely to make irreconcilable claims of their own legitimacy based on their rival popular mandates. Linz contrasts parliamentarianism with presidentialism in this key respect. In parliamentary systems, government is responsible to parliament and not independent of it. There is therefore no basis for such a conflict of legitimation to occur. Parliament is sovereign.

Another problem that Linz identifies has to do with fixed-term limits. Linz argued that a presidential term would inevitably seem either too long or too short depending upon the personality and achievements of the incumbent. There would always be temptations for a popular president to extend his term, or for congress to try to get rid of an unpopular one. However, in the absence of constitutional mechanisms making this possible, the danger would be that frustrated majorities would look for extra-constitutional means either to shorten or to lengthen presidential terms. The result might lead to democratic breakdown. The classic example given was that of the Allende government in Chile (1970–73), which could not be removed constitutionally by a congressional vote of no confidence despite its unpopularity among the majority of Chileans. In the end, congress passed a vote that in effect asked the military to intervene. Subsequently Chile endured sixteen years of dictatorship. Linz and others do admit the possibility of impeachment, but have argued that impeachment is a remedy for criminal misconduct and not for ordinary incompetence.

Linz's argument does identify some important fault lines though his thesis has proved controversial. It might be better to return to his main arguments after considering some additional points made in the literature. Foweraker (1998), following Lijphart (1993) and Stepan and Skatch (1993), points out that party and electoral systems are also relevant to the study of presidentialism. He shows that the common Latin American combination of a majoritarian system of election for president and proportional representation for congress can make it hard to build coalitions, especially in multi-party systems. A beleaguered minority president facing a hostile congressional figure can be vulnerable indeed.

A further institutional point has to do with the existence in much of the region (Uruguay, once more, being a significant exception) of a presidential right simply to decree legislation. Even when this right takes the more limited form of issuing detailed regulations in order to implement a general law, it still goes far beyond the US concept of an executive whose job it is to uphold the law. Interpretative presidential rule-making power is not generally subject to judicial review. With the significant exception of Russia, the notion of a presidential right to decree legislation – and the general absence of an effective system of judicial review – is largely peculiar to Latin America. There is already a good literature on presidential decree powers in the region (Mainwaring and Shugart 1997; Shugart and Haggard 2001). All that needs be said here is that, even where the provisions of Latin American constitutions are meticulously obeyed, they seem to encroach upon any theoretical notion of separate spheres. At the level of pure description, it would be a reasonable conclusion that many Latin American constitutional systems involve an awkward hybrid mixture of Madisonian and Bolivarian features.

Indeed Latin American politicians have not invariably respected such judicial independence as constitutions formally allowed. In the United States there is a powerfully constituted judicial sphere that regulates the presidential system by (among other things) determining which of the other branches of government has the right to do what. In Latin America there have been simple cases of non-enforcement. In Argentina in 2002 the supreme court declared a key aspect of the government's economic policy illegal. President Duhalde simply declared a stay of execution of 180 days on the verdict, while asking the Argentine congress to set about impeaching the supreme court. In Peru, under Fujimori, congress impeached independent members of the judiciary who opposed the government on the issue of presidential re-election, and some important judicial decisions were simply not enforced (OAS 2000).

In an interesting recent article, Cox and Morgenstern argue that Latin American constitutions typically confer powers on Latin American presidents that are quite different from those enjoyed by the

US president. They conclude that 'most Latin American presidents have greater powers of unilateral action, greater ability to "penetrate" the internal legislative process of the assembly, and more variable political support than their American counterpart' (Cox and Morgenstern 2001, p. 179). They show that there have been many occasions in which presidents and their opponents have interfered seriously in what would in the USA be regarded as the autonomous legislative process.

This interference has sometimes taken the form of law-breaking, including the bribery of congresspeople. Brazil's Cardoso is a paradigm example of a respected, constitutionally minded president. However, there were serious suggestions that the change in the constitution permitting his re-election was effected, in part, by bribery (Martino 2000). In Argentina, the important labour law reform of 2000 certainly seems to have been secured in part by bribery. In Peru and Venezuela, to say that Fujimori and Chávez did not much respect the autonomy of the legislative process is to put it mildly. The Fujimori presidency belatedly ended when his security chief Vladimiro Montesinos was caught on video in the act of bribing a congressman to change sides. In the case of Mexico, checks and balances did not really exist even in principle until 1997 due to the constitutional and meta-constitutional powers of the president (Weldon 1997).

The conclusion being drawn from this discussion is that, while it might not be convincing to assert an entirely a priori argument that pure presidentialism is bad for democratic consolidation, there do seem to be historical-institutional factors that can interact with formal institutional rules to produce this result. The weakness of independent law enforcement and the clientelist system of public-sector appointment (to be discussed in the next chapter) are likely to exacerbate these problems. Empirically, severe conflict between president and congress has been common in democratic South America (less common though not unknown in Central America). In Peru, a president closed congress in 1992 and the same president was impeached by congress in 2000. In Venezuela one president was impeached in 1993, and there was also a major crisis in presidential–congressional relations in 1994 – one might call it a near miss. The next Venezuelan president in 1999 used very questionably constitutional means to force the closure of an elected congress and its replacement by an assembly. In Ecuador one president was removed from office by congress in 1997 on the ground of mental incapacity. A new constitution was agreed in 1998 and new elections were held. Less than three years later, in January 2000, a different president was removed from office by the military. In Argentina in December 2001 two presidents were forced to resign in close succession due to lack of political support from congress, local governments, and the people more generally. There were also presidential impeachments in Brazil and Paraguay during the 1990s. In Colombia one president survived impeachment despite a consensus that he was lucky to do so.

The idea that the spectre of Bolivar has not yet been removed from politics is strengthened when we look at another aspect of presidentialism – namely term limits. Whereas unpopular or weak presidents have tended to face premature removal from office, popular and ambitious figures have frequently sought extensions to their term. Re-election provisions might not matter so much in countries where effective systems of checks and balances exist in the first place, but they matter a great deal when law enforcement is weak and there is enormous patronage power in the hands of the president of the day.

Taking these two things together, there are several Latin American countries in which there were more instances in the 1990s and early 2000s in which presidential terms were either truncated or extended than instances in which presidents served the full term (and no more) for which they had been elected. The former category includes Argentina, Peru, Venezuela, Ecuador and Brazil, whose experiences are summarized in Box 1.

Although Cox and Morgenstern raise interesting points, their idea that Latin American presidential systems have evolved into a kind of semi-parliamentarianism (Cox and Morgenstern 2001) therefore gives more coherence to what has happened than there is in practice. As noted, there are several countries in which politics has tended to become less institutionalized and more plebiscitary. Deinstitutionalization is not a feature only of the presidency either. Central to the philosophy of representative democracy is the notion of strong parties characterized by some degree of ideological coherence (Mainwaring and Scully 1995). Coherent parties are absolutely central to effective parliamentary government, though perhaps not quite so important to presidentialism. However, in much of South America parties are weak and in some countries weakening further. There is some relationship, though not a perfect one, between the strength of party systems and the ability of countries to avoid Bolivarian polarization. The problem is that the direction of the relationship is not clear. Bolivarian figures in Peru and Venezuela were able to destroy party systems that – at any rate in the Venezuelan case – seemed very strong.

Another feature of Bolivarian presidentialism is that some of the most dominant South American presidential figures also adopted radical and unexpected changes of policy (Stokes 2001). Menem in Argentina, Fujimori in Peru and Pérez in Venezuela all introduced economic shocks after clearly promising not to do so. It could well be argued that they had little choice in the light of economic circumstances.

However, this is not really the point. This is that some Latin American presidential institutions have lacked both the respect for process expected of presidential democracies and the strong party systems and substantive policy predictability that would be necessary to an effective system of parliamentary government. The latter conditions probably help with democratic consolidation under presidential systems as well.

Unbalanced presidentialism and democratic non-consolidation

As noted, not all of the region's presidential systems are identical. Some Latin American countries have found ways of making their institutions work in a coherent way. Most authors would accept that this was generally true of Uruguay and Chile where, as we have seen, effective means have been devised of linking the presidency to congress and the party system. Impressionistically, these countries would seem to score higher on other indicators of democratic consolidation too. Uruguay has much less of a patronage state than other countries, while Chile also has a relatively efficient state bureaucracy – certainly much more so than Venezuela (Angell and Graham 1995). Bolivia, while it is less obviously consolidated, has found an effective way of managing constitutional conflicts. Where institutions are capable of working effectively over a significant period, it is likely that they will eventually acquire the popular acceptance that is necessary for democratic con-solidation. However, this work is concerned mainly with non-consolidated democracies and, on the other side of the equation, there have evidently been countries in which the role of the presidency has been the subject of severe political conflict. The cases of Peru and Venezuela are discussed in later chapters. There is also an issue of presi-dentialism, albeit a somewhat different one, in the case of Mexico – also discussed in a later chapter.

However, unbalanced presidentialism can have a certain amount of boundedness as well. One reason for this is that it may be a system that is very difficult for anybody to control in the long run. This feature may give it an ultimate resilience that may help prevent outright demo-cratic breakdown. Unbalanced presidentialism may therefore help to underpin non-consolidated democracy in both directions – making both democratic consolidation and democratic breakdown less likely. Linz originally believed that intractable presidential–congressional conflict would be a threat to democracy itself. One possible reason why this has not happened is the feasibility of simply deposing a president or closing a congress and electing a new one. If a president is impeached or even deposed non-constitutionally, for example, at a time of economic crisis, then new elections can be ordered and political life might soon get back to normal. (Dealing with non-political aspects of the crisis is another matter entirely.) Extraordinary political situations are only one presidential election away from normal ones.

Another factor making for resilience is that presidentialism can work after a fashion even without functioning political parties. The traditional parties virtually disappeared for a time in both Peru and Venezuela during the 1990s and have subsequently shown signs of decline in Colombia, but unbalanced presidentialism meant that elections could continue to be held and effectively contested. It is likely that presidential systems work less well in the absence of effective parties – but they can still work after a fashion. The way that presidentialism has evolved in South America since the mid-1980s has therefore made the 'Allende' scenario – in which unresolved conflict between president and congress brings down the whole democratic system – less likely.

As a result unbalanced presidentialism has tended to develop into an institutionally soft and rather flexible system. It is in practice based much more on the state of public opinion and the political judgements of insiders than on the way in which formal rules are interpreted. The idea of an institutionally soft presidentialism fits in well with the notion of non-consolidated democracy.

Without doubt, economic and social problems have also made it harder to develop a more balanced presidential system. Democratic Latin America has suffered from some severe development crises that have made institutional consolidation more difficult, an issue discussed in a later chapter. It is not surprising that development crises tend to become political crises. The enforced resignations of Mahuad in Ecuador in 2000 and de la Rúa in Argentina in 2001 followed very severe recessions. Ecuador's GDP contracted 9.2 per cent in 1999. There were also severe crises in Peru in 1992 and Venezuela in 1999 – in which cases it was the national congress that suffered the worst of the political consequences.

Political partisanship and the (un)rule of law[2]

It has already been noted that an important aspect of democratic non-consolidation in much of Latin America has to do with weak

---

[2]   The term (un)rule is borrowed from Méndez et al. (1999).

law enforcement and the absence of a spirit of constitutionalism. Effective enforcement is of course essential to a system based on rules. Recent studies of the role of the judiciary in Latin America, however, confirm that the legal and judicial system as a whole remains a problem (Méndez et al. 1999; Prillaman 2000; Panizza and de Brito 1998 on Brazil; and Rodríguez Veltzé 2001 on Bolivia). Most Latin Americans understand perfectly well that their law-enforcement systems work badly and resent the fact. For example, a poll in Brazil in 1989 found 58 per cent completely agreeing and 26 per cent partially agreeing with the statement that 'In Brazil the justice system only functions to help the powerful' (Linz and Stepan 1996, p. 176; see also Lagos 1997). At least some Latin American democracies have been characterized by O'Donnell as 'democracies that are democratic qua polyarchies but are not democratic, or are very incompletely so, as seen from the angle of the rule of law and the legal state' (1999, p. 325).

There is probably no legal system in the world that does not somehow favour those with money, education and familiarity with legal procedures. However, the structured inequality of the legal process in Latin America is often extreme, possibly because inequality in the distribution of income itself is extreme. Apart from corruption, judicial behaviour involves issues of social exclusiveness and racial, gender and class prejudice. In the minds of most office holders, the people are not a citizenry with rights but supplicants to whom one might or might not offer favours. Indeed there are large areas of life, in poor rural areas and even urban slums, which are governed by the para-legality of direct organizational power. Gangsters are controlled by their paymasters. So are the police. Politicians depend upon illegal as well as legal aspects of power. O'Donnell refers to this as the 'privatization' of law enforcement.

In the context of this discussion, which is about high politics, it is important to note that we are dealing with apparently lawless systems that are only partially lawless. Laws and formal rules do matter, but they do not matter all the time or even predictably. The problem is not so much an absence of law (there are plenty of lawyers, judges etc.; Jones 1999) but the inability of law to provide an effective focal point that can regulate most political behaviour. Law enforcement shares the arena with informalized systems of decision-making and, sometimes, with open law-breaking. As a result, overtly lawless behaviour has sometimes been rewarded and sometimes punished. In Venezuela, for example, Carlos Andrés Pérez narrowly avoided losing his congressional immunity to prosecution for corruption in respect of his behaviour when president during 1974–9. Notwith-standing this fact, he was elected president for a second time in 1988. However, he was then impeached for corruption and removed as president in 1993. He later served a short sentence under house arrest. As we shall see, this outcome had more to do with a politi-cal bargain than with the autonomous process of law enforcement. No Mexican president has been impeached, but the arrest and con-viction for murder of the brother of ex-president Salinas was a dra-matic demonstration that the law did sometimes have teeth and that illegality did not always pay. However, the way in which members of the top Mexican political elite behaved in 1994 indicates their subjective belief – based on a sound reading of Mexican history – that the criminal law would not be applied to them no matter what they did.

The partisan use of law is deeply grounded in Latin American history. There seems little doubt that we are dealing here with cultural factors that have preceded and survived democratization. The proverb 'obedezco pero no cumplo' (I obey but I do not comply) dates back to colonial days. An even more cynical saying, 'to one's friends, one does justice, but to one's enemies one applies the law', was attributed to Benito Juárez, the great Mexican liberal of the nineteenth century. The Brazilian counterpart proverb is 'to one's friends, everything. To one's enemies, the law.' This, too, dates from a period of formally represen-tative government that was not exactly a consolidated democracy. Selective law enforcement is capable of surviving the transition to democracy and seems in fact to have done so.

If respect for independent law enforcement is to be learned, then it is also evident that the law needs to be made sensibly enforceable. As the phrase 'to one's enemies, the law' makes clear, this is not always currently the case. Historically speaking the law has not been designed to facilitate governance but to register social attitudes – often attitudes reflecting distrust of policy-makers. In fact there is a great deal of empirical evidence that most of Latin America suffers from a culture of distrust (Lagos 1997). This culture of distrust leads to the use of rules as means of keeping potential enemies in check. However, because gov-ernance would be quite impossible in a pitiless world of pure antag-onistic law enforcement, trust is built up between groups of people (kinship groups, *camarillas* and so on) on the basis that they connive to help each other, to some extent irrespective of the law. Governance tra-ditionally takes place through people rather than through procedures or formal processes. The result tends to personalize the entire political process and leads to a lack of respect for law.

Public opinion as court of last resort

In Thomas Hobbes's original 'state of nature', conflict and anarchy led to the rise of Leviathan. A similar argument would suggest that presidentialism without law would be likely to break down and be replaced by authoritarianism. Yet this, so far, has not happened. It is suggested here that this is because of informal understandings to the effect that, in cases of crisis, the solution preferred by the majority of the population should be the one adopted. Political conflict is often decided on the basis of popularity, with due process a very secondary consideration.

Many examples can be given of political behaviour that was technically illegal but which achieved its objectives due to popular support. Mexico's Carlos Salinas (president 1988–94) was for most of his term a popular president, despite the fact that his presidency was characterized by considerable corruption and other forms of illegality. Even more to the point, his presidency was seen by many as illegitimate in the sense that, according to the polls, the majority of Mexicans did not believe that he had truly won the 1988 elections. Whether this perception is accurate is beside the point. The point is that many Mexicans were prepared simultaneously to believe that Salinas had come to power through rigged elections and to approve of his presidency. It is true that people did not know the full details of what Raul Salinas, the elder brother of Carlos, was up to at the time: Raul was later imprisoned for murder and drug trafficking. It is also true that the 'tequila crisis', which broke just after the end of Carlos Salinas's presidential term, had a very sobering effect on Mexico, and the reputations of both Carlos Salinas and the PRI suffered lasting damage.

In Peru there is a somewhat similar story. Alberto Fujimori's popularity went up in 1992 after he, as president, called in the military to close the national congress. It is true that Peruvians did not then have access to the Montesinos videos in Peru, which appeared to show that several generals were bribed to act. However, virtually all adult Peruvians will have been aware that the closure of their national congress by force was illegal but they still approved it. Similarly in Venezuela Hugo Chávez was elected to the presidency in 1998 despite leading an unsuccessful military coup attempt in February 1992. There is no suggestion that Chávez was supported purely and simply because he had been a coup leader, but his previous record unquestionably helped him.

Cases where constitutional observance was actually unpopular may not be typical of the region but they are certainly not isolated. Lino

Oviedo, a former military officer, was for a time in 1999 the most popular political figure in Paraguay despite his participation in a coup attempt in 1996. He later escaped to exile in Brazil in order to avoid being charged with offences including the murder of the vice-president. His popular support within Paraguay did not generally come from people who mistakenly considered him a law-abiding figure – quite the contrary is true. According to Latinobarómetro in 2001 (quoted in *The Economist*, 26 July 2001) 35 per cent of Paraguayans surveyed agreed that 'democracy is preferable to any other kind of government', while 43 per cent took the view that, 'in certain circumstances, an authoritarian government can be preferable to a democratic one.' Furthermore, an observer of the Lino Oviedo phenomenon concluded that, 'after many years of poor economic performance, increasing poverty, rising unemployment, failing banks, increasing crime rates and corruption and weak political leadership, many Paraguayans were disillusioned, ready to punish a political elite unable to solve their problems, and eager to trust anybody who promised to bring back stability' (Abente-Brun 1999, p. 99). These are not very different from the motives of Peruvians who supported Fujimori in 1992 or Venezuelans who voted for Chávez in 1998.

In Ecuador, when – as we have seen – a military movement overthrew the elected president in January 2000, opinion polls showed that most Ecuadorians supported the near coup (Fitch 2001). In Bolivia, General Hugo Banzer – a military dictator during 1971–8 – was elected to the presidency in 1997. It is admittedly true that Banzer has generally played the democratic game in Bolivia since democracy was restored in 1982, but it is still noteworthy that an overtly dictatorial past involving some human-rights abuses was not generally held against him. Finally there were the conflicts and crises that brought down successive presidents in Argentina in December 2001. However much one might blame extreme circumstances in this case, the fact is that rioters brought down an elected president and changed the governing party.

The argument that politics in non-consolidated democracies may sometimes involve a considerable plebiscitary element is clearly borne out in the cases of Peru and Venezuela. In Peru, the closing of congress in April 1992 was followed by several sets of fresh elections, and a new constitution was approved in a direct plebiscite in October 1993. In Venezuela, Chávez called four quite different plebiscites in his first eighteen months in office – including one that approved a new constitution. Outright plebiscitary politics has been less noteworthy in other cases, but there have been significant examples of local or congressional elections that were granted considerable plebiscitary significance. For example, the serious defeat of de la Rúa's Radical Party in the October 2001 congressional elections emboldened opposition politicians to seek his removal. Mexico's Salinas drew the opposite lesson from the victory of the PRI in the 1991 mid-term elections. This was that the PRI had essentially recovered from the shock of the 1988 election results and the ballot rigging that accompanied it.

Institutional and organizational power

While public opinion plays an important part in determining the outcome of conflict in Latin America's non-consolidated democracies, the active participants in contesting for power tend to be autonomous or semi-autonomous organizations. Even when politics seems at its most personalistic, successful personalists need organizational support. Politics is therefore organized according to competing sub-institutionalities. Organizations (including branches of the state) tend to act as rule-makers in their own interest. Relevant cases include the Mexican PRI, the dominant political parties in Punto Fijo Venezuela, the military in Peru and Venezuela, trade union organizations in some countries, and even organized criminals.

This enables us to distinguish between consolidated and non-consolidated democracy on the basis of the definitions of institutions and organizations in the work of Douglas North (1990, p. 3). North defines institutions as 'the rules of the game in a society or, more formally, the humanly devised constraints that shape human interaction' and organizations as 'players'. This definition permits a fairly simple model of how consolidated democracy works. At the top there are a set of institutions that determine fundamental issues of power – these rules relate to elections, the protection of rights and judicial review, and citizen freedom to organize and participate in politics. In most democracies today these over-arching institutional arrangements are entrenched in constitutions or other forms of basic legislation – though this was not always so in the past. For a democracy to be consolidated and healthy, its political institutions have to be seen as legitimate both by participants in the political process and by the general public. There is a general belief, normally based on evidence, that these rules are independently enforced in a genuinely disinterested way. Rule-breaking does sometimes occur, but this is seen as wrong and scandalous, and those detected breaking the rules can expect to be punished.

At the second level of power there are major organized interests, such as political parties, trade unions and business organizations, which accept the 'rules of the game' and seek to achieve advantage by participating in the political process through means permitted by law. It is inevitable that tensions between organized interests and institutions will sometimes emerge. However, at any particular time organizations have to operate substantially within sets of rules that they do not make themselves. Rules change according to the outcome of legislative or judicial processes and, within reasonable limits, according to the will of the people. Organizations do have some rule-making power *vis-à-vis* their own members and sometimes even *vis-à-vis* members of the general public. However, this rule-making power is subject to the overall institutionality of the state. The key point is that both those who enforce and those who wish to change the rules of the game must themselves observe them.

In non-consolidated democracies, contenders for state power do not necessarily obey impartial rules. Following Mainwaring and Shugart's useful distinction between partisan power and constitutional power (Mainwaring and Shugart 1997), partisan power can be stronger than constitutional power. Constitutional power still carries some weight. If it did not do so then democracy would break down. However, the formal rules are often avoided, evaded, 'informalized' and sometimes openly broken. Organized interests use informal and formal rules as bargaining tactics in their dealings with each other. This kind of partisan behaviour can characterize both those that control the state and those in opposition.

However, organizations can and do impose discipline on their own members while resisting the notion that the state should apply discipline impartially. Non-consolidated democracy might therefore be conceptualized as a system in which partisan organizations are not fully subject to institutions, but instead have de facto and often informal rule-making powers of their own. In North's parlance, the umpire or referees also participates as a player, and players on the opposing side may also try to act as umpires or referees if they can.

This situation, once it is allowed to develop, tends to self-reinforce. Successful political movements that are suspected of excessive partisanship cannot easily develop legitimate institutions even if they win power. Rules introduced by law-breakers are themselves likely to be seen as temporary and expedient. If ostensibly institutional rules are seen as serving the interest of a particular status quo, then, when the status quo is discredited, the rules will be discredited as well. The state will be seen as being, and probably will be, biased. This, in turn, may result in both a compliance problem and a legitimation problem. Partisan losers will refuse to accept their defeat as legitimate and will try to overturn it by all possible means. Indeed those who do obey the rules and lose out as a result are likely to be seen by others as foolish rather than genuinely principled. For these reasons, there are likely to be self-reinforcing effects. State bias encourages law-breaking on the part of non-state actors, and it also encourages formerly outsider organizations that may successfully get control of the state to rebias the state in their own interest.

The survival of non-consolidated democracy does show that a political system based on competitive elections can survive without an overarching institutionality. All that is necessary is for the forces of the state to know whom to defend and whom to repress if necessary. In the past, the minimum common ground was provided by the prospect, or fact, of military veto. Today it is likely to be the force of public opinion, with the military playing a lesser but not always absent role. The fact that a political system can retain a minimum level of consensus even though far from fully consolidated is also significant. Here, again, the key issues seem to be the semi-autonomy of partisan organizations and their ability to negotiate.

It was once supposed by some political scientists that micro-political legitimation depends irrevocably on macro-political legitimation (see, for example, Finer 1962). If this were the case, then maintaining military discipline (to take one example) would depend on a satisfactory form of legitimation at the level of the state. State bias would therefore prove to be immediately self-destructive. To some extent there is indeed a tendency for state bias and partisanship to undermine the legitimacy of democratic institutions – for example, in post-1989 Venezuela. However, while this is a weakness, it is not necessarily a fatal one for non-consolidated democracy as such. Popularity is not the same as legitimacy, but it can sometimes act as a substitute. If public opinion is generally supportive, it is indeed possible to exert political power via discrete organizational cultures without any direct threat to democracy. The result may be specific local institutionalities (made up of a mixture of formal and informal rules) rather than a common overarching institutionality. The military may run its affairs one way, the civilian public service may do so in a different way, the political parties in a different way again, organized crime may develop informal rules of its own, and so forth. The absence of a common legal framework based on provisions of legitimate authority does not mean that such systems are all in danger of disintegration. On the contrary, state bias can be re-created after a change of government or constitution, and often is – even after so-called reformers come to power.

The argument that partisan organizations, including personal followings, can be rule-makers opens another perspective on the observation that the region's non-democratic past continues to influence the democratic present. Contrary to the assumptions of some authors, democratic transition need not result in change to all the rules of the game. All that must change are the formal constitutional rules. If constitutional change forces other parts of the political system to change decisively, then democracy changes everything. However, if organizations can retain a significant degree of autonomy from constitutional rules, then a different interpretation is necessary. The argument that democratic transition inevitably implies rupture is also vulnerable if, under democracy, public opinion is the ultimate arbiter of the real political rules rather than the independently judged terms of the constitution. Organizational rules and popular attitudes may change much more slowly in non-consolidated systems than do constitutional provisions.

Empirically, it is clear that Latin American political organizations that long pre-date the current wave of democratization have maintained themselves over quite long periods of time despite regime change. By way of example we might consider Peronism and the Radical Party in Argentina, Peru's APRA, the MNR in Bolivia, the AD in Venezuela and some of the party organizations of Brazil. Indeed some organizations actually associated with authoritarianism have survived the transition to democracy, notably the Mexican PRI. There is also a tradition of authoritarian personalism that has lingered in several countries and is clearly based on notions of charismatic authority. Fujimori (though himself a civilian) and Chávez are obvious examples. These organizations have certainly changed since the days of authoritarian rule, but they have adapted to democracy by ways other than the unconditional acceptance of new constitutional rules.

3

Authoritarian Legacies
and the Politics
of Appointment

Another way in which we can see clear continuity between pre-democratic and democratic Latin America is in the semi-patrimonial character of its public administration. Market reform has not really changed this except in certain specific areas, for example, where state assets have been privatized. Democratization did not really change it either, except in a small number of countries (such as Uruguay) that did undertake serious reform of their systems of public administration.

Empirically, there is no doubt that semi-patrimonialist bureaucratic practices have proved very resistant to reform. This discussion accepts the argument, put forward by Geddes and others (Geddes 1994), that there is a collective-action problem facing reform, because those who benefit from the existing status quo are likely to resist it. If it is the case that democratic consolidation requires the existence of a Weberian rule-enforcing bureaucracy (Linz and Stepan 1996, p. 13), then the difficulties of reforming semi-patrimonialist systems of political appointment bear directly upon the issue of democratic consolidation.

The reform of state agencies has become an important part of the international 'good governance' agenda. However, IFI officials charged with encouraging such reforms have tended to report pessimistically about their experiences. For example, Geoffrey Shepherd, then a World Bank official, concluded in 1999 of civil-service reform programmes that 'results have been satisfactory in the case of isolated reforms in particular areas, but poor in the case of process and global reforms' (Shepherd 1999). Similarly, Peter Spink (1999) quotes Gerald Caiden's (1991) conclusion that

> the most important fact about Latin America over the past four decades has been the stubbornness with which it has pursued administrative reform, despite so many failures and disappointments. Possibly nowhere

in the world have so many governments announced bold, imaginative reform plans to achieve so little in practice. (Caiden 1991, p. 262; Spink 1999, p. 93)

Weak law enforcement is an additional problem with reform attempts. For example, in its report on administrative reform on Bolivia, the World Bank complained that,

> While there are several ways to characterize the institutional weaknesses in Bolivia's public sector, a concept we find most useful . . . is that of 'informality'. The problem of 'informality' exists when there is a significant gap between 'ideal' or 'desirable' behavioural patterns prescribed in a set of formal institutions (i.e., laws, rules and organizational norms) on the one hand, and actual behavioural patterns that obtain. (World Bank 2000c, p. ii of Executive Summary)

In less antiseptic words, administrative behaviour at the higher levels of government is not much constrained by laws. We have already noted that independent law enforcement is generally weak in the region. In the absence of legal constraint, the power of appointment and promotion becomes even more important. Given the likelihood that politicians and senior politically appointed bureaucrats will form symbiotic relationships, a weak legal system makes it very difficult to deal with problems caused by patrimonialism.

This chapter is only partly about issues of bureaucratic performance. It is focused mainly on the wider issue of democratic consolidation. Poor policy performance is certainly relevant to this, though there are other aspects as well. These include the prospect of increasing returns to power. Other things being equal, one would expect presidential power to be enhanced in cases where the incumbent president had many thousands of bureaucratic positions at his disposal. A state bureaucracy that is composed very largely of political appointees and subject to little or no independent discipline from the law is likely to be biased towards incumbents. However, the political consequences of such a situation might nevertheless be more complex than one might suppose. The tendency for the state to act for the benefit of incumbents might be offset by the anticipated reactions effect mentioned in the last chapter. In other words, political behaviour and institutional mechanisms might be adapted to limit the political consequences of state bias and to inhibit the emergence of hyper-presidentialism. The result might be a kind of frustrated hyper-presidentialism instead.

Public sector organization in Latin America

The political and policy implications of the Latin American experience will be discussed below, but first we need some factual information. In fact most public bureaucracies throughout the world contain some political appointees and a much larger number of professional bureaucrats. However, in many Latin American countries the number of top-level political appointees is very high. Meanwhile lower-level employees tend either to be unionized or to enjoy legal security of tenure – or both. This can mean that they show up at work only to collect payment. More generally, the combination of political appointment at the top and security at lower levels prevents any effective system of internal promotion on merit except in some very specific areas.

In Mexico the number of 'confidence' (i.e., politically appointed) positions at the top of the whole public bureaucracy in late 2000 was stated to be as high as 50,000 by Carlos Rojas, who was the former head of the Social Development Ministry (SEDESOL) (quoted in *La Jornada*, 29 October 2000). According to other sources, the number of 'confidence' positions in the core civil service (excluding nationalized industries and so forth) is much lower – but still estimated at a high-enough 15,000 to 20,000 (Arellano Gault and Guerrero Amparán, 2000). If one takes the conservative numbers provided by the latter authors, there are 15,000 political appointees running a core civil service of around 750,000 total employees, which means the ratio is 50:1. In fact, the Mexican proportion is in reality higher, because many of the unionized public positions are occupied by people who do not turn up for work at all or who act as gardeners, lift-attendants and so on. If one compares the 15,000 or so political appointments with the 200,000 or so mid-level bureaucrats who do much of the routine administrative work, then the ratio is 13.3:1.

Further down the hierarchy there are in Mexico some 500,000 unionized workers in the central government. Unionization is also extensive in local government, nationalized industry and the schoolteaching profession. Unionized workers in central government are denied permission to strike but they enjoy tenure. It is possible but very difficult to remove them. Their pay is very low. Indeed, if a unionized public servant behaved as a Weberian bureaucrat should – turning up to work regularly, working hard and regarding his or her official salary as the main source of income – then he or she would have no chance at all of being able to support a family. The kinds of practice often complained of as abuses – moonlighting, petty corruption, or straightforward non-appearance at work – are structurally inevitable.

One of the effects of the high level of political appointees in Mexico is to make it very difficult to establish a bureaucratic career structure except in a few 'islands' within the bureaucracy which are run in a much more Weberian way (Moctezuma Barragán and Roemer, 2001). Mid-level bureaucrats, basically people without connections, cannot aspire to rise very high in a system with so many political appointees. For those with real talent, the private sector is likely to look attractive by comparison. However, because political appointees are likely to change position frequently, the day-to-day business of administration has to remain in the hands of relatively unmotivated mid-level bureaucrats. Incoming teams of political appointees may not initially know how to do such mundane things as order stationery in the legally correct manner. Mid-level bureaucrats are in fact often the only people with organizational knowledge or memory. They are on short-term contracts and relatively poorly paid. However, in practice they are rarely dismissed because they tend to acquire detailed specialist knowledge that is hard to replicate. They can also acquire considerable discretion over mundane decision-making. This allows considerable potential for minor corruption.

Apart from the problem of high turnover, the top political appointees are not likely to be much interested in issues of day-to-day administration. Their main motivation will be to make the political moves necessary to ensure a good subsequent appointment. According to one very senior Mexican politician,[1] it is quite usual for a *camarilla* to put its most loyal but least talented member in charge of the detailed administration of a ministry while the others concentrate on political matters.

The administrative behaviour of the middle-level official is likely to be governed by detailed law and regulation – more so than in the past. Documents and formal processes dominate procedures. It was once the case that a mid-level bureaucrat could enjoy considerable discretion. However, uncontrolled and sometimes corrupt spending by the Mexican bureaucracy was widely blamed for the budgetary problems and financial crises of the 1970–82 period. Budgetary control has therefore been tightened up. The administrative policing unit – the Contraloría, set up in 1983 – today operates on a fairly large scale, employs several thousand people, and has disciplined quite a large number of mid-ranking public officials.

This has enabled a significant tightening of budgetary control over the public sector. There has been a very significant reduction of the size

[1] Presentation given by Esteban Moctezuma at the London School of Economics on 19 November 2001.

of the Mexican state over the past generation — from over 40 per cent of GDP at the beginning of the 1980s to under 25 per cent of GDP at the turn of the century. Privatization has played a part in this overall reduction. However, much greater administrative austerity is in evidence as well. This has certainly not prevented the public sector being used in a partisan way. For example the PRI's budget for the 2000 election campaign (which it lost) was significantly enhanced by over $70 million from the oil workers' union of the state monopoly Pemex. The union had been lent the money for this electoral contribution by the Pemex management. In 1994 the PRI's presidential campaign was financed by donations from those who benefited from the bank privatizations, and to some extent as well by donations from individuals linked to the narcotics trade (Philip 1998). It is not hard to guess what these donors believed that they were purchasing.

However, one unintended consequence of having repressive systems of investigation is to encourage bureaucratic rigidity. The Contraloría makes little distinction between unorthodox behaviour designed to achieve a worthwhile objective and actual corruption; its enquiries tend to start from the premise that somebody is evidently guilty of something. To be fair, this is sometimes a reasonable perspective. Mid-level bureaucrats who have committed administrative irregularities are indeed sometimes punished, and the process is seen as somewhat legitimating the popular will to have honest government. But it does not make the administrative system any more flexible or responsive to public needs. The system is also demoralizing because the Contraloría has rather a poor record of decisively combating genuine 'big fish' corruption.

High-level officials and politicians who enjoy presidential protection rarely went to gaol, although the system did tighten up somewhat after the 1994–5 'tequila crisis'. The administration of justice as well as routine bureaucratic behaviour was largely segmented between a high politics of pro-system corruption (which has remained largely protected) and a low politics of unauthorized personal peculation, which is now more likely to be detected and punished.

In 2000 the Mexican government changed, but the system of political control has not changed very much as a result. It is fair to say that the presidential power of appointment was used with some discretion both before and after 2000, largely because of well-placed fears that any over-enthusiastic appointment of political allies would result in macro-economic destabilization. The general Mexican pattern remains one in which virtually the entire upper bureaucracy has become dependent on the presidential will. One cannot regard the system as purely patrimonial. At the mid-level, law and administrative rules often do apply – sometimes rather rigidly. However, at the upper levels, the power of appointment was – at least until the late 1990s – virtually everything.

The Venezuelan pattern at the beginning of the 1990s was in some ways similar to that in Mexico. The number of political appointments in Venezuela in the early 1990s was around 4000, but there were another 5000 positions – designated as consultancies – which were in effect high-level political appointments (Moctezuma Barragán and Roemer 2001, p. 79). This amounts to 9000 political appointees out of the 417,000 civil servants officially reported to exist in 1991. If one assumes that a significant proportion of this latter figure did little more than collect their salaries, then the proportion of political appointees to others is similar to that in Mexico. There is certainly evidence that the Venezuelan bureaucracy, like the Mexican, paid salaries to quite large numbers of people who did not turn up to work at all (Grindle 2000, p. 80).

The Venezuelan system, despite the existence of alternating parties and competitive elections, seems also to have been almost as presidential in its methods of appointment as the Mexican one. Between 1958 and 1989 there were no elections for local governorships at all. These were appointed positions, with the entire bureaucratic structure appointed from the centre. The difference in Mexico, where competitive elections existed in theory but where the PRI always won them, is not self-evident. Grindle quotes one of her interviewed experts as saying that 'Presidentialism in Venezuela . . . is based on the control of positions and the ability to distribute those positions' (Grindle 2000, p. 48).

However, in Venezuela, much more than in Mexico, the whole process of public administration was overlaid by party politics. The authoritarian system in Mexico, in which the official party was dependent on the government, kept this process somewhat in check, but the Venezuelan pattern, in which the dominant parties acted as patronage machines, exacerbated it. It also contributed to the country's economic problems after 1980. The party machines and the legal tenure of civil servants prevented any significant shrinkage of the state but could not prevent major declines in public sector pay due to the adverse economic situation.

By the 1990s, the Venezuelan administrative system could be characterized as operating at two levels. At the lowest level it provided a subsistence minimum of income to a significant number of people who owed their position and any prospects they might have had to political connections. These tended to come from rural areas and provided vital political support to the traditional parties in poorer parts of the country: this can be seen as a system of mass clientelism. At the highest level the state was run by an elite of several thousand people to whom the law did not really apply: one might call this elite clientelism.

This essential immunity from law enforcement was facilitated by the party politicians' control over the judiciary. In 1992 the World Bank reported that the Venezuelan judicial system was in crisis (Buxton 2001, p. 32). Judges were appointed by political parties on a partisan basis in order to protect their own interests. There were even cabals of judges who worked together at the service of politicians. In 1992 the attorney-general Ramón Escovar Salom accused a leading AD politician, David Morales Bello, of running a so-called tribe of David within the judicial system (*El Universal*, 26 March 1992). Buxton concludes that 'a dual system of justice developed, one for the politically unconnected poor and another for the well-connected and wealthy elite' (2001, p. 32). In 1995 a radical journalist published a book entitled *How Much is a Judge Worth?* The system was not reformed, but the journalist was gaoled for contempt of court.

Apart from the problem of corruption, which was deep rooted and all-pervasive, the system was unresponsive to popular needs due to sheer incompetence. People were appointed to positions that were far beyond their capacity, and faced with neither incentives for good performance nor penalties for poor performance. Largely as a result of this, Venezuela appears at the bottom of most intra-regional indicators of relative effectiveness of public spending on social welfare (Angell and Graham 1995). Election results were often problematic because the public officials selected to work for the electoral authorities were simply not educated enough to be able to add large numbers (Buxton 2001).

It is entirely likely that fluctuating oil revenues added to Venezuela's problems. When oil prices were high, it was hard to resist pressure to increase the number of low-level appointments into the bureaucracy. This led to bureaucratic ineptitude. This, in turn, led to frustration, and successive governments in the 1970s tended to bypass existing bureaucratic structures and set up new organizations and new state companies altogether (Villalba 1987). However, entrenched political interests tended to respond by adopting the rhetoric of reform, moving into new sectors including state enterprises, and carrying on much as before (Karl 1997, pp. 138–40). State enterprises became a most efficient means of transferring national budgetary income to networks of corrupt suppliers, employees and contractors. In the end many state agencies became financial black holes through which Venezuela's oil income disappeared into Swiss banks or the Florida property market.

Venezuela's oil economy was also managed in a different way in the 1980s to that of Mexico where, under conditions of economic crisis, many state companies were either closed down or privatized. In Venezuela the continued flow of oil revenue and the more pluralist political system slowed down the pace of reform. The penetration of the state by particularistic political interests probably had worse consequences because Venezuela continued during the 1980s to try to offset adverse economic conditions by maintaining a system of price and exchange controls. In addition, the Venezuelan political elite sought to control the military by clientelistic means. This policy ended in evident disaster, as will be discussed again in a later chapter.

During the 1960s and 1970s a climate of abundance and an increase in the size of the public sector may well have attracted support to the democratic system as a whole. The shrinking of resources available to the public sector after 1983 subsequently led to zero-sum or negative-sum politics. Public opinion tended to turn against incumbents. Because Venezuelan elections after 1983 were keenly contested, public-sector workers were able to mobilize in opposition to fiscal austerity and market reform much more effectively than they were in Mexico, where political alternatives were blocked off by the semi-authoritarian state (Murillo 2001). However, this mobilization did nothing to prevent continuing economic decline.

Bolivia is an interesting case to compare with Mexico and Venezuela because it is not a major oil-exporting country and it enables us to control for the effect of the 1970s oil boom. Yet we see a broadly similar pattern. One observer of Bolivian politics has recently pointed out that

> Bolivia's democracy is heavily dependent on presidential leadership. One feature that explains the success in implementing the most important reforms after 1993 is that they were all undertaken at the behest of strong leaders with full presidential support. (Muñoz 2001, p. 98)

One sees a pattern of patronage at top levels of the bureaucracy in Bolivia similar to that in Mexico and Venezuela. In Bolivia, too, there are both high-level political appointees and consultants. The latter tend to enjoy higher salaries and status than others in the bureaucracy, (World Bank 2000c, p. 30). Even the World Bank could not find a reliable figure for the number of consultants working in Bolivia – putting the number at somewhere between 2500 and 4200 (ibid.). This is in addition to a considerable number of *confianza* positions. The World Bank was also quite clear in its belief that the top-level political appointees, and indeed party politicians more generally, were able to influence the bureaucratic behaviour even of those who were not formally subject to political appointment.

In Bolivia the relationship between politics and administration relates to a somewhat different presidential system. Bolivian politics is closer to being semi-presidential than purely presidential. The outcome has led to a process of government by coalition that has helped prevent the kinds of political drama that characterized Venezuelan politics in the 1990s. Bolivian governments have shared patronage power with their coalition partners (World Bank 2000c, p. vii). In essence, patronage positions have been used as 'side payments' to win legislative support for reform initiatives of other kinds. Unfortunately such a tendency may have been a recipe for private-sector affluence and public-sector squalor.

This author is not aware of any comprehensive and recent study of the structure of the Peruvian bureaucracy. However, earlier academic studies differentiate that country to no more than a limited degree from the other cases considered here. Before 1968 the Peruvian bureaucracy was small and its functions relatively few. It was not seen as a source of independent activity. Kuczynski (1977, p. 75) blamed this on low pay and 'the tradition of the economic elite of not participating in government at the civil service level.' Peru's former prime minister Pedro Beltrán recorded in his memoirs one remarkable experience following his appointment in 1959. He was visited in his office by an official from the Central Bank who asked him what the rate of inflation had been in the previous month. He replied that it was the job of the bank to tell him. 'No', said the bank representative, 'you tell us what the rate should be and we publish it' (Beltrán 1977).

However, the military government of General Velasco made a real effort to reform the state. The purpose of the reforms, as might be supposed, was to make the state a more efficient instrument of executive power. There is no space to discuss the reforms in detail (Cleaves and Pease García 1983; Hammergren 1983). The point is that, to the extent they worked, they helped the Velasco government execute a genuinely ideological but partisan and top-down agenda. It was also a state expanding agenda, since it involved reforms that required a great increase in state control over the economy. To a great extent the civilian bureaucracy was placed under the control of the military, with some 300 military officers actually working in the 'civilian' public sector at any one time (Cleaves and Pease García 1983, p. 220). At the beginning, these reforms looked as though they might achieve some genuine efficiency gains. However, once General Velasco became ill at the beginning of 1973 and military disunity prevented the emergence of clear alternative leadership, then any efficiency gains faded away. The bureaucracy just became a resource-consuming locus of partisan conflict.

It is likely that the expansion of state employment during 1968–75 made the Peruvian military government less unpopular than it otherwise would have been and helped it stay in office. However, its policies of land reform and property nationalization were inherently controversial both within the military itself and within broader Peruvian society. So was its instinctive authoritarianism. The Velasco government did not therefore get the popularity bonus for which it hoped. Financial stringency started to impact on Peru from around 1977, and evidently reduced the popularity of the government. The effect of stringency was the reduction of real wages in the public sector. In addition, the government in 1979 offered incentives to people who wished to resign from the public sector. As later become clear, the most capable bureaucrats were happy to accept incentives to move on, and the general quality of public administration suffered as a result (Sagasti 2001, p. 224).

After the ending of military rule, the Peruvian state faced a whole series of adverse circumstances, including major insurgency from Sendero Luminoso and the MRTA, economic decline, hyperinflation and international debt default. The democratically elected presidents governing Peru during the 1980s made the occasional effort at administrative reform. There was a plan to develop a career civil service, elaborated in 1982, and the government negotiated a loan from the World Bank to do this. However, although the plan might have been a good one, it was obstructed by renewed economic difficulty in Peru and by various political obstacles.

The García government (1985–90) moved in a different direction to that of many others in the region at that time. It was heterodox in its economics and expansionary in its aspirations. As before, an expanding state was in the interest of the president of the day, who was under pressure to find public positions for his supporters. Data from the Library of Congress indicates that the total number of state employees increased from some 282,400 in 1985 to 833,000 in 1990 (Library of Congress, Federal Research Division, 2002: country studies, Peru). This seems an enormous increase, and the figure may be too high, but there is no real doubt about the general trend. After around 1987 economic disaster struck, with hyperinflation and a complete decline in the capacity of the state. The military, as we shall see in a later chapter, worried about a decline in governability. Certainly the García government's extreme combination of a rapid expansion of state employment and a decline in everything else was not a basis for popular support.

As in Mexico and Venezuela, the fact that the bureaucracy was only really responsive to pressure from above led to a political temptation to centralize further. Crabtree concludes that 'the system of government which evolved under García was both highly personalist and highly centralised' (Crabtree 1992, p. 62). President García distrusted the bureaucracy that he inherited and sought to bypass the usual channels by relying – in as far as he relied on anybody at all – on a limited circle of advisors. The same was true of Fujimori in the 1990s, only more so. In fact, as we shall see in chapter 8 below, Fujimori ran the Peruvian state in a relatively professional way but clearly in an authoritarian spirit.

Anybody looking for a sharply observed rather than a measured discussion of how political parties and public servants interacted in Peru in the 1980s could do worse than consult Vargas Llosa's political autobiography *A Fish in the Water* (Vargas Llosa 1994). In Vargas Llosa's account, public officials and politicians behaved as a kind of mutual benefit society. Party politicians drew such support as they possessed from control over state patronage. They made little attempt to relate to ordinary people and every attempt to pursue particularistic interests through gaining access to the resources of the state. State officials were often arrogant, corrupt and incompetent. They related to the politicians, and not to the public. While public bureaucrats were unpopular for this reason, they still formed a powerful voting bloc. Vargas Llosa was the front-running presidential candidate for the 1990 elections until his campaign featured a televised commercial that involved a direct attack against the state bureaucracy. The loss of support that arose from this may well have cost him the election.

Fujimori's government followed the neo-liberal pattern in which there was considerable reform to the economic aspects of the state. There were many privatizations. However, Fujimori's government was positioned to avoid the worst political consequences of continuing budgetary austerity. This is because the García government, in its chaotic mismanagement, had defaulted on 'soft loans' from the international financial institutions (IFIs). Peru, being one of the poorer countries in the region, is eligible for some loans on very easy terms. Fujimori was able to mend fences with the IFIs and could then use soft loans in order to expand the role of the state in certain policy areas. Privatization receipts also helped considerably. However, proposals to reform the Peruvian state to make it less patronage-based and more professional were made and rejected. In fact two IFI loans, one by the Inter-American Development Bank and one by the World Bank, earmarked to promoting public-sector reform, were approved and then cancelled as it became clear that the Peruvian authorities would not comply with the appropriate requirements.

There is insufficient space here to discuss the other countries of the region. However, it does seem that only a few countries, Uruguay and

Chile particularly, have sufficiently autonomous states to be able to prevent, at least to some extent, the politicization of appointment systems and the development of systems of mass clientelism. In Chile the size of the public bureaucracy was decisively reduced under General Pinochet. According to Nunberg and Nellis (1995, p. 19) the number of centrally employed civil servants fell in Chile from 305,000 in 1973 to 130,000 in 1990. This was done without external financing. Uruguay also has a reasonably professional civil service. In Uruguay the number of high-level political appointments is much lower – the number in 1998 was no higher than 324 (Panizza 2001). It may well be that the much lower proportion of political appointees at the top of the bureaucracy is a part of the explanation for Uruguay's more con-solidated democracy. However, the Mexican/Venezuelan/Peruvian pattern in which the political elite controls the state is the more usual one in the region. Hagopian (1996), for example, documents the way in which democratization in Brazil led to the gradual suppression of some kind of technocratic state and its replacement by one that was far more dominated by traditionally minded (i.e., patronage-minded) politicians.

Politics, state bias and policy performance

It is necessary to acknowledge that the system of presidential appoint-ment can facilitate top-down changes in policy direction. Autocratic presidents in Latin America have been able to achieve at least some significant policy objectives. One could not possibly explain the deter-mined pursuit of market-oriented reforms across the region in the late 1980s and 1990s without recognizing that political appointees can sometimes make very capable public servants. As we shall see in a later chapter, the ability of the Mexican president to appoint the upper bureaucracy made possible a major change in the direction of economic policy after 1982. In Mexico the political system between 1982 and 2000 was in the hands of a market-oriented technocracy that pursued (in Centeno's felicitous term) 'democracy within reason' (Centeno 1994). In performance terms, the Mexican system of appointment facilitated reform in areas where technical skill at the very top was the most important factor. This would be true of macro-economic management, tariff reform, membership of NAFTA, etc. Here political authoritarian-ism, top-down patterns of policy-making and technocratic leadership can work as a coherent package. However, where reform requires the motivation of a large number of able and public-spirited people – in areas such as health, education, law enforcement, indeed the so-called second generation of reforms in general – then the system performed worse. Moreover, the Mexican public bureaucracy is poorly regarded by public opinion as a whole – a factor that is part of the general anti-tax culture in Mexico and therefore a direct source of economic problems (Moctezuma Barragán and Roemer 2001). Some reforms have indeed happened in fields such as education, but the political effort needed to secure them has been significant indeed.

The pattern in other countries of the region is somewhat similar. In the majority of cases, Latin American states are no longer inefficient in any simple-minded sense at the making of economic policy. Manifestly incompetent people no longer stand much chance of becoming economics ministers or directors of central banks. The general level of human capital in top technocratic positions in many Latin American countries compares quite favourably with much of the first world. What seems to be happening instead is a kind of double bifurcation. There is often a very wide difference in ability between those at the very top of the state apparatus and those nearer the middle. There is also a sophisticated technocracy at the head of a few key economics ministries while other parts of the state are much less well regarded.

This pattern of a highly competent upper technocracy in the main economics ministries and a general morass elsewhere does produce severe problems. The idea that patronage systems privilege control over efficiency is basically correct, so long as it does not imply that state bureaucracy is all of a piece. The argument that the state bureaucracy in general performs inefficiently in a range of respects does seem to have confirmation from comparative studies. Thus, in 1996, Shahid Javed Burki and Sebastian Edwards, both senior officials in the World Bank, produced an individual viewpoint on development in Latin America. This was strongly critical of the effectiveness of the public administration in these countries (Burki and Edwards 1996). Among other things, these authors claimed that 'Latin American countries have neglected the social sectors' (p. 18). As a result, the amount of poverty in the region was 'staggering' and the degree of income inequality was among the worst in the world. One of the main explanations for this outcome was the poor quality of the state's provision of education services. In other words, by no means everything could be blamed on macro-economic difficulties. Latin America actually spent more on education than did East Asia – 3.7 per cent of GDP rather than 3.4 per cent. 'Yet the quality of Latin American education is one of the poorest in the world' (ibid., p. 19). Latin American students performed poorly in standardized tests, there was little actual instruction in classrooms as opposed to purely mechanical pedagogic exercises, and the quality of the teaching was poor. Teachers were insufficiently paid by the standards appropriate to serious professionals though not so badly paid that a teacher's position would be regarded as unattractive by a person who did not intend to turn up for work. The problem was that there was little relationship between pay and performance. A significant number of people paid as teachers moonlighted elsewhere and did not show up for work at all, and there was an excessive ratio of bureaucrats to teachers. The bureaucrats, though, achieved little in the way of enforcing educational quality. Meanwhile university education was heavily subsidised – considerably benefiting upper-middle-class young adults who had often been educated at private school.

As far as health is concerned, the authors' conclusion was rather the same. Latin American indices were slowly improving but more slowly than in other parts of the world. 'Today the delivery of health services is worse in Latin America and the Caribbean . . . than in regions at a comparable level of development' (Burki and Edwards 1996, p. 20). Just as was the case in education, this relatively poor performance could not be related to underspending. Latin America spent about 6 per cent of its GDP on health. There is no shortage of doctors or hospital beds. The problem was a lack of general sanitation, drinking water and preventative services. Too much investment was locked up in curative services aimed at the middle and upper-middle class.

Other IFI publications have looked at the performance of the Latin American public sector in the general areas of law enforcement, justice, police behaviour, etc. (Ayres 1998; see also Acha 2001). There is general consensus that poor performance is widespread. Corruption in the police is endemic. Even when not corrupt, the police do not generally know how to secure convictions by civilized means and resort to brutality in order to extract confessions. If prevented from doing this by human-rights laws, then they find it almost impossible to secure convictions at all. Suspects are either left alone or simply arrested and put in gaol on remand. The judicial system, even when not actually corrupt, is slow and inefficient (Prillaman 2000). Relatively few cases come to trial. The entire process hangs upon the decision of whether to grant bail when a case is being considered further. This is a process open to endless abuse. People from poor backgrounds suspected of petty crimes remain in prison for years because they cannot afford bail or bribes while the rich but guilty walk free. As a result of this, crime rates are higher across the region than they have ever been, while there has been an enormous but ineffective increase in imprisonment – not necessarily of the guilty.

The performance of the state in these sectors shows that the reasonably efficient pursuit of market reform has not been matched in other sectors of policy. IFI overviews of the progress of market reform during the 1990s are much more positive than those on administrative or social reform (Inter-American Development Bank 1997). There was quite an impressive litany of deregulations, privatizations, trade reforms and so forth. In a number of countries, notably Mexico, one could see a sharp contrast between some economic sectors of the state – which were impressively reformed – and the 'old corruption' that continued to be practised in those parts of the state that the reformers did not get around to reaching. Some reforms, moreover, actually made things worse because they did not pay sufficient attention to the problems of semi-patrimonialism. This is particularly true of decentralization, where functions were at times transferred from corrupt and inefficient central government to even more corrupt and inefficient local regimes.

This bifurcation of administrative behaviour between islands of efficiency and oceans of patrimonialism is not simply a continuation of authoritarian practices. It has also suited a broader set of elite interests. State bias permitted insider dealings of all kinds that helped economic elites to prosper during the transition to democracy and free-market economics and therefore helped secure elite acquiescence to such changes. This has enabled semi-authoritarian market reformers such as Fujimori and Salinas to strengthen some patrimonial aspects of the state while appearing to conduct reform, for example, via privatizations welcome to domestic elites and the international financial community.

State bias and democratic consolidation

We can now return to the broader political theme. On the face of it the power of an incumbent president to appoint large numbers of senior bureaucrats who can operate without much legal accountability should allow the executive to dominate the political process. However, this does not universally seem to be the case in practice. A patronage public sector has sometimes helped to strengthen executive power, but at other times it has not prevented pronounced executive weakness.

There seem to be three major reasons why state bias has not strengthened the political power of incumbents more than has actually been the case. One of them is that heads of government find it hard to motivate and mobilize the bureaucracy, except in rather limited areas of policy. Trade unionization, legally granted tenure and the absence of a meritocratic system of promotion can make for an impressive degree of bureaucratic inertia. Even in Mexico, whose presidency was until recently one of the most powerful on the globe, there was frequently expressed presidential frustration at the behaviour of the bureaucracy. There were also many administrative reforms, which scarcely achieved their effect (Torres Espinosa 1999). It is reasonable to suppose that elected heads of government in Latin America have not generally welcomed the kind of bureaucratic performance reviewed by Burki and Edwards (1996). It is likely that very poor performance by state agencies may be negative for the popularity of incumbent governments.

A second factor, which may now be in the process of changing, has been the general restrictiveness of rules governing presidential re-election. Until around 1990, most Latin American countries limited the right of incumbent re-election. However, within the last decade, constitutions have been changed to permit presidential re-election in Brazil, Peru, Venezuela and Argentina. Consecutive presidential re-election remains forbidden in Mexico, Chile, Uruguay and Bolivia. The reason why 'no re-election' provisions were originally introduced in the region was as part of a genuinely innovative attempt to come to terms, though in a second-best way, with state bias. If incumbents could not be re-elected, they would have no incentive to use the potential advantages of a biased state for their future political benefit. (The idea that they might use their advantages for financial benefit was taken for granted.) The result would be to reduce the extent of political boss rule.

Clearly presidents in the first term of what they hope will be a two-term incumbency (or the second term of three) have every incentive to use the state to facilitate re-election. By the same token, opponents of a government will be aware that the end of a term may not lead to the departure of the incumbent. They will therefore have more to lose from the success of any particular president and will have every incentive to resort to disruptive behaviour to undermine him. It may be that the decision of some countries to permit immediate presidential re-election will prove destabilizing through increased partisanship. This suspicion will be backed with some empirical evidence when we consider the cases of Venezuela and Peru in greater detail later in the work.

In policy terms there are advantages as well as disadvantages in permitting immediate presidential re-election. For many years, it was quite common for Mexico to suffer from severe economic difficulties in the final year of a presidential term due to the fact that many people close to the outgoing government would tend to loot the public treasury in preparation for political retirement. However, as a means of limiting the potential for ambitious presidents to destabilize precarious institutional systems, the 'no re-election' provision clearly worked well.

It is instructive that the provision proved so important in Mexico, where the Mexican PRI routinely manipulated state machinery in order to guarantee election victories, and where the outgoing president routinely chose his successor. The Mexican case suggests that there is no close substitute for a 'no re-election' provision. In Mexico, it was always possible for outgoing presidents to try to promote a favourite and thereby retain power indirectly. However, attempted manipulation of the system in this way did not generally work. In Mexico former presidents have not generally been as influential as at least some of them hoped and expected.

In other countries, the existence of strong party systems has often prevented outgoing presidents from choosing their successors. This was evidently the case for many years in Venezuela (Coppedge 1994). Where outgoing presidents do not choose their successors, the degree of pro-incumbency bias in the system is likely to be less. Sometimes factions and tendencies within political parties are on such bad terms that the incumbency effect can work in reverse. Argentina's Duhalde, who as Peronist candidate lost the 1999 presidential elections to the Radical Party candidate, complained publicly that outgoing President Menem – who was also a Peronist – engineered his defeat. Menem seems to have calculated that his own eventual return to power would be more likely if his own party lost the 1999 elections. In Peru in 1990, it seems as though the outgoing president, Alan García, backed the independent candidate Alberto Fujimori rather than the candidate of his own APRA party, though it is likely that this was due to his calculation that APRA could not win.

Patronage and fiscal control

The third major factor preventing state bias from leading to hyper-presidentialism has been the region's economic difficulties and the general change in the direction of economic policy since 1982. Although figures are not always reliable, it seems clear that the period from 1945 to 1982 saw a general increase in the number of state employees in Latin America as a whole. At times this increase was very rapid. In Argentina, for example, the number of employees in the central government bureaucracy increased from 394,000 in 1955 to 684,000 in 1976, while the number of public-enterprise workers increased from 148,000 to 431,000 (Williams 2001, p. 172). The incoming democratic government in 1983 was appalled by the size and complexity of the public administration that it had inherited (Ferraro 2002). In Bolivia the number of public sector workers increased from 66,000 to 170,000 between 1970 and 1978 (World Bank 2000c, p. 1) – mostly under the dictatorship of General Banzer. As these examples indicate, an expanding bureaucracy was no guarantee of either democracy or stable authoritarianism.

However, the adoption of economic stabilization policies has generally required either a reduction in the size of the state or at least a limit on its growth. These policies have made it harder to increase the efficiency of the public sector because fiscal adjustment reforms (i.e., mainly reducing the number and salaries of public-sector workers) can often conflict with 'good governance' reforms. For example, voluntary severance policies can be fiscally effective in the short term but very damaging to the performance of a public agency in the longer run. Economic stringency may thus have reduced long-term policy performance in the region and so made democratic consolidation more difficult.

Moreover the much harsher global economic climate post-1982 has reduced the political advantages from controlling a clientelist bureaucracy. Yet it has done nothing to make conflicts over public spending less partisan. Instead, heads of government tend to find themselves impaled on the horns of a serious dilemma. If they are serious about expenditure cuts, there will be resentment in the bureaucracy and also from disappointed aspirants for government favour. If they are insufficiently serious about fiscal stabilization, they risk severe macroeconomic problems. These will have a negative effect on presidential popularity.

One policy measure that seemed for a time as though it might somehow resolve this problem was radical privatization. This had the advantage of reducing the size of the state while also offering a windfall gain to privatizing governments. Even then the politics of privatization was not completely straightforward. It was often the case that unionized public-enterprise workers would look for political allies in order to block privatization processes (Murillo 2001). In Peru in June 2002 there were even some serious anti-privatization riots that led to the resignation of the finance minister. Nevertheless, broadly and in general, the privatizations that took place in Latin America, especially during 1990–95, did help some incumbent governments maintain popularity by offering them windfall gains that could be used on public projects. Yet this was essentially a limited process with a finite ending place.

Another possible answer to financial stringency was decentralization. However, the evident danger here is that the same problems of clientelist appointment at the top and rigid unionization lower down the scale would recur at local level. Moreover there was at times a 'moral hazard' problem, in the sense that local authorities could incur financial liabilities in the hope that central government would bail them out. Bailouts did not always happen, but problems with state and local government played a significant part in precipitating the Brazilian devaluation of 1999 and the Argentine default of 2001.

Direct reductions in the size of the central bureaucracy were politically painful. They were also difficult to achieve due to constant political pressures to do favours for client groups or political allies. Although presidents may appear to have had absolute powers of appointment, they were often the prisoners of others' expectations – at times, unreasonable ones. One reason for the collapse in political support for the party systems in both Venezuela and Peru is that party politicians could not so easily seek access to the government in order to do favours for their friends and thus shore up their political base.

A brief conclusion

Pluralist political scientists have routinely disdained 'winner takes all' politics. However, several Latin American countries have a kind of 'winner takes all' state. On the face of it, this should increase the power of the executive. The fear that over-powerful executives may be able to maintain themselves in power by the use of patronage is not altogether misplaced. There have been circumstances in which presidential power over appointment has proved a key political resource – notably in post-1982 Mexico. However, the more general point is that biased states have not necessarily led to stronger or more autonomous executives. This is partly because of an 'anticipated reactions' effect. Fear of endlessly re-elected presidents has been an important factor fuelling the intense partisanship in political life that was discussed in the last chapter.

Another factor that has worked against the concentration of power has been economic. Economic reform since 1982 has somewhat reduced the extent of mass clientelism in Latin America. Semi-patrimonialism may well have tended to strengthen authoritarian government in the days before capital mobility became so easy. However, it has not necessarily strengthened incumbents in democratic systems under globalized economic conditions. Democratic governments have very often found themselves pressed by international conditions to undertake popularity-reducing spending cuts instead. A related point has been that the poor policy performance of semi-patrimonial systems has impacted negatively on popular support for incumbent governments, as well as representative institutions.

Nevertheless democratically elected presidents have generally sought to retain patronage systems out of a (possibly misguided) belief that this was to their advantage. By doing so, they have worked against the achievement of one important criterion of democratic consolidation, namely the development of an impartial rule-based state bureaucracy.

4

Civilians, the Military and Democratic Transition in South America

No argument from path dependency can ever be absolute. It would be altogether excessive to claim that the whole of Latin America has always been governed by some kind of unchanging logic of power, explicable in terms of Catholicism, Iberian heritage, collectivist political culture or whatever. Nevertheless the partial nature of the democratic transition is undoubtedly a factor that helps us understand the difficulties facing any kind of institutional consolidation in Latin America. It helps in both South America and Mexico, though the two are not equivalent. The Mexican case is considered in a later chapter, while this chapter discusses mainly South America. Of the factors that have inhibited democratic consolidation in South America, one is the political role of the military. This is not solely because of its historical role – though this is a factor – but because it remains a focal point for partisan contestation. The military can be brought into political conflict even when their direct seizure of power is not on the agenda. To understand the potential political role of the military we do need some historical context.

The emergence of despotic power in South America

Nineteenth-century South America did not follow any single path. The semi-homogenization of South American politics is essentially a twentieth-century phenomenon brought about in large part by changes to the pattern of military organization. Nineteenth-century South American politics was a variable mixture of authoritarianism and anarchy, patrimonialism and law. Patrimonialism was probably the most important single basis of political organization, yet it was tempered by the existence of some kind of formal legal and political framework that sat alongside the politics of rebellion and despotism. Nineteenth-century South America did, though, develop a presidential system of government and a patrimonial system of state behaviour somewhat checked by administrative law.

The professionalization of the military in the early years of the twentieth century led to the concentration of what Mann (1986) has called 'despotic power' in the hands of the state. However, it also complicated civil–military relations to the extent that these became the key aspect of the political systems of most South American countries. Colombia excepted, every South American country experienced some kind of military takeover during the 1920s or 1930s, at least one military coup after 1945, at least a decade of military rule at some point between 1945 and 1983, and quite a lot of electoral politics as well. The dominant forms of rule were either elected government with the military in the wings or else military government with some eventual prospect of elections. Even Colombia experienced several years of military rule during the 1950s.

Before the military acquired effective command of a monopoly of force within particular South American countries, politics was much more uncertain and variable. At the risk of generalizing rather widely, coercive authority was precarious across Latin America during the nineteenth century. Revolts and political upheavals were frequent, and landlord power was the source of such political stability as there was. Local political practice was patrimonial, corruption was endemic, and financial misappropriation (followed by default) was a part of the system (Miller 1996). The main sources of social power were to a great extent private and based on control over land, physical force and (to an extent) spiritual authority.

The absence of a state monopoly of force was the result partly of economic weakness (armies have to be paid) and partly of the nature of military technology at that time. Individual caudillo figures could sometimes deploy lightly armed semi-civilians (generally agricultural workers on horseback) against the national state. The national budget was often inadequate to pay for a standing army of sufficient size and sophistication to defeat insurgents. Moreover state governors sometimes enjoyed financial resources of their own which could be used to mount military operations against the centre. Conflicts of this kind could be very bloody. For example, the Venezuelan Federal War of 1859–64 saw the deaths of some 40,000 men at a time when the regular army stood at 3500 (Dunkerley 1979). Even if they achieved success, caudillo governments could not necessarily find the money or the men to remain in power once they had seized the national capital. Sometimes they were themselves overthrown by insurgents. A famous example was the victory of Peruvian civilians led by Nicolas de Pierola in 1895. In 1911 revolutionaries also overthrew Mexico's Porfirio Díaz. However, it becomes much harder to find examples of insurgent military victories over an established state in South America after the outbreak of the First World War. (This statement does not apply to either Central America or the Caribbean.)

It is clear that there was a close relationship between precarious coercive authority and the entrenchment of patrimonial and lawless political practices. It is also clear that the precariousness of despotic power made it hard for countries in the region to create any developmentally effective state. Patrimonial practices were virtually inevitable. From around 1880 to around 1930 South American economic policies were generally laissez-faire but not liberal. Elites, generally landed elites, controlled the state and used its powers selectively. Even reformist elites did not behave in a very different way. Economic historians of the region mostly agree with Bulmer Thomas that 'the state has usually been relatively weak and little more than an expression of the class interests of the dominant groups' (Bulmer Thomas 1994, p. 426).

However, during the 1920s and 1930s the essential parameters of the political system of most South American countries changed. The claim here is that this period saw the development of civil–military systems that were effectively bounded but never fully institutionalized. There are significant parallels between this system and the pattern of non-consolidated democracy in South America since 1980 but also some differences. What has to be explained is how the post-1920 political systems worked in practice and what kind of legacy they handed over to post-1982 democracies.

The development of a civil–military system in South America

Once the military came to monopolize force, which was generally the case by 1920, the range of possible political changes in a society was reduced. Moreover, another possible catalyst for political upheaval, namely major war, was largely absent as well. With some significant exceptions, South America remained internationally peaceful. Political stability nevertheless required the military to remain united and disciplined. Even after 1920, a split in the military could make the state vulnerable to defeat by force – something that happened in Bolivia in 1952 and (in a different context) Spain in 1936. (South American elites closely followed political events in Spain and were influenced by them.) In South America, however, organizationally self-destructive forms of military indiscipline were rare. This allowed the army to intervene in politics while limiting the politicization of the army.

The development of increasingly bureaucratic military organizations that could successfully claim a monopoly of force did not immediately lead to military rule. During the 1890–1925 period, civilian rather than military rule was the norm across the region. There were elections and some degree of political pluralism, though this was mainly urban and middle class by nature, and suffrage was both restricted by law and limited by informalized kinds of illegality (Mouzelis 1986; Rueschemeyer et al. 1992). There was some limited development of electoral competition. Rueschemeyer and his colleagues characterize Uruguay as a democracy in the 1920s and the other countries of South America as either constitutional oligarchic or semi-authoritarian. In 1920 only Peru and Venezuela, of all the major South American countries, were ruled by the military, and Peru (though not Venezuela) had already had significant experience of elective government. However, by the end of 1930 Chile, Brazil, Argentina and Ecuador had joined Peru and Venezuela as military ruled societies. The military later intervened in Uruguay and Bolivia, though it extricated itself from power in Chile in 1932. Only in Colombia did civilians continue to dominate the political process throughout the 1930s.

While most readers of this work are likely to identify civilian rule and democratization with progress and military rule with the opposite, this was by no means the general view in the 1920s. For many intellectuals, influenced by the apparent success of authoritarian rule in Mediterranean Europe, military government was regarded as progressive. Military officers themselves considered the bureaucratic and to some extent meritocratic practices of their own organization (at least at officer level) as superior to the clientelist practices of civilians. Those officers who had originally begun their careers in newly professionalized military institutions were resentful at the clientelist way in which civilian presidents still sought to control promotions at the highest levels of the army. Tensions within the army sometimes brought the military into politics. The military was, indeed, the first politically significant institution in South America to reject a pattern of organization on clientelist principles.

The 1920s also witnessed some pressure to professionalize other aspects of the state even though progress was not enormous. The Kemerer mission to Latin America in the 1920s was associated with a policy of creating what might be called islands of efficiency – individual ministries run on more-or-less Weberian principles – within a state that was run more generally on patrimonial lines. A number of politically influential military officers also came to be influenced by ideas of national capitalism fomented by protectionism and public investment. These were not ideas with much appeal to the landlords who controlled the political process in rural areas. In some countries, notably Brazil, the military came to be associated with projects of national capitalist development that appealed to at least some intellectuals more than democracy did.

The military was also jealous of its professional reputation in the eyes of the public. This could be hurt if it was called in to break strikes or suppress anti-government demonstrations – as sometimes happened. In fact South American civilian elites in the early part of the twentieth century and earlier tended to be class conscious and racially prejudiced. As a result, electoral democracy came to be associated more with the rights of property and private influence and with suspicion of the state rather than with any strong commitment to universal rights or state impartiality. In common parlance, civilian conservative politicians were generally seen as 'oligarchic'. A common military reaction was to blame civilian oligarchies and the clientelistic states that they ran for any current discontents and problems. Military officers, and not only they, often saw military rule as an improvement.

The officer corps in most of South America gradually became a bureaucratic elite and not especially a fighting elite. Its political ascendancy generally reflected peacetime conditions. Where armed conflict did break out within the continent, there were internal political consequences. Only the Chaco War (1928–34) between Bolivia and Paraguay was fought with a sufficient intensity to change domestic politics radically. There was a revolution in Bolivia in 1952, while General Stroessner in the 1950s established a personal ascendancy over Paraguayan politics that lasted until the late 1980s. The Peruvian–Ecuadorian conflict of 1941 had rather fewer political consequences, and the major countries in South America avoided significant conflict with each other.

Patterns of authoritarian politics in South America after 1930

The development of a civil–military system of rule came about as the result of a pragmatic response to changing political circumstances. It created a way of conducting politics that greatly influenced the way in which most countries in the region would evolve politically up until the 1970s and even beyond. As with post-1980 non-consolidated democracy, the civil–military system was bounded but the boundaries were wide. As to proof of the effectiveness of boundaries, no South American country had a Communist revolution, as happened in Cuba, or major popular upheaval, as happened in Mexico and Nicaragua. No South American country saw a genuine Fascist takeover and only Bolivia and Paraguay fought a major war.

Extreme personalist dictatorship was also comparatively rare in South America. Paraguay's Stroessner and Venezuela's Gómez remained in power for decades, and Pinochet managed sixteen years in Chile. However, these were exceptions. Gómez came to power before the development of military professionalism in Venezuela, Stroessner's rise owed everything to political disarray at the end of the Chaco War, while Pinochet was not as autonomous of the rest of the military as his length of time in power might suggest.

What essentially prevented transformation into Communism, Fascism or extreme personalism was the fact that the officer corps was both willing and able to resist them. While it may seem strange to put personalism in the same category as Fascism and Communism, military officers generally had almost as much to fear from personalist dictatorship as civilians did even if the personalist was an officer. The way in which the Argentine military proved so determined to keep Perón out of power after 1955 can be explained only in terms of their dislike for his personal style of rule (Potash 1982; 1996). Many other aspirant personalists – such as Odría and Velasco in Peru, Pérez Jiménez in Venezuela, and Vargas in Brazil – were removed when enough military officers were convinced that they were outstaying their welcome (see Huntington 1968).

Some form of corporate military rule was acceptable to most of the military most of the time, but the majority of officers were also willing in principle to accept a restricted and limited form of democracy. As a result military rulers tended to alternate in power with civilians during the 1930–80 period. When it appeared as though democracy was in danger of being 'subverted' – as, for example, in Brazil in 1964 or Chile in 1973 – then the military would remove a democratically elected president and impose a dictatorship. Dictatorships, in turn, would eventually give way to civilian rule. However, the notion of alternation between dictatorship and democracy does not take in the entire picture. Just as there was alternation in power between civilian and military presidents, so there were also considerable civilian influences over military regimes and considerable military influence over elected governments. Most elected governments were very strongly aware of the possibility of a military veto that could be cast at virtually any time. Much the same was true of military regimes themselves, which fell from power when a strong enough coalition of military officers and civilians was able to bring about a change of government.

While this situation can be described as a system, it was clearly a system with wide boundaries. The rules pertaining to the survival or otherwise of particular governments were essentially informal and to some extent unpredictable. Military coups occurred when enough senior officers and civilian allies (the civilian aspect was important) decided that the current political situation was undesirable and that change was necessary. However, while coups often involved military officers who acted virtually as full-time politicians, it would be mistaken to suppose that civil–military relations were always hyper-politicized. The most active military politicians were not always the most successful. A coup could not succeed without a critical mass of supporters, who almost invariably needed to include non-activists. There were periods in the history of individual countries in which there was indeed intense political conflict. There were, though, quieter periods as well, and sometimes it looked as though democracies were consolidating or dictatorships deepening when nothing more was really involved than a temporary period of quiet.

Because the rules of the system were significantly informal, they could not be entirely predicted. It would be wrong to say that military coups would occur only when there was a genuine threat of civil conflict. Any such threat would surely bring in the military, but there were many coups that took place for barely consequential underlying reasons and merely reflected the balance of power between rival civil–military coalitions. Political life therefore necessarily involved a high degree of uncertainty.

Personal and political differences influenced the policy orientations of both civilian and military rulers – but only within limits. By far the most important limiting factor was a commitment to the organizational hierarchy of the military. This took a lot of ideology out of military-political behaviour. In retrospect some kinds of military politics in the 1930s could be seen as semi-Fascist, but the anti-oligarchic and anti-patrimonial motives of some military officers should not be ignored either. Some individual officers certainly had Fascist sympathies during the 1930s and even the early 1940s, but the officer corps as a whole was never willing to share power with blackshirted paramilitaries. In general, though, the military hierarchy became more conservative as time went on in reaction to threats from the civilian left. These included APRA-led violence in Peru and the 1933 sergeants' revolt and 1935 Communist revolts in Brazil. The latter events led to a tightening up of both military discipline and political control: the Brazilian Estado Novo was imposed in 1937. The basic point here was the integrity of the command structure. Any form of civilian radicalism that threatened to undermine military discipline was utterly unacceptable to any high command. Popular mobilization that the military could control was indeed acceptable – but any such movement could never be very popular or very mobilizing. Anything that threatened senior officers' control over the military institution was a direct threat to the state and could not be tolerated.

Military professionalism continued to develop after 1945, with staff college professionalism playing a significant part in the politics of military government in Brazil and Peru in the 1960s (Stepan 1971). The main effect of this was to make the military high command more collegial and harder for a single individual to dominate. Broadly speaking, the more experience of military government a South American country had endured, the keener the officer corps was to keep the military president of the day under control. Military presidents were not autonomous of the opinions of senior military officers. They could themselves be deposed by other military officers and often were. When General Onganía, the president of Argentina from 1966 to 1970, removed an army commander, the dismissed man complained bitterly that 'Onganía adopted a *Franquista* model in his treatment of civilians, but he behaved like a president of Switzerland in his treatment of the military' (quoted in Lanusse 1977). Two years later, Onganía was removed by his fellow officers.

In order for a military president to command the obedience of other senior officers he had either to be popular with the general public or find a persuasive alternative way of establishing his rule. For this reason, most military governments in the region sought to find ways by which they could credibly demonstrate their popularity or, at least, acceptability to the general public. Paradoxical though it may seem, popularity with civilians was a possible resource that military officers could use in intra-military political competition, though the value of this resource could prove extremely variable.

Chile's Pinochet was more of a sultanistic figure than many other military presidents (Remmer 1989), but Chile before 1973 had far less experience of military rule than Argentina, Brazil or Peru. Even in the case of Chile, Pinochet was forced to promulgate a constitution and call a series of plebiscites. When he lost one of these, in 1988, the military leadership publicly accepted defeat on Pinochet's behalf while he himself was still considering whether it would be possible to ignore the adverse result (Angell and Pollack 1990). In most cases military rulers sought some form of backing either from direct manifestations of popular support, or from plebiscites or some continuing system of elections, or from putting a fixed-term limit on the time that they intended to stay in power.

The Brazilian military (1964–85) allowed congress to remain open and permitted regular, if supervised, elections. They also allowed direct election for municipal government and, after 1982, state government. When these seemingly tame politicians finally decided that they wanted the military regime to end, then it did. The post-1973 Uruguayan military government sought to legitimize itself by plebiscite in 1981, but lost the vote. In Peru General Benavides (after 1933) and General Odría (after 1948) converted themselves into fixed-term presidents, in one case by running unopposed for the presidency and in the other by ignoring unfavourable election results. In both cases they gave up power at the end of a (lengthy) term in office. Most famously of all, Juan Perón resigned from the military and successfully ran for presidential office as a civilian. There is therefore plenty of historical precedent in South America for authoritarian rulers to seek popular support after having seized power, and sometimes to have done so successfully.

At a wider societal level it is clear that a political system bounded at the extreme but informal and unpredictable in its day-to-day aspects was acceptable to the region's elites, such as large landholders and the traditional church. There were also business supporters of authoritarianism, and at times even middle-class supporters as well (for the best political sociology of South American authoritarianism, see Rueschemeyer et al. 1992). It is also clear that authoritarianism was seen internationally as an acceptable form of government. However, the development of 'staff college' professionalism within the military and the growing political sophistication and militancy of some aspects of civil society tended to reduce the flexibility of military rule in the 1960s and 1970s (Stepan 1971). Military governments seized power and behaved in ways that were unexpected and unheard-of in terms of their durability, harshness and unwillingness to respect previous limits. Chile's Pinochet imposed a harsh form of neo-liberalism. The 1976–83 Argentine junta waged a 'dirty war' against its own citizens and then in 1982 invaded the Falkland Islands. Peru's General Velasco moved in a different direction, and decreed large-scale expropriations of land and other privately owned property. Many influential civilians who would once have endorsed military governments fairly uncritically became alarmed by these unexpected developments and withdrew support from the concept of military rule. However, this was a gradual process, and the majority of the region's military governments still had some civilian support even at the very end.

Semi-democracy within the civil–military system

While South America's civil–military system certainly involved a lot of military government, it also included something that looked somewhat like democracy but was certainly not consolidated democracy. One key obstacle to the consolidation of such democratic processes as there were can be summed up in a phrase: Jose Luis de Imaz declared that civilian politicians always tended to 'knock on the doors of the barracks' when disappointed by trends in civilian politics (Imaz 1964). If one looks at the entire history of military intervention in South America between 1925 and 1976 it is impossible to find a successful coup that did not enjoy influential civilian support. In some countries, the senior ranks of the military and the leading party politicians seemed to be almost permanently engaged in a game of conspiracy and counter-conspiracy. At times, as for example when the inoffensive if ineffectual Argentine civilian Arturo Illia was overthrown by the military in 1966, almost the only person in the country unaware of what was being planned was the president himself (Potash 1996).

Democratic politicians who were vulnerable to overthrow by the military could not easily apply formal and impartial rules to the political system or the administrative process. Geddes (1994) has found a clear relationship between the insecurity of the incumbent government and the degree of partisanship in administrative appointments. It is therefore not surprising that civilian governments tended to operate administrative systems that were significantly based on patrimonialism and political partisanship. Nor could they attempt any ambitious programme of reform without taking the risk that the enemies of reform would combine with political malcontents and ambitious military officers to overthrow the system. Civilian governments were typically in office but not really in power.

The administrative process, meanwhile, remained dependent on the political process and the government of the day. It could not be subject to law because there was no fully established constitutional authority that could be the ultimate source of law. A judge could not defy a general with any hope of ultimate success, and it was generals who mostly arbitrated the political process even when elected civilians formally ruled. Civilian rulers were constantly required to seek approval, or at least acceptance, from those who did not share their most basic political principles. Otherwise there was danger that opponents of the government could take to the streets in the hope of bringing in the military. In such a context, authority came first, popularity second and constitutional forms of politics a poor third. Neither civilian nor military leaders could expect to survive a period of sustained or severe unpopularity, or a period of violent upheaval. This made state-strengthening reforms very difficult to achieve. It also made it very hard for governments, whether civil or military, to undertake development policies without being subject at all times to informal vetoes from such interests as were affected. Again, the military was the final arbiter.

The political instability generated by this kind of system was a theme that much preoccupied political scientists writing during the 1960s. Then, too, there was a considerable academic discussion of how far and to what extent rules actually governed political activity. Several authors focused on the lack of political force behind notions of rules, laws and procedures in South America – or indeed any accepted restraints on power. Yet this absence of restraint did not (at the time) seem to lead to the totalitarian or extreme authoritarian forms of rule that might have been expected to emerge from an institutional vacuum. This led some observers to suggest that there were implicit (unwritten) rules governing the use of power which were more important than formal, constitutional, rules (Anderson 1967).

Impunidad – in other words, the non-investigation of abuses that occurred under authoritarian regimes – became a structural necessity in this kind of system, or else the military would simply have refused to co-operate with civilians. Observance of the law therefore became subordinated to a kind of 'separate spheres' arrangement. The military might discipline their own, but they would not allow civilians to do so. The ever-present threat of renewed intervention provided a real deterrent to genuine political accountability. Nor could the military regimes themselves impose, create or develop an alternative form of institutional rule due to the essentially provisional nature of military regimes themselves.

The civil–military system and the semi-patrimonial state

Despite the informalities and uncertainties of their political systems, many South American countries did see some significant increases in the sophistication of the state after the 1920s. This change was very largely bound up with changes in the direction of national economic policy. Latin America's laissez-faire orientation was not abandoned immediately when the Depression came. However, while allowing for exceptions, it is generally clear that from the late 1930s the intellectual climate in the region started to change. Progressive-minded intellectuals started to advocate industrialization fomented by the state. There remained a few genuine intellectual or political liberals but not many. Liberalism increasingly came to be seen in the regional context as a socially reactionary 'oligarchic' doctrine that reflected the interest of landed interests rather than offering a genuine philosophy of life or strategy of development. At the worst, economic liberals came to be seen as *entreguistas* – people of doubtful patriotism whose main aim was to make money out of selling cheap raw materials to the industrializing countries of Europe and the USA. For this reason, after around 1940 very few elected governments identified themselves with genuine laissez-faire policies. Even many of the region's military dictatorships – notably those of post-1964 Brazil and post-1968 Peru – pursued a state-interventionist and pro-industrial policy. Mexico, although politically different in that it was not ruled by the military, also adopted a policy of state-sponsored industrialization.

There was therefore a significant change in the character of the state after around 1945. Many countries of the region – though to varying degrees – started to build up a class of state technocrats associated with industrial development. The process was probably most significant in the case of Brazil, though Mexico (with its different political system) followed close behind. However, this process did not lead to any fundamental reform of the existing state but to an accretion of state roles and functions. New spaces were indeed created for technocrats whose mode of operation was more professional and less patrimonialist than the old-guard politicians. Technocrats did play a key part in many economic agencies in the region after 1945. There were a very significant number of political appointees as well. However, the political appointees tended to co-exist with technocrats who were appointed to run particular agencies such as the central bank and (mostly) state development banks. Technocrats were also actively engaged in managing state enterprises. These technocrats negotiated with both foreign and domestic capital, tending to build up 'developmentalist' coalitions that helped promote industrial development (Evans 1979). The state in many South American countries therefore became at least somewhat technocratic without becoming fully formalized.

However, while the military continued to operate as a bureaucratic hierarchy in itself, military rulers generally did little to bureaucratize the public administration. They tended either to put military officers in charge of the key state agencies or to ally themselves with politicians and to run the public administration 'politically' – that is to say, along time-honoured patrimonial principles. A stable public administrative system can certainly survive alongside an unstable political system (France in the 1950s would be an example), but only if the former has first been created. As we saw in the previous chapter, this was not the case in Latin America.

It is interesting that where stable authoritarianism did develop for a significant period, autonomous development strategies were perhaps more likely to be attempted. The clearest examples are Brazil from 1964 to around 1982 and Chile under Pinochet from 1973 to 1989. The developmental benefits of the Brazilian strategy of 'triple alliance' state capitalism – featuring state capital, private capital and foreign capital – were subsequently lost as state autonomy weakened during democratization (Hagopian 1996). It was also unfortunate for Brazil that there was, from the mid-1980s, a general loss of confidence in the state-led pattern of industrial development without any real commitment to an alternative market-reforming strategy.

The Pinochet regime in Chile was authoritarian liberal, but there can be no doubt that it did pursue a coherent strategy. When it reversed that country's previous protectionist and state interventionist model (a model that had long preceded Allende), most observers attributed this to social reaction rather than economic vision. Previous attempts in Latin America to reverse the pattern of protectionist national capitalism – for example, by Onganía in Argentina and Castelo Branco in Brazil – had been brief, economically inconclusive and politically unsustainable. The neo-liberal Chilean model, too, started badly at first – Chile suffered at least as much from the 1982 recession as other countries in the region – but Chile started to outperform the other countries in the region from the mid-1980s. Without the class polarization of the 1970–73 period, even an authoritarian regime in Chile might well have lacked the political autonomy necessary to carry out the intense economic adjustments after 1973 or to sustain a radically deflationary line of economic policy after 1981. By the time that the Pinochet government eventually fell, the original economic model became a positive resource for the reconstructed democracy. It was quite late in the day before the Chilean left or even moderate left became persuaded of the merits of maintaining a free-market economic policy. However, the achievements of the Pinochet dictatorship in maintaining fiscal orthodoxy were largely maintained under the slow and initially limited transformation to democracy in that country.

A third military regime that could be regarded as aggressively developmentalist rather than simply system-maintaining was that of Velasco in Peru. This, too, was regarded by most observers as unusually autonomous, although this was often explained in terms of the decline in the power of the landed elite and a temporary weakening of US economic hegemony rather than the strength of the Peruvian state (Stepan 1977; Gilbert 1977). Unfortunately Velasco's state-led development strategy led quickly to deficits and debts and had eventually to be abandoned under pressure from the IMF.

Transitions, pacts and democratization

Military rule tended to transform itself in a harsher, more authoritarian way from around the late 1960s. This harsher pattern of politics alienated some civilian conservatives who were once willing to accept a moderate form of authoritarianism and may indeed have welcomed one. When the Brazilian military introduced press censorship in 1972, the head of the powerful Mesquita family, the owners of the *O Estado de São Paulo*, sent a telegram to the justice minister congratulating him on turning Brazil into a banana republic. This unease did not usually have much immediate effect on military rule, but it did make it less likely that the military would quickly be invited back into government once they had finally been persuaded to return to barracks.

There was a much more significant change after the military seizure of power in Bolivia in 1980 and the Argentine invasion of the Falklands in 1982. Following on from the already described tendency to greater political harshness, there was now an even stronger sense on the part of at least some people who might once have accepted military intervention that the military had broken out of the previously accepted informal limits. The Bolivian case involved a close political alliance between military officers and drug traffickers, an alliance that triggered a powerful negative US response. The Argentine government broke an international taboo and faced both isolation from its former allies and hostile military action from Britain. In both cases the military regimes fell, but both cases (particularly that of Argentina) suggested to many people that military rule was ceasing to be part of a long-established pattern of politics and was instead becoming unpredictably dictatorial.

The debt crisis then broke in 1982. This damaged the economic reputations of the authoritarians who still ruled in South America, their popularity and eventually their external autonomy, since there started an endless set of debt renegotiations in which the international community could indicate a preference for democracy. The US government position towards democratization changed after 1982, partly because of the Falklands War. Until then there were those in Washington who believed that the cause of anti-Communism justified some US support for friendly authoritarian governments. However, changes in the patterns of international politics then shifted Washington's position towards democracy.

Democratic transition across the region took place only gradually. Around twelve years separated the Ecuadorian transition from the one in Mexico. This gradualism had several consequences. One is that the early transitions could not necessarily be considered definitive. The previous pattern of civil–military government had featured many cases in which the military called elections and returned to barracks: not everybody expected them to stay there when they did so. Not many Ecuadorians and Peruvians believed that they had seen the back of military rule permanently at the beginning of the 1980s, and significant numbers of Brazilians and Argentineans also half-expected the return of the military. Some of them still do. If democratic transition is to be considered a cognitive process (involving a genuine belief that the military will not return to government) then it is enormously helped if there is a single, dramatic act of change. In South America, however, the early processes of democratization could not easily be distinguished from politics as usual.

Moreover, the majority of transitions from military to civilian rule also involved some pact-making between civilians and the military or, at the very least, a military input into the transition process (Schmitter et al. 1986). The essential logic here is that successful transition required the defeat of military hard-liners who were content with the idea of permanent military rule. The hard-liners could only be defeated by military soft-liners. However, the military soft-liners could only hope to prevail if their opinions were acceptable to the majority of senior officers. They would not be able to 'sell' ideas that the military as a whole would not accept. For example, a major movement in Brazil in the early 1980s in favour of direct presidential elections (rather than indirect elections that the military could dominate) was simply ignored and defeated. The pacted nature of the transition meant that the retreating military were able to demand concessions in return for abandoning power, thereby making it even less clear that the earlier civil–military pattern of politics had been transformed for all time.

As a result, democratic transition did not self-evidently involve a paradigm shift in the cognitive processes of those who had been active in politics previously. What tended to happen in some places was that actual or aspirant military dictators ran out of allies. However, whereas military populism was not invariably unpopular, the extreme repressiveness of military governments in the southern part of the region did cause a significant rejection of the concept of military rule among a broader public. Revelations of terrible human-rights abuses in some countries did indeed shock and revolt educated public opinion at any rate. There is therefore a significant difference between civilian orientations towards the military in those countries whose previous military regimes were not particularly violent (Peru, Ecuador, perhaps Venezuela) and those in which they were (Argentina, Uruguay, and Chile) (on Ecuador, see Fitch 2001). Later chapters on Peru and Venezuela are concerned with countries in which military-political activism was not necessarily unpopular as such.

In conclusion: democratic South America's institutional inheritance

This chapter has sought to add a historical and civil–military dimension to the discussion of post-1980 non-consolidated democracy. It is not equally relevant to all countries. Mexico did not experience military rule in the same way, while some South American countries experienced military rule in the 1970s in a manner that sharply reduced the chance of its returning within living memory.

In South America before 1982, democracy was not self-reinforcing but was bounded by the threat of military intervention. It could well be argued that this kind of bounding made democratic consolidation impossible because there would always be some politicians and military officers with an interest in defecting from the system and bringing it down. (This is precisely what most concerns us in respect of post-1982 democracy.) Rule-breaking was a potentially advantageous political strategy, almost a normal one at times. Admittedly coup attempts did not happen every year, and did not succeed even when they did take place, but the risk was always there. As a result, civilian governments either had to be extra cautious in order to avoid offending anybody or else they had to cultivate their own allies within the military. As we shall see in later chapters, this situation did not change in every country following the most recent wave of democratization.

It is also clear that there was no dramatic institutional rupture when democratization finally did occur. The military would not have allowed one and were generally able to exert at least minimal control over the process of transition. South American democracy was not put in place by the collapse of authoritarianism – not even in Argentina, where the military, though severely discredited, could not be described as completely out of the game in 1983. Any such rupture might have helped to consolidate democracy – we cannot be sure that it would have had this effect – but nothing of the kind took place. Haynes has recently argued that 'the consolidation of democracy requires a protection of elite interests, not their undermining' (Haynes 2001, p. 53). There are good reasons for this assertion. There are obvious dangers in creating an anti-democratic and alienated elite. However, there is a problem with pacted transitions as well. While elites may have adapted to the external appearances of democracy, they did not necessarily democratize in spirit. The adaptation was sometimes rather superficial, and traditional modes of wielding power continued much as before. The price of adopting democracy at all was the acceptance of a form of democratization that made subsequent democratic consolidation harder to achieve.

5

International Influences and Democratic Consolidation

We have now gone through our checklist of non-consolidated democracy in Latin America. The system is presidential but not securely based on any universally shared concept of how presidentialism should work. Institutional checks and balances tend to act as focal points for partisan conflicts rather than forums for disciplined conflict resolution. However, elections are routinely held and genuinely contested. Unpopularity and the fear of unpopularity are constraints on government both at the end of presidential terms and during the course of them. Limits on presidential re-election sometimes matter as well, though the role of re-election can be variable.

Some semi-autonomous organizations (such as but by no means only the military) often retain a significant rule-making autonomy and constrain governance. Pacted democratic transitions did not invariably rupture the pre-1982 tradition in South America in which civilian rule often involved the military and military rule often involved civilians. As a result of this and other continuities, organizational behaviour has often changed less as a result of democratization than might have been expected. Other legacies from the past include selective and partisan law enforcement and the existence of biased states based on patronage. However, frequently recurring economic difficulties and the discipline imposed by global financial markets can limit the political benefits derived from incumbency.

We now turn to potentially transformative influences, asking why these have not proved stronger and whether there is any prospect that they will exert greater influences in the future. This chapter examines first the way in which certain forms of institutional consolidation have taken place in other parts of the world and compares the Latin American experience. It then goes on to look very briefly at international political influences. The next chapter complements this discussion by considering mainly economic and global financial issues.

The rule of law and political institutionalization

If we start from the premise that law enforcement is weak and biased in Latin America and should be strong and impartial in consolidated democratic systems, then we have a destination but not a route map (Ciurlizza 2000). Democratization can be negotiated on the basis of shared interests. However, democratic consolidation requires the self-reinforcement of institutions, and this cannot be brought about through maximizing strategies alone. The essential difficulty is that there is a collective action problem. Consolidation requires that both public opinion and powerful political actors agree to be bound by rules, the operation of which is not necessarily in their own interest. In the World Bank's words, 'good governance requires the power to carry out policies and to develop institutions that may be unpopular among some – or even a majority – of the population' (2002, p. 99). Why should people who have enough power not to need to be bound in such a way agree to this? The social contract philosophers once sought to explain this in terms of mutual self-interest and negotiation. Yet this is not at all the way in which democratic institutionalization, when this has happened historically, has come about.

Zakaria (1997) has written a provocative and interesting piece on a closely related point. His work contrasts liberal with what he calls illiberal democracy. He does not define liberalism in terms of self-reinforcement, but one would expect to find that illiberal democracies were inevitably non-consolidated. It is hard to see how Zakaria's illiberal democracies could be institutionally self-reinforcing.

Zakaria asks how constitutional government came to be entrenched in some parts of the world though not, for the most part, in others. His approach is historical. If we define constitutionalism as the belief that political power ought to be effectively bounded by an independent interpretation of law, then it was invented within English politics in the seventeenth century. This is not the place to discuss whether English medieval constitutionalism (expressed in Magna Carta and the thirteenth-century parliament) was an authentic forerunner of seventeenth-century constitutional development or whether Athenian democracy ever had much to do with our present systems of government. What is clear is that there is no unbroken line of constitutional development in the Anglo-American world before the late seventeenth century. However, such a line can be traced clearly enough after 1689.

The English Bill of Rights of 1689 did significantly limit executive power. To that extent it was a constitutional document even though it did not directly question either the principle of monarchy or the supremacy of the crown in parliament. It did limit the royal preroga-tive. Arguably the jury system limits parliamentary sovereignty in the sense that a jury can make whatever decision it pleases even though a judge must do his or her best to interpret the law. The most progres-sive ideas in the Bill of Rights – the formal division of power and the direct subordination of the executive to the law – were further and unambiguously extended into a system of judicial review via the US constitution and the *Marshall* vs. *Marbury* case in 1801. The US consti-tutional settlement has endured as an institutional fact, whatever objec-tion philosophers might have had (and still have) to the doctrine of national rights upon which eighteenth-century liberalism was based. Mann refers to the invention of the supreme court as 'a stroke of genius' (Mann 1993, p. 156), and it certainly made a difference to the way in which the US political system worked.

Shortly afterwards most Latin American countries became indepen-dent of Spain or (in the case of Brazil) Portugal. The new republics all adopted presidential systems, in most cases with a bicameral congress, but they did not adopt the system of judicial review implicit in the US constitution. They mainly adopted the French legal system instead. In fact Latin American republics have generally acted on the basis that the law is the servant of the executive and not the other way around. As we saw in earlier chapters, this tradition has remained in place until the present day. Ciurlizza states that, 'in republics with highly presi-dentialist characteristics, the judiciaries are the "Cinderella" of the state' (Ciurlizza 2000, p. 218). He also quotes a World Bank poll carried out in 1996 which shows very little public esteem for the judiciary in any country in the region except Uruguay (ibid.).

Of course it would have been very difficult, perhaps impossible, for any Latin American republic to retain a tradition of independent law enforcement under the circumstances of the time. What is clear, though, is that the republics of Latin America did not establish judicial power in the same way that the American republic clearly did and the British constitutional monarchy did after a fashion. This difference is signifi-cant in that it shaped the entire character of subsequent democratiza-tion. Today the problem is less likely to be physical oppression of judges by the state (though even this is not unknown) than low budgets, little public esteem for the judiciary, the greater attractiveness of non-judicial careers and the risk of financially or politically motivated corruption.

If we are to regard path dependency as an important part of the explanation for the divergence of the two systems, then it is significant that the setting up of liberal institutions in England and, later, the United States followed periods of violent conflict. Reform was not accomplished purely by men of goodwill sitting around a table. An English king lost his head in 1649, another lost his throne in 1688 and the British lost their American colonies after 1776. There was also a civil war in the USA during 1861–5, prior to which the USA somehow combined some liberal institutions with slavery. Whatever the 'social contract' philosophers might have said, liberal institutions were the product of armed conflict. Conflict was not, of course, a sufficient condition. There was evidently an ideational relationship between British Enlightenment liberalism, religious conflict, doctrines of rights, and the protection of property and judicial autonomy. However, the path from the articulation of these ideas to their institutional embodiment passed through a period of warfare, the outcome to which was, without benefit of hindsight, very uncertain.

The British and American traditions were gradual in the sense that there was a logical progression of steps from despotism to liberal democracy. The USA accepted English constitutional freedoms, extended them via its war of independence, extended them further following the civil war, and then did so again via the progressive movements of the early twentieth century and the desegregationist and civil rights movements of the 1950s and 1960s. The British counterpart was the gradual extension of the vote in 1832, 1867, 1884 and 1918. This tradition is commonly counterposed to the French pattern of violent struggles between revolutionaries and reactionaries between 1789 and 1871 that also eventually culminated in the establishment of a form of parliamentary democracy. Nobody supposes the establishment of constitutional democracy in France to have been anything other than contested and violent, but the same is actually also true of Britain and the United States – at least until the second half of the nineteenth century. It is just that it happened in a series of steps.

A similar pattern of conflict, changing political ideas and the institutionalization of law enforcement can be seen in the intentional use of law to check executive power in Western Europe after 1945. Here, too, a complicated set of factors was involved in reform, but the military defeat of Fascism and the subsequent military occupation of Europe were absolutely necessary. The USA and Britain regarded the development of a strong and enforceable doctrine of rights in continental Europe, quite reasonably, as necessary to avert a renewed Fascist threat to European and world peace. (The British authorities were rather discomfited when, a generation later, the British state was itself subjected to an internationally interpreted doctrine of human rights.) The Allies also believed, again reasonably, that any restoration of majoritarian democracy in Europe without entrenched constitutional liberalism might not necessarily be robust against populist anti-democrats. The European Court can be seen as a part of a package, which included the formation of NATO and the European Union, deliberately designed to re-institutionalize Western European politics away from the failed post-1919 model of parliamentarianism within nation-states. One of the most powerful US 'proconsuls' in post-war Europe, John McCloy, defined his achievement thus: 'we made unthinkable another European civil war' (quoted in Brinkley 1998, p. 196). A crucial step in this policy was the express subordination of government to independently interpreted law. The Western European model, like the British/American and French models, was therefore one in which the establishment of an independent principle of individual rights followed a military outcome.

It therefore seems that one historically trodden path towards consolidation is now closed. Nobody is seriously suggesting that Latin America today needs a war or a civil war. In an earlier period, conflict helped the cause of reform by making demands for a return to the status quo ante essentially taboo. Any Englishman who advocated a return to absolute monarchy after 1688, any American who advocated a return to the British Empire after 1783, any German who advocated Nazism after 1945 was regarded as a potential traitor. It was not just a matter of battles and dates but of major change in the political culture brought on by violent and cataclysmic events. There is an obvious point of contrast between these changes and the pacted and gradualist pattern of democratization in most of Latin America since 1980.

Diffusing institutional development: Southern Europe and Latin America

The pattern of democratization and constitutionalism in Southern Europe is admittedly different. Here the transition to democracy did involve an incremental pattern from the mid-1970s onwards, and constitutionalism came on board as well. On the face of it, there is a possible comparison with Latin America. There had been violent conflicts in the past in both Latin America and Southern Europe, but this had not created either liberal or democratic governance. However (at the risk of generalizing rather sweepingly), conflict in the USA, Britain and France led mostly to the victory of the more progressive forces, while in Spain, Portugal and Latin America it led more frequently to the victory of social reaction. Iberian and Latin American liberals were not especially liberal. When the democratic transition in Southern Europe eventually prompted the establishment of a doctrine of rights and genuine institutional consolidation, this occurred via adaptation rather than conflict.

Unfortunately South America is not as well placed today to take advantage of potentially positive international influences as Southern Europe was after 1974 (Mexico may be another story). In Southern Europe, the influence of institutional transfer from the European Union was very significant. This is not at all to deny that democratization in Southern Europe occurred primarily because the people wanted it: this is true of Latin America as well. However, the subsequent consolidation of democratic institutions undoubtedly involved an international dimension. Membership of the European Union clearly influenced the way in which institutional procedures consolidated in Southern Europe by offering a mixture of incentives and constraints. This would not have worked if the will to consolidate institutions did not exist in the first place, but it helped overcome the collective action problem. Politically powerful business and other elites were given an incentive to subordinate themselves to the rules of the democratic process because they could hope for real advantages from accession to the European Union. On the other hand, the European rules that were applied to elites were applied to potential counter-elites also. This meant that elite groups still afraid of Communism could be offered some degree of security in return for giving up the advantages of arbitrary power. In addition, the countries of Southern Europe stood to receive large-scale financial help as well as trading advantages from accession to the EU. Their effect was to prevent the emergence in Southern Europe of the Latin American pattern of democratization without economic progress.

The transformation in Southern Europe was effective because it occurred across a broad front. Democratization meant far more than just the adoption of electoral practices. The political culture changed as well. The proof of this is that any Spaniard, Portuguese or Greek who called for the re-establishment of military rule plus withdrawal from the European Union would be seen as eccentric indeed. It is also a matter of note that the Spanish judiciary, which did not successfully prosecute a single Spaniard for abusing human rights under the Franco dictatorship, has been impressively active in the pursuit of General Pinochet and some other human-rights abusers in Latin America.

When we compare Iberian Europe and Latin America, we can see the difference made by governance reform in the first case but not the second. At the popular level, most Latin Americans undoubtedly believe that both corruption and the abuse of power are morally wrong. They also want better law enforcement. However, this does not necessarily mean that Latin American political systems are characterized by state impartiality and a genuine government of laws or that they are likely to become so by popular demand (Panizza and de Brito 1998). On the contrary, popular disapproval of corruption and law-breaking in Latin America is often tinged with fatalism, and so it reasonably might be given the difficulties of bringing about genuine institutional change to date. European electorates might respond with the same disaffection as Latin American ones do if they had to evaluate the same politicians, the same state failures and the same problem with the non-enforcement of law.

Good governance and institutional change

It would of course be an exaggeration to deny that international influences have played any part at all in shaping Latin American institutional development. It is evident that Latin American countries, like those of Southern Europe, operate within an international system – the nature of which is in constant flux and has changed considerably in the past twenty years. It is also true that Latin American governments are signatories to at least some international laws and conventions on rights. Officially virtually all democracies, including those in Latin America, accept that human rights should be protected (Robertson 1999). There is an inter-American system of human rights, based on the charter of the Organization of American States. The Inter-American Commission on Human Rights in 2000 reported very negatively on the situation of human rights in Peru (OAS 2000), a report that played its part in weakening Fujimori's political position. The arrest of General Pinochet in London in October 1998 was also a very significant development and shows a strengthening tendency in international human-rights law.

It is also the case that the IFIs, notably the World Bank and the IDB, have since the beginning of the 1990s accepted that they should be involved in institution-building (World Bank 1992; 1997; 2000a; 2002). There have been a considerable number of initiatives in this respect. However, there have been problems too. The World Bank itself has been ready to acknowledge that governance reforms are harder to achieve than reforms to macro-economic policy (World Bank 2000a).

In fact, as we shall see in the next chapter, economic stabilization has not been securely achieved in the region either, and failure to achieve this has made the task of institutional reformers even more difficult. It is clear that conflicts over priorities led to some sharp differences of viewpoint between the IMF and the World Bank and the IDB at the end of the 1990s. The cause of the tension is that (as we shall see in more detail in the next chapter) few Latin American countries have reliably achieved sustained macro-economic stability. There is little doubt that macro-economic difficulties can prejudice institutional reform efforts. A supporter of the IMF might point out as well that institutional reforms, if not carried out with complete financial discipline, could be risky from the macro-economic viewpoint. Attempts to gloss this conflict by making a conceptual distinction between 'first generation' reforms (primarily macro-economic) and 'second generation' reforms (primarily institutional) are not entirely satisfactory. Some so-called first generation reforms (such as privatization and enhanced tax collection) involve institutional prerequisites while, as noted, second generation reforms can be undermined if first generation targets of macro-economic stability are not achieved – as often they have not been.

Even apart from this macro-economic problem, there are real difficulties standing in the way of effective IFI-led governance reform. The scepticism voiced by IFI executives in respect of civil-service reform was noted in an earlier chapter. However, there have also been strategies of reforming the judiciary, decentralizing administration, reforming tax collection, regulatory reform and other things as well. There is not the space here for a detailed discussion of all major IFI attempts to reform governance. There are many World Bank documents available and their tone is admirably free of unjustified complacency (see, for example, World Bank 2000a, 2000b). However, it is worth just mentioning a few of the problems that they currently face.

To begin with, IFIs lend mainly to governments or to bodies that have to work with or retain good relationships with governments. If a government is not committed to a process of reform, because this would threaten its political interests, matters become very complicated indeed. The World Bank has suggested that civil society and the private sector can help to press individual governments for reforms, but this does not really offer much hope of overcoming the original collective action problem. In principle, IFIs can try to change the incentive structures facing governments but in practice this is a difficult thing to do constructively.

For example, an IFI could in principle refuse to lend to a particular government in protest against its policies. In fact the World Bank refused to finance a judicial reform project designed for Peru in 1995–6, leading to its cancellation in 1998. However, this is something that can only be done exceptionally. At least some IFIs (notably the IDB) really have to lend at any rate to the larger Latin American governments if they are to remain credible as operations. It often happens that IFIs, NGOs and national aid agencies compete to lend. If a borrowing country is solvent, then competition between potential lending agencies makes it easy for a government to borrow for a project that it sees as a political priority. This can mean that particular IFIs, in order to find borrowers, need the political support in borrowing countries of precisely those elite interests that would have most to lose from the imposition of effective governance reforms. According to personal information from a former World Bank official, the head of the Mexican Administrative Development Ministry (SECODAM) was reluctant to deal with the World Bank in the late 1990s because the latter had been critical of SECODAM's anti-corruption record in the past – as well it might have been. However, the British government did provide initial finance to help SECODAM with a consultancy project dealing with civil-service reform, though in the end no such reform occurred. It might seem absurd to lend money to a corrupt anti-corruption agency with the aim of reducing corruption, but such an agency could probably get the money if it wanted, provided that its national government was solvent.

Then there are prudential issues relating to any question to do with borrowing and lending at positive rates of interest. This is less of a problem in very poor countries because here loans are typically offered on very soft terms. Even here conditionalities do not always work as lenders would wish. However, there is much less leverage in the case of middle-income countries, including most of Latin America, because the development banks have to lend at rates of interest that are not far below market rates. For this reason, prudent borrower countries might be wary of committing loan funds to open-ended institutional reform projects whose immediate returns are not clear.

There are, of course, variations in the amount of leverage that different IFIs have. Broadly speaking, leverage comes from the ability to influence the short-term macro-economic prospects of a borrower government. Even here there are complex moral hazard and game theoretical implications. Nevertheless the IMF is in a better position than the international development banks to negotiate toughly because a government's failure to reach agreement with the IMF might well bring immediate pain. This is much less true of the development banks. Few people would sell Argentine pesos short as a consequence of the non-completion of a project to reform the civil service or the judiciary.

Finally the whole notion of lending money for institution-building is based on the assumption that either the lenders or the borrowers know what good government looks like. There is surely a sense in which they do. However, there is a sense in which good governance has to be based on a coherent philosophy of how institutions should work. More than one such philosophy is possible, and this is the problem. The idea of transferring an idea of 'good practice' across a range of countries tends to ignore the point that cultural factors matter. The World Bank is quite well aware of this difficulty (World Bank 2000a) and it does not cause insuperable difficulties for all forms of lending. A possible way of resolving it is to move from a strategy of 'best practice' to one of 'good fit' in which specific local conditions are taken into account when designing institutional changes. However, a 'good fit' concept would work best in a positive-sum world when political forces could work together to resolve problems in a non-partisan way. The problem with non-consolidated democracy is that it already tends to suffer from an excess of political partisanship. There is every likelihood that well-meant foreign involvement might under such circumstances trigger a hostile response from potential losers, who might wrap themselves in the national flag in order to express their opposition.

Finally first world politics can be an enemy to effective IFI activity in Latin America. There was a time in the early 1990s when it made sense to talk of a 'Washington consensus' because the vast majority of Latin American governments were market-reforming democracies. However, it is sometimes the case that official Washington would prefer not to have to deal with a particular government, or alternatively that it badly wants the government to triumph over a potential threat. This need not preclude institution-building under all circumstances, but it does complicate the task when there is an elected Latin American government at odds with the international consensus or when official Washington badly wants to work with a particular electoral candidate. It also complicates the task if there is a general withdrawal of interest in the task of reforming Latin American democratic institutions due to crises and conflicts in other parts of the world. Overall the 11 September 2001 attacks on New York and Washington seem to have diverted US and European attention away from Latin America.

There are a whole set of complex issues here that lie far beyond the scope of this discussion. This author's impression (it is no more than that) is that IFI thinking about the politics of development is becoming much more sophisticated, but that there remain complex political problems that make it hard for IFIs to act as effective agents of transformation. Nevertheless, if one considers the direction in which autonomous law enforcement has evolved in Latin America, then one cannot dismiss the importance of international influences entirely. The prosecution of military officers and others who were involved in human-rights abuses during previous periods of dictatorship has been a very limited affair, but before 1980 nothing of the kind happened in the region at all. There has been a considerable increase in judicial activism since the 1980s (Méndez 1997), and NGOs such as Amnesty International have become more influential. There have also been significant attempts by the IFIs to strengthen judicial autonomy and effectiveness in the region. While much of the work done has been essentially technocratic (Ciurlizza 2000), some of it has had genuine political impact. The creation of an ombudsman's office in Peru under Fujimori would be an example. This office put some real constraints on the Peruvian security forces and played a part in the dramatic events of 2000.

The international environment in the 1990s

The case studies considered in the second part of this work relate to a period in which international constraints on governance were relatively loose but global economic constraints much tighter. International incentive structures related much more to macro-economic than governance issues, and they mattered more to countries close to the United States (notably Mexico) than to more distant countries. The United States has been intimately financially involved with Mexico at least since 1982 (some authors would go back much further). Mexican economic and financial policies were deeply shaped by the 1982 bailout of Mexico, the 1986 Baker Plan, the 1999 Brady Plan, Mexico's entry into the NAFTA and the renewed bailout in 1995 that followed the 'tequila crisis'. There is no suggestion that the US government used any of these cases to seek openly to change the policy preferences of the Mexican governing elite. Market-oriented technocrats have run Mexico since late 1982 and were responsible for organizing the transition to democracy. However, given this underlying policy orientation, US policy (reflected to varying degrees in the policies of the IFIs) certainly changed the specific incentive structures facing the Mexican authorities. For example, Mexico had little chance of being able to join the NAFTA without credibly promising to democratize.

International influences were rather less in both Venezuela and Peru. However, in both cases a return to overt authoritarianism during the 1990s may well have been prevented by the anticipation of a US veto. It is in fact quite a strong conclusion (in the light of so much literature about democratic consolidation) that both the Venezuelan and the Peruvian militaries might possibly have imposed an overt form of non-democracy without a strong international veto. Evidence for this claim will be presented in the subsequent chapters. Yet there was not the same degree of direct international involvement in positively shaping institutions in either case.

If it is to be effective, international influence must remain clear and constant. The US and British role in appearing to support the failed Carmona coup attempt in Venezuela in April 2002 did not help the cause of consistency. Of course international politics varies unpredictably and it might be dangerous to assume that the US administration or the first world in general will remain steadfastly committed to the cause of democracy in all developing countries.

Another necessary condition for international influence to work well is that there should be no total crisis or breakdown in any domestic political system. As and when rioting on the street becomes a sufficient problem, the subtleties of international influence upon incentive structures are likely to be lost. International influence upon Southern Europe operated under general conditions of economic growth and rising prosperity. This has not generally been the case in Latin America, where a really disastrous development failure might bring about far more difficult political consequences than we have yet seen.

6

Democracy, Market Reform and Development Failure

Latin America's post-1982 development performance has not been impressive. Institutional problems are certainly a part and may be a large part of the explanation for this. The argument that institutional weaknesses (i.e., intense political conflict, inadequate law enforcement, patrimonialism) are likely to be bad for economic progress is in principle widely accepted (World Bank 1997; 2002). There is plenty of empirical evidence to substantiate this point. For example, the World Bank has shown that there is a clear statistical relationship between economic success and public confidence in the judiciary (World Bank 1997). Studies by Evans and Rauch (Evans and Rauch 1999; Rauch and Evans 2000) have also shown that states whose core economic agencies are run according to Weberian principles of bureaucratic rationality tend to achieve better economic results than those where this is not the case. Alesina et al. (1999) have suggested that countries with formal budgetary rules have more reliable fiscal outcomes than those where everything is left to the political process. Baldez and Carey (2001) concur. These conclusions seem statistically robust.

While democratization in the abstract should not be blamed for poor development performance in Latin America, non-consolidation clearly is a relevant factor. In the absence of institutional consolidation, not only has democratization failed to resolve some of the region's historically inherited problems, it may have introduced new sources of difficulty as well. Since there does seem to be a relationship between economic failure and democratic breakdown in non-first world countries (Przeworski et al. 1997), this is an evident concern. Furthermore, globalization may have made the effect of these inherited institutional weaknesses more damaging than they once were. It would be hard to claim that economic policy-making in at any rate the majority of Latin American countries is carried out less professionally today than in the

1960s, but the results are for the most part worse. It seems reasonable to blame this on adverse conditions, at least some of which are international in character.

Democracy and market reform in Latin America

Tables 6.1 and 6.2 sum up the region's recent economic history in slightly different ways. Table 6.1 covers the real 'Washington consensus' period during which democracy and market reform were the main norms in the region. Figures for GDP growth in the 1990s are not generally impressive when we remember that most countries in the

Table 6.1   Average annual GDP growth, per capita, 1990–2000

Country	GDP growth minus population growth
Chile	5.3
Costa Rica	3.4
Peru	3.0
Argentina	3.0
Uruguay	2.6
Bolivia	1.7
Mexico	1.5
Brazil	1.5
Colombia	1.1
Ecuador	−0.3
Paraguay	−0.4
Venezuela	−0.5

Source: World Bank, *World Development Report 2002*, 232–3, 236

Table 6.2   Percent GDP growth in selected Latin American countries, by period

	1900–29	1929–45	1945–72	1972–81	1981–96
Argentina	3.8	3.4	3.8	2.5	1.9
Brazil	4.2	4.4	6.9	6.6	2.4
Chile	2.9	3.0	4.1	3.6	5.4
Colombia	4.5	3.8	5.1	5.0	4.0
Ecuador	nd.	3.3	5.3	7.0	2.6
Mexico	3.4	4.2	6.5	5.5	1.5
Peru	4.5	2.8	5.3	3.4	0.4
Venezuela	5.0	4.2	5.7	4.7	2.2
All of Latin America	–	–	5.3	3.7	2.2

Source: Thorp (1998, p. 15)

region experienced negative per capita growth in the 1980s. A small number of countries did perform well in the 1990s, though of all the larger countries only Chile has done so in a sustained way. During the period 2000 to 2002 the region will have enjoyed little if any per capita growth due to the disaster in Argentina. Table 6.2 also shows that Latin American economies on the whole grew fairly rapidly during the 1945–81 period before slowing subsequently. Some allowance has to be made for the effect of the gradual decline in population growth, and there was also some tendency for economic growth to slow during the 1970s. Even so it would be hard, certainly in retrospect, to claim that the general rate of growth achieved in the region during 1945–81 was unsatisfactory.

Latin America went into severe economic crisis in 1982. The crisis followed a build up of heavy foreign debt during the 1970s and a series of events including Argentina's unsuccessful military adventure in the South Atlantic in April and the near default by Mexico in August. Capital flight, although not new in the region, reached historically unprecedented levels during 1980–82, and this seriously aggravated the crisis. In Mexico, Venezuela and Argentina the total value of capital exported by private Latin Americans may have equalled or even exceeded the public debt contracted by governments (Mahon 1996). Growing public indebtedness unintentionally subsidised capital flight. Unfortunately the 1982 crisis struck when several Latin American countries were at a sensitive stage of their process of democratization. It was therefore necessary for the region's democracies to manage some severe economic problems. On the whole, they did not do this successfully.

Explaining development failure is never straightforward, and this work is not primarily a discussion about economics. However, there is a reasonable consensus that the region's underlying situation can be characterized more or less as follows. To begin with, its savings ratio is not high. Gross internal savings across the region as a whole remained fairly stable during the 1990s, at between 21.7 and 20.3 per cent of GDP (Villareal and Villareal 2002). This is much lower than savings rates to be found in Asia. Investment as a proportion of GDP is essentially similar, and is not only well below the rate of the Asian 'Tigers' but also significantly below the level reached across the region before 1970 (Ocampo 1998). While savings and investment are in rough balance, the region's high level of debt and foreign direct investment ensure that there have to be considerable capital outflows. These therefore have to be covered by capital inflows. In order to comply with external commitments, and also to maintain an investment to GDP ratio that is more or less in line with the existing savings to GDP ratio, it is necessary for the region to continue to attract external savings amounting to around 3 per cent of GDP. Even if this could be done, the growth performance likely to result would probably not be remarkable.

It could well be argued that this is an inevitably precarious situation in view of the uncertainties inherent in the global economy. However, there is a specific domestic aspect as well. Latin American democratic institutions have not generally been geared to the requirements of a capital-importing region in a globalized world. There is nothing new about the region's tendency to import capital, but the institutional requirements of such a situation have changed since 1982, while the region's actual institutions have not generally changed as necessary. In some respects, though not all, democratization might actually have made things worse. There are all kinds of problem here – regulatory failure, unreliable law enforcement, poor fiscal control, the suspicion that domestic publics might be disinclined to support orthodox economics and, perhaps most of all, the intense partisanship of the electoral process.

These problems may well have been overlaid in the early 1990s by some positive 'good news' shocks. Washington's Brady initiative allowed significant debt reduction, and some countries then adopted aggressive privatization policies that attracted a lot of fresh capital into the region. However, the 1994–5 'tequila crisis' was a powerful shock in the other direction, and the negatives were reinforced when fresh crisis returned to the region following the Russian debt default of 1998 and the Argentine default of 2001.

This discussion rather abstracts from the inherent merits or otherwise of market reform itself because of its concern with institutions. Fundamental disagreements about development strategy raise very wide issues that cannot all be considered here, but it does seem hard to dispute that continuing institutional problems associated with non-consolidated democracy can undermine the value of market reforms. It has been authoritatively argued that market reforms such as deregulation and privatization might have been positive for growth (Inter-American Development Bank 1997). Certainly the success of the market-reformed Chilean economy is evident. Yet it is also obvious that market reform was not a sufficient condition for rapid economic progress in the region. One reason for this is that deregulations and privatizations have made demands on institutional structures that Latin America's semi-patrimonial bureaucracies were not always able to meet. Privatization plus poor regulation can be an even more damaging formula than inefficient state ownership. The classic example is Mexico, where the Salinas government earned some $12.9 billion by privatizing the banks while the successor Zedillo government had to spend $65 billion in rescuing the banking system from collapse. While problems in the Mexican banking system might well have been unavoidable in the light of the 1994–5 devaluation, it is clear that the privatization of the banks did not bring the developmental benefits hoped for.

The rest of this chapter seeks to discuss certain aspects of the relationship between democratization, democratic consolidation, globalization and Latin America's economic performance. This is a vast and complex field, and it is not possible to deal with every issue in detail. All that is attempted is substantiation of the claim that democratic non-consolidation has worked against the achievement in most Latin American countries of a satisfactory synthesis of democracy and effective economic policy.

Good governance and institutional reform

It is generally accepted that successful development requires an effective developmental state (Leftwich 2000). Developmental states do not have to be democratic, and they may be quite varied in terms of what they do and how they do it. However, it is hard to see any major contradiction between some of the requirements of developmental effectiveness and the main institutional aspects of democratic consolidation. Consensus on the role of the core executive, a genuinely autonomous legal system, and a state run in large part on Weberian criteria are all likely to be good economics as well as good politics. Moreover a culture of respect for law may achieve even more than narrowly defined law enforcement. The problem of law without cultural backing is that it tends to become over-restrictive and arbitrary. Public servants who are subject to a thousand and one restrictions in respect of legal observances are not likely to be as efficient as they might be. A culture of trust in which the force of law is used only exceptionally and as ultimate sanction will work very much better than a culture of total regulation.

A climate of law enforcement is also essential for complex systems of regulation that are necessary to control financial and other markets in an era of free-market economics. Here democratic non-consolidation can be a problem. If politics is corrupt and lawless, then why would one expect regulation to be honest and transparent? It is in fact likely that the superior economic performance of Chile and perhaps Uruguay has to do with the fact that these are countries where, according to common consent, the rule of law is more respected and more consistently applied than in some other countries in the region. Respect for law helps to reduce transaction costs. This has a virtuous circle effect because of the mutually reinforcing effect of economic success, democratic legitimation and further institutional development.

The idea that the non-consolidation of democracy rather than democratization itself has been economically damaging to some Latin American economies seems plausible. However, it does not explain why Latin America's economic performance has deteriorated since 1982. Here we probably do need to bring in the issue of globalization, but with an important nuance. From a functionalist perspective globalization 'required' certain institutional changes within the region, which mostly have not happened. The general pre-1982 pattern of authoritarian (or at least semi-authoritarian) politics and national capitalism would not have worked well subsequently because international conditions changed. Indeed it contributed significantly to the debt crisis of 1982. However, those changes that took place within the region in and after 1982 – the debt crisis, democratization and economic liberalization – did not involve institutional consolidation. This has proved damaging. The discussion briefly considers Chile as a case where some degree of institutional consolidation has actually occurred. Before doing this, however, we need to review the general picture.

Democratization and structural adjustment

The early 1980s saw a change in the dominant ideas of several first world countries, including the USA, in favour of free markets. There was a renewal of confidence in markets and market-oriented solutions to problems, and a loss of confidence in the role of government. This changing paradigm certainly influenced thinking about development. (On USAID, see Adams 2000, p. 90.) With respect to Latin America, this market-oriented perspective seemed to be confirmed by the 1982 debt crisis. This was blamed on too much industrial protection, the neglect of exports, bad public investments, and insufficient macro-economic control. These criticisms were by no means altogether unfounded.

This new market-oriented paradigm was, initially, not much concerned with politics. At the beginning, too, there was a tendency to regard the region's post-1982 problems as essentially temporary (involving liquidity rather than solvency) and capable of solution by orthodox stabilization measures. By this was usually meant simple economic stabilization and adjustment. While the arguments in favour of economic stabilization may have been obvious to most Washington-based economists, they were at first strongly contested in some of the region's largest new democracies (notably Brazil, Argentina and Peru) where governments preferred to try heterodox alternatives. In all of these cases, the democratic process was an important part of the explanation for governments' preference for heterodox over orthodox policies. In Mexico and Chile, where the governments remained authoritarian, orthodox policy proved intensely controversial domestically and might not have been enforceable under more democratic conditions. Unfortunately, for reasons too complex to explain here, most heterodox policy initiatives adopted by the region's democracies failed. They led to economic decline and very high rates of inflation. Once hyperinflation developed, orthodox remedies were much more widely accepted.

Of all the countries that underwent some major adjustment programme only Chile, the most authoritarian of all the major capitalist Latin American countries at that time, achieved significant economic recovery during the 1980s. Even Mexico, the other country where policy was orthodox and government authoritarian, continued to face severe economic problems during the rest of the decade. Colombia, whose more conservative borrowing strategy made its debt problems less severe at the outset, was the only country other than Chile to achieve positive per capita growth in the 1980s. If one were to consider only the relationship in the 1980s between democracy and successful economic stabilization policies, one would have to come to the conclusion that this was negative. While it is certainly true that it was mainly (not entirely) authoritarian governments that built up the region's debt in the first place, democratization as such was evidently not a sufficient solution to the resulting problem.

From structural adjustment to Washington consensus

The initial emphasis on stabilization and adjustment therefore evolved at the end of the 1980s into something more complex. By the beginning of 1989 the US government had become persuaded that it should take an active role in helping Latin America overcome its economic crisis. Under the 1989 Brady plan, limited debt write-offs were allowed on the understanding that the governments taking advantage of the plan went further down the road of free-market economics. There developed what became known as the Washington consensus (Williamson 1990). This consensus was firmly in favour of free markets but advocated fundamental 'structural reform' (freer trade, privatization, etc.) and not just economic stabilization. 'Washington consensus' values also gave the World Bank, the Inter-American Development Bank and to some extent the IMF an extended role in providing 'conditionalities' and pressing for policy change.

The political model of the Washington consensus was more interventionist than that of the 1980s stabilization orthodoxy. Washington was willing to use its influence to help Latin America recover. Democratization of some kind was seen as a prerequisite for being allowed to participate fully in the global financial environment. Before 1982 it is not at all clear that US policy in the region generally favoured democracy – there were some notorious incidents where the reverse was the case. However, the decline in Cold War politics gradually allowed the USA to distance itself from authoritarian but anti-Communist governments or (for example, in the case of Mexico) to press for change. In the early 1990s world of Brady plans, conditionalities and political risk assessments it was clear that the form of government adopted in a Latin American country would influence the way in which it was viewed internationally, and this, in turn, would influence its cost of capital. As a result, business interests that in the past might have responded to social or economic crisis by indicating a preference for authoritarianism now had no real choice but to accept some democratic principles.

The expectation that only democratic Latin American countries would participate in the new international financial order admitted of many compromises. Salinas was allowed to take Mexico into the NAFTA, while Fujimori found his policy of reintegrating Peru into the international financial community only temporarily upset by his closing of congress in April 1992. Indeed, the issues of development and/or economic management and the question of democratization were generally considered apart from each other. For example, Edwards (1995), in a work published under the auspices of the World Bank, praised the economic policies conducted by Pinochet's Chile and was silent about its politics. Latin American countries were expected to be both market-oriented and democratic, but the two were not seen as being intimately connected. Democratization was seen fundamentally as a moral prerequisite, not as a source of efficiency as such. Efficiency gains would come from the market reforms themselves.

During the 1990–95 period, 'Washington consensus' policies were on the agenda in most Latin American countries. There was far less policy variation in the region (Cuba of course excepted) than there had been in the period 1930 to 1990 – during which time there was generally at least one government to be found going in quite a different way from any general policy orthodoxy. From 1990 to 1995 there were significant trade reforms, deregulations and privatizations. The adoption of such measures coincided with some improvement in the region's growth performance and some economic optimism. It was authoritatively claimed that market-oriented reforms would help achieve resumption in growth (Inter-American Development Bank 1997). The most aggressive privatizing and liberalizing governments did indeed temporarily achieve some quite positive economic results.

Unfortunately, though, this period of economic improvement and the optimism that it produced did not last. The so-called tequila crisis which hit Mexico in 1994–5 made it clear that macro-economic stability, which was once seen as the essential prerequisite for further reform, had not been definitively achieved. The 'Asian flu' crisis of 1997 and Russian debt default of 1998 brought with them further macro-economic destabilization. Brazil devalued in January 1999. In 1999 Latin America went back into recession – if we define recession as a year-long period of negative per capita growth. The hoped-for recovery in 2000–01 was aborted by new financial worries associated with a slow-down in the USA, and in late 2001 a new crisis developed in Argentina and culminated in a disastrous default. So what went wrong?

Macro-economic stability and its problems

It does seem clear that macro-economic stability was never truly achieved on a sustained basis across the region as a whole. There have of course been some genuine achievements, but it is not at all the case that Latin America as a whole had achieved so-called first generation reforms (mainly macro-economic adjustments) and could safely move to 'second generation' reforms (mainly institutional reform). Given the enormous amount of policy effort that has gone into fiscal stabilization since the 1980s, this conclusion has to be regarded as an unpleasant surprise. The debt crisis was widely regarded as having been solved by 1990 through a mixture of debt buybacks on the secondary market at a large discount, and the agreed rescheduling and partial forgiveness of the 1989 Brady Plan. The perception that the debt crisis was largely over by 1990 was entirely understandable. While in 1982 the region suffered from excessive indebtedness according to almost any reasonable standard, this was less obviously the case in 1990 or even 2000. Yet debt and deficits are still an important part of the problem.

One thing that seems to have happened, at any rate since the 1994–5 'tequila crisis' in Mexico, is that global financial markets have become much less tolerant of any kind of macro-economic weakness and have

Table 6.3 Public-sector debt as a percentage of GDP in 1999, selected countries

Country	%
Mexico	22.4
Chile	36.1
Venezuela	37.5
Colombia	39.7
Poland	42.9
Peru	45.8[a]
Argentina	50.8
Ukraine	53.0
Turkey	57.7
South Africa	57.9
Brazil	75.2
Panama	80.1
Russia	114.4
Ecuador	129.0

[a] A comparatively high proportion of Peruvian debt, 18 per cent according to Fitch/Ibca (1999), was contracted via the IFIs at concessional rates due to that country's low per capita GDP.

Source: Goldman Sachs, quoted in the *Financial Times*, 26 April 2001

sometimes reacted to exaggerated fears. Gavin and Hausmann (1998, p. 35) refer to the 'in many ways less forgiving context' in which Latin American countries are judged *vis-à-vis* their first world counterparts. Alarm bells start to ring at a much lower degree of debt than might be supposed. Table 6.3 indicates that there was in early 2001 a problem with public-sector debt in some Latin American countries, but the story of over-indebtedness does not hold up across the region as a whole. Nor is there as much correlation as one might have supposed between the absolute level of debt and market confidence in the debtor country. It is true that Chile and Mexico had relatively low debts and relatively low interest rates and that Ecuador had already defaulted on very high levels of debt. However, Venezuela, Colombia, Peru and Argentina had levels of debt that were not so very different from that of Poland – and yet (as table 6.4 below shows) these levels had to be serviced at much higher rates of interest. Argentina in late 2001 defaulted on levels of debt that were not, on the face of it, excessively high. In 2000 there were first world members of the European Union whose level of public debt was higher than that in most Latin American countries.

Why should the financial markets seem so intolerant of what did not appear to be obviously excessive levels of debt? To discuss this, we need to look at a range of factors. One of these is that Latin American economies have suffered from an over-dependence on commodity exports. The problem is not simply that commodity exports are apt to fluctuate sharply and may indeed tend downwards in the long run. They also introduce policy problems via the way in which resources are typically allocated within commodity exporting countries. One possibility is that they may acquire high real exchange rates inhibiting the growth of other exports (the so-called Dutch disease problem), plus an unhelpful cultural belief that the country concerned is naturally lucky and wealthy, plus a low tax base except for commodity taxation (Karl 1997). Above all, there may be a tendency for electorates to set their expectations high, for candidates for office to promise much and for governments to aspire to use the state to spread the benefits from commodity wealth. This is particularly a problem when the price of the commodity is booming. 'Our problem is to learn to manage abundance', said Mexican President López Portillo in 1981. 'We must sow the oil', said the Venezuelan economist Uslar Pietri in the 1940s. In Argentina the success of Peronism in the 1940s relied on much the same mentality – 'take advantage of good times and redistribute.'

It is self-evident that people who do think in this way are setting themselves up for subsequent disappointment. That certainly can be a problem for the politics of economic adjustment. It is also the case that the combination of remembered abundance and an unsound but popular pattern of resource allocation can be hard to change when times turn bad. Economic reforms that are inevitably seen (with some reason) as damaging to living standards in the short run are likely to be strongly resisted. People defying a fall in the income to which they have become accustomed are particularly likely to organize and mobilize. Even without much access to organization, discontented people can treat bad economic news – such as the announcement of an increase in public-sector prices – as a focal point for anti-government demonstrations. A classic example of this was the Caracas rioting of February 1989. O'Donnell once called this phenomenon in Argentina a 'defensive alliance' (O'Donnell 1988). Democratic patterns of politics may allow such alliances either to block macro-economic stabilization policies or to reduce the benefit from them by creating political instability and thus raising the prospect that hard-won macro-economic stability might be unsustainable. Such prospects are obviously bad for investor confidence.

Market-oriented reforms were supposed to reduce some of these problems by encouraging export diversification. To some extent, they worked. According to IDB figures, Latin American exports doubled during the 1990s – from $142 billion to $299 billion. This seems a good enough number but, if we exclude Mexico and Chile, the proportionate increase is much less, from $92 billion to $147 billion (i.e., just under

60 per cent) (Inter-American Development Bank 2000). Even so, this export performance was certainly not a disaster, and some countries that suffered from severe financial problems at the turn of the millennium – notably Argentina – actually achieved quite reasonable rates of export growth during the 1990s. Argentina's exports doubled during the course of the decade, admittedly from a very low base.

Abstracting from a lot of complex detail, some countries did have problems with the export prices of their most abundant commodities. The real price of oil, copper, tin and many soft commodities fell during the 1980–2000 period. This certainly helps to explain particular difficulties facing some countries at some times, notably oil exporters such as Ecuador and Venezuela, but does not seem a strong enough explanation to carry general weight for the region as a whole.

Another possible explanation has to do with faulty exchange-rate policies. This, too, is something that involves political and technical factors. There certainly were occasions on which markets quite reasonably suspected Latin American governments of trying to maintain over-valued exchange rates for reasons of domestic popularity. The exchange rate was used as a counter-inflationary anchor in Mexico under Salinas (1988–94), in Brazil under the Real Plan (1994–8) and under the Argentine currency board regime (1991–2001). Exchange controls were also used to postpone devaluation in Venezuela during 1994–6. All of these policies ended badly. Severe economic adjustments following their collapse, plus some resulting contagion effect, certainly explains a significant part of the region's poor growth performance since 1990.

Gavin and Hausmann's (1998) study of fiscal policy emphasizes the importance of both political and technical matters. Between 1990 and 1995, Latin America's non-financial public-sector spending on debt servicing was 13.7 per cent the total – compared to 7.9 per cent in the advanced industrial economies. Not only is an additional 5.8 per cent of the budget a significantly large number in political terms, but it also indicates a problem of confidence. Why should countries in the region have to pay so much? One factor is that the Latin American state is comparatively small, around 25 per cent of GDP compared to the 50 per cent so generally typical of Europe (Gavin and Hausmann 1998, p. 35). This makes any debt burden more onerous as a proportion of public revenue. Tax collection is more difficult in Latin America. This is partly due to the high proportion of people employed in the informal sector and to the level of poverty more generally, but there are also institutional problems on account of state bias and patrimonialism. Well-placed supporters of governments have not always had to pay their taxes in Latin America, whereas government opponents generally have had to do so. Erratic or low tax collection would make it rational for lenders to demand a higher rate of interest from Latin American governments.

Could overall fiscal policy be blamed as too loose? Gavin and Hausmann found no real evidence to suggest that Latin American fiscal policies during the 1990s were excessively loose in general terms, but they did find that there was considerable volatility. There were several reasons for this. One was that commodity export revenues tend to fluctuate, and these are an important source of government revenue in some countries. Another is that changing international conditions mattered. However, the Gavin and Hausman study found mainly that fiscal volatility was associated with elections. Incumbent governments tried to spend more at election time, and this led to fiscal destabilization. Here, again, we have clear evidence of a political and institutional problem. In most first world countries, governments have much less freedom to manipulate the economy at election time because independent central banks are likely to take counteracting measures.

Lessons from Chile

The argument that globalization as such is not entirely to blame for the region's problems, and that institutional variances are indeed important, can be substantiated with reference to Chile. The experience of Chile under the Pinochet dictatorship and later during democracy in the 1990s highlights a contrast with many other countries in the region. Chile experienced a crisis in 1982 of at least equal severity to that faced by most other Latin American countries: the most repressive period of the Pinochet dictatorship was also the least economically successful. Institutional weaknesses stemming from the under-regulation of the excessively bullish financial sector were an important aspect to Chile's vulnerability to crisis (Congdon 1985). However, the Pinochet dictatorship then vigorously adopted a 'short term pain' strategy and moved away decisively from an economic culture of borrowing and importing capital to a more 'Asian' policy of covering investment through savings. In 1981 it reformed its social security system, moving from a 'pay as you go' system to one in which savings had to be paid in and then managed by large privately owned but state-regulated pension funds. However, it made the necessary adjustments so that this reform did not undermine budgetary stability.

Indeed the macro-economic policy response to the 1982–4 crisis was to get the budget back into surplus at almost any social cost. As a result the country suffered an enormous recession in 1983 – growth was a negative 13.4 per cent. However, the authorities later regarded this policy as a success. Chile's finance minster, Buchi, later recorded (*Economic Reform Today*, summer 1991, p. 28) that 'domestic savings needed to be increased to replace the external savings that failed to materialise.' Since 1985, moreover, the Chilean budget has remained generally in surplus, and its public financial position is very stable (Baldez and Carey 2001).

As soon as the Chilean economy began to recover and state assets could find buyers, orthodox fiscal policy was followed by a radical programme of privatization. In the mid-1980s there were further changes in tax policy in order to encourage saving and discourage consumption. Moreover the real value of the exchange rate was held down in order to encourage export profitability. This, in turn, encouraged reinvestment out of retained profits. As a result of increases in both public and private savings, the overall savings ratio in Chile rose from around 16 per cent in 1980 to some 23 per cent in 1992 (Edwards 1995, p. 228). At the end of military rule, the outgoing Pinochet regime legislated the setting up of an independent central bank in a constitutional form in which it was entrenched against subsequent political change.

Although an enhanced private savings ratio, an independent central bank and tight control over public spending may not be the only reasons for Chile's superior economic performance since 1980, they are surely part of the explanation. Chile has, until recently, used controls on capital to discourage short-term *inflows* and so avoided exposure to the 'post-tequila crisis' which hurt other countries in the region. Chile's foreign debt, at just over 2.1 times exports at the end of 1997, is below the regional average. Moreover Chilean legal and bureaucratic institutions seem to work better than those in most other countries in the region, which is also part of the explanation for its superior creditworthiness. Largely because of these reforms, Chile has been granted an investment grade by the international assessment agencies, and its existing level of debt is comparatively cheap to service.

It does seem significant that the more authoritarian Chilean experience with market reform should have proved more successful than those of some of the region's more pluralist political systems. It is too simple to regard this as a dictatorship vs. democracy issue, if only because authoritarian regimes in Latin America have quite frequently presided over fiscal problems and debt crises. Moreover Chile democratized at the end of the 1980s, and its improved economic performance has evidently been sustained under democratic government. It can certainly be argued that the design of the Chilean constitution was helpful to strong presidential power and deliberately biased against demands for high spending (Baldez and Carey 2001). It may indeed be that direct self-restraining legislation in respect of budget deficits can work well in other countries of the region. Institutional design certainly does matter.

However, this does presuppose that the collective action problem that lies at the heart of the issue of democratic consolidation has been overcome. The Chilean executive has remained bound by law and would be subject to sanction if it were detected violating budgetary law. But in other countries of the region this is not invariably the case. Venezuela's Chávez has openly violated budgetary legislation and has not so far been subject to judicial sanction as a result. The most optimistic conclusion to draw from the Chilean case is that law-bound Latin American governments can achieve budgetary stability and can expect some economic benefit from that fact. The post-1990 Chilean experience therefore, in a sense, measures the cost of democratic non-consolidation elsewhere.

The reputational consequences of institutional problems

Unfortunately institutional problems, once established, have reputational consequences, and table 6.4 is eloquent. This table relates to a key index of investor confidence measured on several occasions during early and mid-2001. This seems a reasonable period to have chosen, since it relates to a spell of relative tranquillity before the outrage in New York on 11 September and the onset of the Argentine crisis in November. Figures for 2002 were much more unfavourable.

The general pattern is clear. Within the major Latin American countries, only Mexico could borrow at interest rates less than 5 per cent above their US counterparts – though smaller countries such as Uruguay and Chile could do so. Table 6.4 shows that limited investor confidence is not exclusively a Latin American problem, but it also shows that it is not a total 'emerging markets' problem either. If we take a spread of 5 per cent or less as a mark of trust, we see that the markets generally trust Korea and Poland, as well as Mexico. However, Argentina, Brazil and Venezuela have to line up alongside Turkey and Russia, which are not much trusted. Ecuador shares a position with Nigeria as being one of the financially least-trusted countries on the globe. Argentina spent 2001 on a mainly downward trend, and its spread reached an impossible 35 per cent in November.

Table 6.4 Emerging market bonds index: selected country spreads, selected dated, 2001 (hundred basis points)

	6 April 2001	23 April 2001	4 May 2001	1 June 2001
Nigeria	17.53	14.71	16.30	15.43
Ecuador	14.56	15.38	14.02	14.00
Russia	10.73	10.47	10.42	9.30
Turkey	10.37	9.79	8.90	8.23
Argentina	9.00	10.49	10.67	10.19
Venezuela	8.58	8.52	8.39	8.40
Brazil	7.92	8.42	8.26	8.62
Bulgaria	7.76	7.91	7.75	7.09
Peru	6.89	8.16	8.05	7.75
Colombia	6.38	6.16	6.48	6.04
Panama	4.56	4.26	4.22	3.98
Mexico	3.93	3.75	3.66	3.20
Qatar	3.38	3.06	3.01	2.76
Korea	2.20	1.82	1.86	1.43
Poland	2.09	1.73	1.85	1.65

Source: Reuters, published in IDEA, LatAm Markets Today, various issues

One factor that may have raised the cost of capital in much of Latin America has been the growth of the evaluation industry. Twenty years ago most companies or banks made their own assessments of political risk. These assessments were therefore non-standard and sometimes even eccentric. However, because ordinary fund managers do not generally know a very great deal about the countries with which they are dealing, they have increasingly tended to rely on the judgement of a small group of professionals. Near the top of the professional tree are the three internationally recognized risk-rating organizations Standard and Poor, Fitch, and Moody's. These agencies produce regular reports on most countries in the world and on many companies as well. Most Latin American countries perform relatively poorly in these assessments. Early in 2001 Chile and Uruguay had achieved 'investment grade' status according to all three agencies, while Mexico was positively rated by Moody's and less so by the others. As we can see from table 6.4, though, Mexico is one of the region's few genuine winners. In fact Mexico received an investment grade in 2002 while Uruguay lost its rating due to its exposure to the Argentine crisis.

As for the other countries, according to Fitch/Ibca in 1999, Argentina, Mexico and Peru were graded the same as South Africa and below the Philippines. Venezuela scored at the same level as Kazakhstan. Standard and Poor in September 2000 gave Brazil the same long-term foreign currency rating as Turkey, while Argentina and Peru shared a rating with Morocco. (In fact Morocco's spread on government bonds 1 June 2001 was 4.49 – which is much lower than that of either Argentina or Peru.) According to Standard and Poor, Ecuador shared a C (essentially a default grade) with Russia. These are not flattering ratings. Overall, while Latin America was not quite at the bottom of the international league table, the majority of countries in the region performed relatively poorly.

Political risk assessments have to reflect to some extent as well as shaping market judgements. These judgements can be naïve or plainly mistaken. It may be that Latin America is currently suffering from some kind of lenders' bias, based on the region's historically earned reputation for over-indebtedness and default. However, table 6.4 also shows that investors are capable of making genuine evaluations of different countries and do not simply regard emerging markets or even Latin American markets as an undifferentiated whole. Clearly once a country is distrusted by markets, then the high cost of capital can interact with low growth to produce a vicious circle. In 2001 Argentina had to face a prohibitively high cost of capital because it was in recession, and it was in recession because it had to pay far too much for its capital.

Globalization and financial crises

Latin America has come off rather badly in the post-globalization financial architecture. Apart from the fact that they started out in the 1980s with a great deal of debt and a bad reputation, most Latin American countries (not Peru or Bolivia) suffer from being neither very rich nor very poor. First world countries and, as we have seen, some emerging economies are seen as creditworthy and can borrow cheaply, while very poor countries enjoy significant financing on concessionary terms. Of the major Latin American countries, however, only Peru and Bolivia enjoy significant concessionary finance and only Chile and Uruguay were during the 1990s more or less trusted by the markets. That leaves a lot of cases that fit into neither category. It is of course clear that there are power-political as well as institutional-economic aspects determining respective interest rates. The United States has helped Mexico out of financial difficulties on at least four occasions in the past twenty years. By the same token, association with the rest of the European Union has been very helpful to several Southern European countries with debt problems. Turkish membership of NATO is also a relevant consideration in this context. South America (as opposed to Mexico) does not fit so easily under any politically significant protective umbrella, as Argentina discovered during 2001–2.

An important reason why risk assessments are so important to markets is that financial globalization has not so far brought its own institutional structures along with it. Finance capital requires effective institutional systems. It does not create them. During the 1990s at least, there were no clear international 'rules of the game' that might have replaced local ones when it became necessary to determine (for example) what would happen when debtor countries fell behind with their payments. Nor was there any direct way of dealing with corruption in developing countries in cases where domestic legal systems were inadequate to cope. Pragmatism was everything. There was plenty of world-trade law, and there was a rapidly developing field of international human-rights law (Robertson 2000), but there was no real counterpart in international financial law. In November 2001 the IMF formally proposed establishing a set of procedures in order to create a system that would allow borrower governments to declare themselves bankrupt if necessary. However, until that time, the consequences of bankruptcy were considered to be chaotic and rather punitive – and so was the reality that faced Ecuador after 1998 and Argentina in 2002 when those countries did indeed default on their debts. In the absence of an agreed and credible set of international rules, investors and lenders had to deal with the vagaries of local legislative frameworks and, behind these, local political systems.

The result of this situation was the worst of both worlds. Creditors and investors prepared to take the risk of supplying money to countries with unreliable political and legal systems were therefore almost bound to demand high rates of return as compensation. These, in turn, made default more likely. The point is not to blame global factors for the problems posed by poorly functioning domestic institutions but to point out that globalization without the development of appropriate international institutions has amplified the difficulties.

The knowledge that the international financial system can be both destabilized and destabilizing has been painfully acquired. One reason why Latin American governments were allowed to borrow as much as they did from the international banks in the 1970s was the belief that – in the notorious phrase of one prominent banker – 'countries don't go bankrupt.' As was later discovered, there was nothing to stop borrower governments failing to service their loans either through actual default or simple non-payment. This lesson was learned the hard way in the 1980s. In principle, attempts to attach the assets of non-paying governments via courts in creditor countries might have had interesting consequences, but no Latin American government had to face such a situation. Instead, creditor organizations either attempted to sell their non-performing loans to less risk-averse organizations at a discount or else they sought to negotiate deals with defaulted governments. Sometimes they sought to persuade first world governments such as the USA and international financial agencies such as IFIs to organize bailouts of some kind. This clearly happened in Mexico in 1995, though it seems that US government policy responded to official US concerns more than to the lobbying of adversely affected interests (Parker 2001).

In the early 1990s there was a belief that the IFIs could prevent a recurrence of the debt crisis of the 1980s. The idea was that they would identify good macro-economic policy in an emerging economy. Once such policy had won the IFI seals of approval, markets would be encouraged to lend. IFI confidence would also help keep interest rates low, thus permitting economic progress. This, in turn, would facilitate macro-economic stability and so the virtuous circle would continue. In many ways, this was a good idea. Unfortunately, though, it did not always work. Essentially the IFIs have very limited leverage over debtor governments and international financial markets, and such leverage as they did have tended to diminish during the course of the decade.

Nor did IFI involvement resolve the fundamental question of who should pay the price in the event that things went seriously wrong. Critics were soon heard complaining of what they called 'moral hazard'. In other words, if the IFIs were too gentle with failing governments, then emerging economies that managed their financial affairs irresponsibly and lenders who extended credit irresponsibly would not learn the error of their ways. They would just continue lending and borrowing on unsustainable conditions. In the end, the United States government might find that it had to assume liability for much developing-country debt. This was a problem that could be confronted at the end of the 1980s with the argument that Latin America's worst problems lay in the past and that 'Washington consensus' reform would avoid any recurrence. The Mexican 'tequila crisis' of 1994–5 raised US national interests directly, and so the US bailout could be defended on national interest grounds. However, each fresh crisis led to an 'I told you so' reaction from some first world critics of financial globalization. Of course it is not clear from a moral standpoint why poor people in relatively poor countries should be expected to suffer in order to 'educate' corrupt or incompetent policy-makers in the error of their ways. However, the only way to avoid the moral hazard problem is to ensure that lenders lend and borrowers borrow at their own risk. IFI conditionalities could possibly help build confidence in the short run, but the limits of what they could do became clearer as problems continued to recur.

It may well be true that the IFIs were, in the 1990s, given a role that afforded only a limited possibility of success. Moreover, in the absence of effective institutional structures, either at global or national level, IFI decision-making was almost bound to reflect political criteria to at least some extent. However, when their policies came to be seen by markets as 'too political', their ability to boost confidence was impaired. Why, the critics asked, did the IFIs not insist on earlier devaluations in Mexico and Brazil? One immediate factor here was that the US government generally approved what the Mexican government was doing politically in 1993–4, as was the case in Brazil in 1997–8, and wanted to help. When difficult elections were held in Mexico in 1994 (involving the left-wing Cuauhtémoc Cárdenas) and in Brazil in 1998 (involving the left-wing Luis Ignacio de Silva – known as Lula), official Washington wanted the left-wing candidates defeated. There is at least a suspicion that the IFIs were encouraged to provide excessively positive reports on economies that needed adjustment so as to make sure that adjustment did not take place before the elections (on Brazil, see De Souza 1999). As a result, according to this suspicion, financing was found for Mexico and Brazil until the elections were safely over, and the peso and the real were then devalued. It is conceivable that stories of Washington pressing IFIs to change policy towards Russia or Latin America on political grounds were exaggerated. The point is that they might have been true, and were widely believed to be so.

Problems of contagion

The so-called contagion factor was also a significant contributor to the problems posed by globalization. Latin America was quite successful at attracting foreign capital during the 1990–94 period (Held et al. 1999). However, the 'tequila crisis' caused enormous damage to the rest of the region in 1995. According to World Bank figures, net capital inflows to Latin America were $60 billion in 1993 but fell to minus $7.5 billion in 1995 (World Bank 2000a, p. 74). Argentina, which had nothing to do with the original problem, saw a fall of one-sixth in its banking deposits during the first quarter of 1995, while the Argentine central bank lost $5 billion in reserves over the same period. Although there was some subsequent recovery in both Mexico and Argentina, there was an additional contagion effect three years later due to problems in the Asian and Russian markets. The Asian crisis did significant damage to the Andean countries of Latin America and contributed to Brazil's decision to devalue in 1999 – a decision which once more exported recession to Argentina and Uruguay. During 1999–2002 there was another wave of capital flight, and it was obvious that emerging markets had not successfully stabilized. In 2002 the Argentine default caused serious economic pain in Paraguay, Uruguay and Brazil.

Financial globalization impacts upon the private as well as the public sector. However, private-sector failure is likely to bring in government, which may then have to assume the costs of other people's mistakes. Certainly one of the most serious negative consequences of globalization plus regulatory failure has been bank failure, which is a common enough problem across the whole developing world and not just in Latin America. According to the World Bank, 'between 1977 and 1995 69 countries faced banking crises so severe that most of their bank capital was exhausted' (2000c, p. 74). Within Latin America, cases include Argentina in 1981, Chile in 1982, Venezuela in 1994 and Mexico in 1995. The costs in economic growth were in all cases very large.

A brief conclusion

The relationship between globalization, democracy, free markets and institutions is complex and has been very much studied. It is therefore necessary to be modest about claiming too many profoundly original insights about the Latin American experience. However, this discussion can be summed up follows.

To begin with, under current global conditions at any rate, macro-economic stability seems absolutely fundamental to sustained economic progress in any economy that does not rely significantly upon command and control. Governments that cannot convince markets of their commitment to macro-economic stability can face alarming economic difficulties. The hyperinflations that occurred in Argentina, Peru, Bolivia and Brazil at the end of the 1980s are discussed in a later chapter. No doubt there will be sequel works examining the deep recessionary crisis that hit several countries during 1999–2002.

Macro-economic stability can be facilitated by appropriate institutional design in consolidated systems because the formal rules will mainly be respected. What complicates matters in non-consolidated systems is that the formal rules need not determine what governments or other political actors do. A further problem with democratic systems is that it is entirely possible for ingenious and irresponsible political authorities to set up 'short term gain, long term pain' systems of economic management. In Latin America this has happened rather a lot. We have noted that anti-inflationary policies that relied on maintaining a potentially or actually over-valued currency failed badly in several countries in the region. Macro-economic management evidently involves technical aspects that are beyond the scope of this work, but it is clear that some of the most damaging decisions made by the region's policy-makers were based on strategies designed to produce quick results for electoral advantage.

A technocratic response to the region's macro-economic problems would be a concerted policy of fiscal stabilization, raising the domestic savings ratio and retaining a competitive exchange rate. The problems associated with trying to do this in a democratic framework have already been mentioned, and there is a real danger that – after many economic disappointments – public opinion in the future may simply be unwilling to accept yet further attempts to impose macro-economic stability. There is, of course, something unsatisfactory about a world order in which a wealthy country such as the USA can afford to borrow heavily (as it did during the 1990s) because it is seen as creditworthy while poor countries have to run surpluses because they are seen as financially insecure. However, it may be that a determined effort to push economic policy in the direction of saving and exporting – or to retain that policy where it already exists – may be the only shot now left in the locker of Latin American democratic governments.

7

The Politics of Crisis in the 1990s: A Comparative Perspective

So far this discussion has taken an essentially region-wide view of Latin America's political institutions, offering specific examples as appropriate. It has also, in general, given somewhat more weight to historical-institutional factors in explaining political outcomes than to global economic factors – though the latter should by no means be ignored. The subsequent chapters of this work discuss individual countries, seeking to put the general factors already discussed into varying local contexts during a particular historical period.

This chapter aims to link these various case studies to the general theme of the work, by asking how far the institutional crises and breakdowns that are the subject of the next three chapters can be understood in comparative terms. The method is to compare a group of countries that suffered from economic crises during the years 1985 to 1992 and ask why some of them (notably Peru and Venezuela) suffered constitutional breakdowns while others did not. What generally seems to have happened is that crisis situations changed the distribution of partisan power within particular countries. In some cases the resulting conflicts could be played out within existing institutions, while in other cases the new pattern of partisan contestation led to open breaches of the formal rules. This occurred both in Peru, where crisis management led to an excessive strengthening of executive power, and in Venezuela, where failed crisis management dangerously weakened the executive.

This chapter discusses six countries, Bolivia, Brazil, Argentina, Venezuela, Peru and Mexico. The latter three are considered again at more length in later chapters. All of them suffered from severe economic crisis in the 1980s. Hyperinflation or something very close to it developed in four of the six – Bolivia, Argentina, Peru and Brazil. Relative inflation rates can be seen in table 7.1 below.

We can divide the six countries whose evolution is discussed in this chapter into three groups, according to the way in which economic crisis impacted upon their political institutions. In Brazil and Bolivia they were transcended with surprisingly little long-term political effect. It did for a time look in Brazil as though hyperinflation might bring in the kind of personalist presidentialism seen in some other countries. However, Fernando Collor, who aspired to such a role, was impeached in 1992, and this style of politics ended then. Subsequently a more consensual style of politics was adopted, on the whole with reasonable success. Bolivia did not see a presidential impeachment, though it did see the semi-voluntary curtailment of a presidential term. This difference may have had something to do with the system by which congress chooses the Bolivian president rather than the electorate doing so directly (Mayorga 1997), which ensures that no candidate can be elected president without the support of congress. The pattern of policy-making in post-1985 Bolivia and post-1992 Brazil was essentially based on coalitions. In both countries the exercise of some executive power by decree did not undermine the general trend for policy-making to be based largely on coalition-building.

In Venezuela and Peru, economic crises played a part in bringing about constitutional (though not necessarily democratic) breakdown. In both cases, the long-term effect of crisis was the displacement of some form of representative democracy by very strong personalist leadership. In both cases, too, a longer-term consequence was to make the political system significantly more militarized. Observers generally found the Venezuelan outcome surprising, though there was much less surprise at constitutional breakdown in Peru. It is certainly worth asking why there have not been more cases of hyper-presidentialism in the region.

Mexico and Argentina are in an intermediate category. Economic crises had institutionally significant consequences in both countries but, during the 1990s at least, not system-changing ones. (It is too early to assess the political impact in Argentina of the 2001–02 crisis.) The Mexican system did not break down after 1982 despite facing recurrent economic crisis. Instead there was a clear, though not entirely smooth, transition to democracy in the period 1982 to 2000. However, there was one striking event in Mexico, the rigging of the 1988 presidential election, that is crucial to what followed. The ballot-rigging did not ultimately derail the process of democratization, but it did determine the elite strategy of democratization and what one might call the political economy of democratization. Mexican membership of the NAFTA (North American Free Trade Agreement), which is likely to have been a path-breaking step, would have been hard to imagine without the victory of Salinas in what seems to have been a rigged election. What is surprising is not so much the fact that the 1988 election was rigged – this might have been predicted from previous Mexican official behaviour – but that so major a step did not prevent President Salinas from enjoying the domestic and international benefits of legitimacy.

In Argentina in 1989 there was hyperinflation and military unrest, and national democratic institutions seemed under severe threat. However, during Menem's generally successful presidency, military unrest was suppressed, inflation declined sharply and economic growth resumed. By the late 1990s it appeared as though Argentina had come through a major economic and constitutional crisis. Argentine politics in 1999 seemed far more conventional and ordinary than they had been in 1989. It is true that Menem had clearly exceeded his legal presidential powers in some important ways, but not by enough to threaten the democratic system (Jones 1997; McGuire 1997). Moreover Menem also reduced the threat of renewed military intervention – which would certainly have undermined democracy – and ended hyperinflation. However, the renewal of crisis in 2001–02 has forced a reappraisal of the case. Subsequent to this it has to be asked whether Argentina's currency board system, established under Menem in 1991 as a key part of his government's anti-inflationary strategy, set the stage for an even more disastrous crisis a decade later (Starr 1997).

At the turn of the new millennium, economic difficulties returned to much of the region. It is possible that the effect of economic troubles on the political process in Latin America will prove cumulative, and that the ability of some republics to survive the 1980s and 1990s economic crises with only limited institutional damage will prove temporary. However, if the pattern detected here in respect of several countries were repeated, then it would seem more probable that Latin American political elites may try to cope with crisis by breaking the formal rules selectively rather than trying to overthrow democracy as such. The outcome may, yet again, be some kind of halfway house between representative democracy and overt dictatorship. If it were not an oxymoron, one might anticipate the deepening of democratic non-consolidation.

Characterizing the economic crises

Before considering political aspects of these crises in more detail we need a little bit of background information. The essential aspects of the various inflationary crises are set out in table 7.1. In Bolivia, Argentina

Table 7.1   Increases in consumer prices in selected Latin American countries, 1985–94

	1985	1986	1987	1988	1989	1990	1991	1992	1993	1994
Argentina	672.2	85.7	123.1	348.3	3086.9	2313.7	171.7	24.9	10.6	4.2
Bolivia	11,749.6	276.3	14.6	16.0	15.2	17.1	21.4	12.1	8.5	7.9
Brazil	226.9	125.0	233.3	690.0	1289.0	2937.7	440.9	1008.7	2148.5	2668.6
Mexico	57.7	86.2	131.8	114.2	20.0	26.6	22.7	15.5	9.7	6.9
Peru	163.4	200.0	66.7	660.0	3371.1	7481.5	409.5	73.6	48.6	23.7
Venezuela	11.4	11.5	28.1	29.5	84.5	40.6	34.2	31.4	38.1	59.9

Source: Inter-American Development Bank, annual reports

and Peru there is a sharply increasing inflationary trend until a crisis point is reached. This happens in 1985 in Bolivia, 1989 in Argentina and 1990 in Peru. There is then a sharp fall in inflation rates. There is also a considerable recovery in economic growth. In Mexico the pattern is somewhat similar though the trajectory is lower, and table 7.1 does not catch the sharp though temporary upward rebound in Mexican inflation when the 'tequila crisis' struck at the end of 1994. Even if crisis management in all of these countries had long-term implications, we can regard these four cases as indicating short-term policy success for counter-inflationary governments. This is in marked contrast to the policy failure of their predecessors.

Venezuela and Brazil are, however, exceptions. Venezuela cannot be said to have suffered from a hyperinflationary crisis, though the peak of 84.5 per cent in 1989 was uncomfortably high. What happened instead is that the government early in 1989 sharply increased a number of public-sector prices in order to try to resolve a fiscal problem that, had it not been addressed, might well have developed into hyper-inflation. It may well be that the politics of launching a pre-emptive counter-inflationary policy may be a lot more difficult from a government's point of view than responding to manifest crisis. However, as table 7.1 shows, the Venezuelan government's anti-inflationary policies were unsuccessful in the medium run and the rate of inflation started to increase again in 1993. It reached a new peak in 1996 and remained troublesome thereafter. There were also severe political problems in Venezuela, where it is clear that the 1989 stabilization package signifi-cantly weakened executive power – an effect that did not show at all in the four successes.

In Brazil there was a double peak in inflation, though the rate fell back sharply after 1994. In Brazil, as in Venezuela, executive power weakened in the 1990s, as manifested by the impeachment of Fernando Collor in 1992. However, this weakening had far fewer long-term consequences in Brazil than they did in Venezuela. This is because Brazil's Cardoso was able to achieve a reduction in inflation and an increase in presidential popularity for a few years in the mid-1990s.

Each inflationary crisis had some specific national characteristics, and it is quite possible that these will have significantly shaped the political consequences. Unfortunately there is not the space to consider specific economic features in detail. What is clear, and not at all surprising, is that governments in office at a time of sharply rising inflation lost popularity. Argentina's Alfonsín (in 1989) and Bolivia's Siles Suazo (in 1985) ended their terms early in a public admission of failure. Candidates from opposition parties subsequently won the presidency in both of these cases. The elections held in Brazil and Peru in 1990 also led to opposition victories. The Mexican PRI suffered a sharp electoral setback in 1988, and resorted to some degree of electoral malpractice to keep power. Only in Venezuela did rising inflation fail to bring about a change in the governing party, and here inflationary problems were much smaller – at any rate when the 1988 elections were held.

It therefore seems fairly clear that rising inflation is bad politics. It also seems clear that presidents who successfully brought down inflation rates mostly did enjoy considerable popularity for a time. Menem, Fujimori, Salinas and Paz Estensoro proved both more popular and more successful than many observers expected at the time of their election. If we regard Pérez as not having had the 'benefit' of an inherited hyperinflation, then only Brazil's Collor clearly lost popularity despite coming to power when conditions were seemingly favourable.

If one assumes that political practitioners are essentially rational, then this presents us with a puzzle. If counter-inflationary politics is mostly good for incumbents, how did it happen that hyperinflationary crises were allowed to develop in the first place? In most cases, the rising rate of inflation in the 1980s did reflect some genuinely serious economic problems and cannot be blamed entirely on mismanagement. The severity of the 1982 debt crisis has already been noted, and the 1980s also saw sharp falls in the prices of some important commodities – such as oil, tin and some agricultural products. Moreover the international policy environment improved after 1989. The Brady Plan did provide the possibility of some debt relief and improved the political odds facing counter-inflationary governments. Despite this, it does seem that mistaken economic policies during the 1980s often made things worse (Dornbusch and Edwards 1991). The underlying economic strategy of figures such as Peru's García and Brazil's Sarney was evidently flawed. Yet these strategies did have their economic advocates and supporters at the time.

The object here is not so much to try to attribute policy failure to particular causes, but rather to point out that international circumstances – in the form of tangible conditions and also intellectual atmosphere – can change rather quickly. Policy responses that may appear unthinkable in one climate can appear entirely logical only a few years later. The story being outlined in this chapter, which is one in which successful crisis resolution could significantly if temporarily increase the power of the executive, relates to a particular time and place. It illuminates the cases of Fujimori and Salinas, considered in later chapters. It is also instructive to see why the fate of Venezuela's Pérez was so different despite a context that seemed in some ways similar. However, the socio-political context of the 1980s was quite different, as is the first decade of the current century.

Economic crisis and presidential politics in the 1990s

Hyperinflation or other forms of economic crisis did not prevent the holding of reasonably free and fair elections in five of the six countries discussed in this chapter; in Mexico, as we have seen, the 1988 elections were not free and fair. As a result of these elections, Peru's Alberto Fujimori, Argentina's Carlos Menem, Bolivia's Victor Paz Estensoro, Venezuela's Carlos Andrés Pérez and Brazil's Fernando Collor took office at a time of extreme economic difficulty. Mexico's Carlos Salinas also took office at a difficult time and, while he may not have been properly elected at all, he too faced some rather similar economic problems.

As noted, the six presidents encountered very different results. Collor and Pérez were impeached and removed from office before the end of their terms. Fujimori closed congress and ruled for ten years, before he was himself finally impeached. Salinas served a full term, allowed the holding of genuinely free elections in 1994, left office as an apparent success, and then found his reputation shattered by Mexico's 1994–5 'tequila crisis'. Menem successfully sought changes in the constitution to permit re-election, and then stood successfully for a second term. However, an attempt to seek a third term failed, and Menem, like Salinas, was blamed for an economic crisis that broke after he had himself left office. Victor Paz served one term (his third as president of Bolivia) and then retired from office. What explains these different outcomes?

The issue of presidential mandates has been considered in detail in a recently published work (Stokes 2001). In fact, there does not seem to be much relationship between the positions taken by the incoming presidents when campaigning for office and their subsequent fate. In Mexico, as we have seen, Salinas probably did not win honestly, but he did make apparent his preference for free-market economic policies. In Bolivia in 1985 the first-placed candidate was Hugo Banzer, a former military dictator whose conservative orientation was not in doubt. However, the choice of president was ultimately made by congress, and this allowed the second-placed candidate – Paz Estensoro – to be elected. Although in most respects clearly a conservative, Paz won the backing of left-wing congressmen with the slogan 'all against the General'. This slogan was mainly about dictatorship rather than economics, however. In Brazil, Fernando Collor de Mello was overtly a conservative, although his appeal contained a considerable heterodox element. He was the main political opponent of the left-wing candidate Lula. Lula polarized the electorate and, although ahead at the end of the first round of voting, lost the presidential runoff to Collor. In none of these three cases should the adoption of orthodox economic stabilization measures have been a surprise.

This was not the case in the other three. In Venezuela, Carlos Andrés Pérez had served as president previously and was generally regarded as a pro-business but economically heterodox candidate. When he imposed sharp austerity measures soon after coming to office, public shock was palpable. In Argentina, Carlos Menem, though careful not to make too many explicit commitments during the campaign, was regarded as a left-wing Peronist. He was not at all associated with economic orthodoxy and clearly won many votes from working-class voters who objected to it. The Peruvian case is rather similar except that Fujimori, unlike Menem, was not backed by a strong party. However, as candidate, Fujimori openly criticized the idea of an economic shock package to deal with Peru's hyperinflation. As will be discussed in slightly more detail below, he emerged late in the presidential campaign from (as it appeared) somewhere on the left as a 'stop Vargas Llosa' candidate. (Vargas Llosa was the candidate of the orthodox 'neoliberal' right.)

In each category, there are two successes and one failure. Salinas and Paz were successful presidents who did more or less as expected. Collor tried to do the same but failed. Of the mandate-breakers, Venezuela's Pérez was a spectacular casualty. However, attempts to explain Pérez's failure on his shift in policy does not explain why Fujimori and Menem broke their election promises but remained popular.

It may, though, be significant that both 'unconstitutional' outcomes – those in Peru and Venezuela – occurred when there was an open breach of campaign promises. It is reasonable to suggest that presidents who act directly in conflict with their campaign promises may, by so doing, contribute something to the partisanship of the political process through the destabilizing of reasonably held popular expectations about the predictability of political life. However, while Stokes (2001) is right to say that the issue of electoral trust is important in building political institutions, there is no simple relationship between presidential promises and the fate of presidential regimes.

Institutional power and economic stabilization

Another hypothesis is that these different outcomes might have something to do with the different degree of formal institutional powers vested in the presidency. In all six cases counter-inflationary policies involved some conflict between the policy-making establishment and vested interests, and therefore required active leadership. Presidents tended to use forms of emergency power, or decree power, or both, to pursue policies that the national congress might have been reluctant to support – excepting the case of Mexico, where the president controlled the political system without the need for these. It might be hypothesized that different formal institutional aspects of presidentialism might help us to understand why counter-inflationary policies sometimes strengthened executive power and sometimes weakened it.

It is indeed true that, in most of the six cases, the effect of crisis was to induce presidents to rely upon decree powers to an unusually great extent. This is true even of Bolivia and Argentina, where there existed on paper a pro-executive majority in the legislature. In Bolivia, Paz first decreed a new economic policy on 29 August 1985 and then declared a three-month state of siege the following month. The state of siege enabled Paz to take direct repressive measures against trade union leaders and to call upon the support of the army. The army itself proved willing to follow the presidential lead. Paz also negotiated the support of ex-president Hugo Banzer. As a result of this alliance with Banzer, Paz enjoyed a congressional majority, and he used this to run the economy during the rest of his presidential term with little input from congress.

In the case of Argentina, there was less policy coherence at the outset. Menem immediately turned to the private sector for help, and moved clearly in the direction of economic orthodoxy. However, quite a lot of political reorganization had to occur before the character of the

Menem government was definitely set early in 1991. During all of this time a great deal of legislation was enacted by decree. The right to decree legislation provided the necessary underpinning for the eventual adoption of a radical set of economic reforms. There was some congressional deliberation of these reforms, but not much. Legally speaking, the most important legislative instrument was the delegative decree, which is a legal mechanism according to which congress gave to the executive the right to legislate in detail without reference back to the legislature (Jones 1997, p. 285). In addition, Menem between 1989 and 1994 issued 336 decrees of 'urgent necessity', compared with some twenty-five such decrees issued during the entire 1853–1989 period. To the extent that there were difficulties with congress, Menem was helped by his control of the judiciary. In April 1990 Menem submitted to congress a proposal to expand the supreme court from five to nine members (McGuire 1997, p. 256), the effect of which was to allow him to appoint the four additional supreme court justices and thereby control the court. Menem's congressional opponents boycotted sittings when this proposal was due to be discussed in order to deny a quorum to the legislature, but the proposal was eventually declared passed on a voice vote.

Mexico's Salinas clearly had enough power in the presidential office to be able to pass his reform programme. Yet he was careful to consult widely. He retained a kind of corporatist arrangement, initiated in 1987, by which business and labour representatives met regularly to discuss economic policy. He was also willing to negotiate with the right-wing opposition party, the PAN, in order to broaden support for his proposals. His negotiation of the NAFTA involved extensive input from Mexican business interests as well as, inevitably, the USA. In some ways Salinas used his presidential powers to the full, notably in replacing a large number of state governors, but he was careful not to be seen as a presidential despot.

This was less true of Brazil's Collor who, like the others, relied significantly on decree power. The Brazilian constitution of 1988 specifically allowed for this. Collor's initial anti-inflationary policies did achieve some early success. However Collor, unlike Paz or Menem, soon encountered major political difficulties. These have been attributed to his failure to build a core political coalition around his policy objectives – though this would have been a harder thing to do in Brazil than in the more politically centralized Spanish American countries (Panizza 2000b). For one thing, state governors and mayors who were beneficiaries of (for them) a valuable revenue-sharing arrangement under the 1988 constitution were unwilling to permit any fiscal recentralization. For another, the weakness of the Brazilian party system made coalition-building time-consuming and politically costly. A different president might have made a greater effort to marshal support. Collor, however, adopted the style of an old-fashioned leader president, even though Brazilian institutions were no longer designed for this kind of leadership.

Another relevant factor in the case of Brazil is that the courts were generally more independent, if not necessarily more capable, than those of Spanish America (Prillaman 2000). Collor had to operate within the limits of the 1988 constitution, which guaranteed job stability within the civil service. Accordingly one of Collor's key policy proposals, reform of the public sector in the interests of efficiency, was frustrated by the Brazilian supreme court. Instead of being able to reduce public employment, and thereby possibly improving the efficiency as well as the cost-effectiveness of the Brazilian state, Collor was forced to rely on wage cuts. These led to an exodus of some of the best-qualified state employees and a weakening of state capacity (Weyland 1997).

Collor later found himself the target of specific and serious corruption allegations, of a kind that would have been difficult for any president to defend himself against once they had seen the light of day. It has been argued that Collor's political isolation made it more likely that he would use corrupt methods to finance his political programme (Weyland 1998). However, it may be that both the political isolation and the corruption reflected political inexperience and naïveté about the way in which Brazilian institutions worked. By early 1992 Collor's presidency was on the defensive, and he was at the end of the year impeached and removed from office by congress. The suggestion that Collor's problems were to some extent self-inflicted rather than being based solely on an institutional lack of power is strengthened when we look at what happened after his fall.

It looked for a time as though no policy issues had been solved by the impeachment of Collor. There was soon a renewed increase in inflation. A subsequent counter-inflationary plan, this time led by Fernando Henrique Cardoso as finance minister, succeeded in 1993 without much political conflict. Cardoso, unlike Collor, proved able to build a coalition behind his economic programme. It has been argued (Mainwaring 1997, p. 104) that it was easier for Brazilian political society to accept effective anti-inflationary measures after around 1993 because similar measures had already succeeded in Argentina, Peru and other countries where strong presidentialism was instrumental. It is also the case, though, that Cardoso was willing to work with the grain of Brazilian politics – accepting that this involved clientelism and some corruption (Panizza 2000a). The Brazilian economy was significantly reformed by these policies but the political system was not.

Venezuela's Pérez also had serious problems with congress. This was partly the result of the fact that his own Acción Democrática (AD) party was narrowly in a minority in congress, and partly the result of poor relations between Pérez and other leaders of AD who had not wanted Pérez to run for president for the second time. Meanwhile the Venezuelan constitution of 1961 gave only limited emergency powers to the president. It was generally assumed that the strong party system would allow necessary changes to be negotiated. However, Pérez tried to impose a drastic stabilization package in February 1989, and this led to serious rioting and a collapse in Pérez's popularity. This loss of popularity made it harder still to control congress.

Close allies of Pérez have indeed argued that the Venezuelan institutional system made his stabilization policies harsher than they needed to be and so contributed to his unpopularity and eventual failure (interview with Miguel Rodríguez, March 1992). The presidency had power to raise public-sector prices (which was the principal means by which the 1989 adjustment was effected). However, it did not have the power to raise direct taxes, privatize state assets or take other 'supply side' measures that might have achieved economic stability at a lower social cost. While this is true, it is also evident that Pérez did not approach his difficult macro-economic task with very much political sensitivity. If his initial stabilization measures had been better timed or more carefully presented, then Pérez would have been less unpopular nationally and better placed to negotiate with congress. Furthermore there were things that the president could have done that might have made the adjustment less drastic – marginally breaching OPEC agreements on oil output, for example – that he did not do. It seems likely that Pérez simply adopted the mental mapping of a fixed-term Bolivarian presidential system and did not sufficiently consider the political dangers that he faced from extra-constitutional forms of politics.

In Venezuela, as in Brazil, the impeachment of a president did not completely end any idea of continuing with 'Washington consensus' policies. Some Venezuelans certainly hoped that the fall of Pérez would have a political effect similar to the fall of Collor in Brazil: in other words, it would allow the continuation of a market-reform programme, but more slowly and more consensually. Rafael Caldera, who was elected president of Venezuela in 1993, was personally close to Brazil's Cardoso and had many similar aspirations. He pursued some market-reforming policies, but did so gradually. Moreover, he demanded special powers through the imposition of a 'state of economic emergency' in July 1994. When congress voted to lift this, Caldera reimposed it the same afternoon, and it was then congress that backed away from confrontation. The idea that Venezuela could still resolve its problems by gradual reform became unviable only when Chávez emerged as front runner for the 1998 presidential elections. Chávez's election was partly the result of political factors that went far beyond economic mis-management, and his campaign was also helped by the fact that Venezuela went back into recession during 1998. Taking the Pérez and Caldera presidencies together, it would seem hard to argue that insuf-ficient presidential power was any very large part of the explanation for the political failure of 'Washington consensus' policies, though it may have played a limited role.

Finally, Fujimori largely made economic policy by decree. The 1979 constitution gave considerable decree power to the Peruvian presi-dency, and Fujimori continued to decree legislation even when his relationship with congress was at its most difficult: 126 supreme decrees were enacted in November 1991 alone. There are some dif-ferences of interpretation over what really happened in respect of presidential–congressional relations between 1990 and 1992. Fujimori certainly complained about congress a lot, but it is not clear whether this was because of any real congressional obstructionism or because he already had it in mind to launch a coup. Some authors believe that Fujimori stoked up an atmosphere of crisis until he sent troops to close congress in April 1992 (Cotler 1995; Tuesta Soldevilla 1996). There is no dispute that the most drastic economic stabilization measures were decreed in 1990 under enabling legislation approved by congress. In September 1991 Fujimori went further and sent a further major package of legislation to congress. Some parts of this package, mainly those dealing with security issues, did not meet with congressional approval, but most of the economic measures did. Congressional failure to approve everything that the president asked led to a sharp worsening in relations between president and congress. Whether this contributed to the April 1992 coup or provided mainly cover justifica-tion for it cannot absolutely be proved, but the balance of the evidence seems to back Cotler's argument that the second explanation is most likely.

Looking at the constitutional politics of counter-inflation and eco-nomic reform in the six cases, we can see two main patterns. In Brazil and Venezuela the presidency did suffer serious political defeats at a time of presidentially led market-reform attempts, though it would be hard to say that these defeats were the result of inherent presidential powerlessness. Political mistakes and corruption explain more. More-over, in both countries there was sufficient presidential power in the system to allow subsequent presidents – Cardoso and Caldera – to pursue gradual reform. Gradualist market reform largely succeeded in

Brazil, though not in Venezuela, where it was ultimately rejected at the polls.

In the other pattern, in Bolivia, Argentina, Mexico and Peru, market reform was accompanied by a period of centralization under a strong presidential figure. The degree of illegality involved in this centralization is in ascending order. Paz in Bolivia seems to have respected the constitution completely. Menem's government in Argentina involved limited breaches of the constitution, but these were not nearly so serious as to threaten constitutional breakdown. In Mexico the fact that public opinion was willing, in retrospect, to turn a blind eye to the 1988 election results was probably necessary for Salinas's ambitious economic reforms to succeed. In Peru, which is the most dramatic case, the closure of congress and suspension of the constitution followed on from an already autocratic style of counter-inflationary policy.

The general conclusions are twofold. One is that Peru is the exceptional case. The other is that there is no strong comparative evidence associating constitutional breakdown, presidential impeachment, the success or otherwise of economic policy, or indeed anything much else with the strength or weakness of formal presidential powers alone. It all depended on how the political game was played. Institutional limits on presidential power may form part of a more complex explanation, but we do need to get a sense of how partisan politics worked as well.

Partisan power in comparative perspective

An earlier chapter pointed out that, in non-consolidated democracies, partisan power could at times prove to be greater than constitutional power. This did not make constitutional rules completely irrelevant, but it did limit the extent to which they could explain outcomes. It therefore seems logical to hypothesize that differences in the distribution of partisan power may prove to be of major importance in explaining the politics of counter-inflation.

In this context, it is noteworthy that Salinas, Paz and Menem all came to office with political bases of support that gave them advantages that Pérez, Collor and Fujimori did not have. The former group could genuinely rely on backing from powerful political parties and allies. The latter group either had limited party support or else (as in the case of Pérez) led a badly divided party. The former group all succeeded in bringing about economic transformation in a more-or-less democratic context while the latter did not, either failing completely or (as in the case of Fujimori) succeeding by means of overthrowing the constitution altogether.

It therefore seems that there are two ways in which crisis politics can be dangerous for constitutional government. One is when crisis-resolving measures are bitterly unpopular and therefore expose a president who is weak in partisan terms (and perhaps constitutional terms as well) to attack from extra-constitutional forces – as happened in Venezuela. (Going a little bit beyond this discussion, this also seems to have been the case with the downfall of Argentina's de la Rúa in 2001.) The other is when the authorities could see some advantage in exploiting crises in order to impose some kind of partisan ascendancy – as happened in Peru and, with some variation, with the Mexican technocracy.

This hypothesis, while promising, needs more substantiation. We have already noted that presidents who enjoyed sufficient partisan and constitutional power to make policy did not find it necessary to challenge the constitutional system. In Bolivia, Paz Estensoro was politically as well as institutionally secure. He was the founder and leader of the MNR (the National Revolutionary Movement). He had already served twice as president. The MNR, which had originally been the effective leader of the Bolivian Revolution, was not in the mid-1980s what it once was; it had fissured several times, and no longer had labour support. Ironically one of the most important fissures came in 1971 when Paz Estensoro supported the military coup of Hugo Banzer against the left-wing military government of Juan José Torres. However, Paz Estensoro in mid-1985 enjoyed control of his own party, an alliance with Hugo Banzer's party, and support from the military. As a result, of the three areas where trouble might have been expected – congress, the military and the trade unions – only the trade unions were hostile. Moreover the role of the Bolivian trade union confederation, the COB, had been so obstructive during 1982–5 that it had by 1985 lost a lot of the political credibility that it had previously earned by standing firm against dictatorship (Ibáñez Rojo 2000).

Argentina's Menem also enjoyed a good combination of partisan and constitutional power. Menem arrived at the presidency after competing for and winning a Peronist presidential primary. As a former governor of La Rioja and a former prisoner under the 1976–83 military junta, Menem had Peronist credentials that were unimpeachable. In 1984 he briefly fell foul of the Peronist union leadership by supporting President Alfonsín over a referendum on a peace treaty with Chile, but his personal independence was respected by many, and by the mid-1980s he had acquired a high personal recognition rating among the general public (McGuire 1997, p. 208). Menem's poor relations with some of the union bosses by no means signified his political isolation. When he came to the presidency, he did so as the head of Peronism.

Although Menem moved rather abruptly in the direction of economic liberalism when in office, his economic break did not reflect any fundamental political break. Although the unions were hostile to much of what he was trying to do, he never faced a united trade union front. Nor did he ever claim to be anything other than a Peronist. It could be argued that the well-known 'Nixon in China' effect helped Menem with his policies. Certainly, amid the complex bargaining that took place between Menem and the various trade unions, there was the continued recognition that he was negotiating with his own side. He was also prepared to negotiate some of the details of Argentina's reorganized corporatist system. These details were highly important to the unions themselves (McGuire 1997; Phillips 1998). Menem also gained the support of Argentine business, which proved entirely supportive of what he was trying to do.

Menem's relationship with the military was more complex. The last two years of Alfonsín's government were marked by considerable military unrest (Norden 1996). Those officers most restive within the military – the so-called *carapintadas* – identified themselves with the left of the political spectrum, in reaction to the many failures of the 1976–83 military regime. Dissident officers also objected to the Alfonsín government's attempt to try senior officers from the previous military junta. There can be no doubt that many of these dissident officers supported Menem in 1989 and that Menem helped his relationship with the military by promising an amnesty to cover criminal acts committed during the 1976–83 period. Nobody has yet proved that relations between Menem and the military went beyond what was constitutionally permissible. Once he was in office, Menem soon made it clear that he would offer much less to the *carapintadas* than they had hoped; the amnesty went ahead but the president in other ways sought to protect his government from undue *carapintada* influence (Norden 1996). Deteriorating relations finally led to a military revolt in December 1990, which failed completely.

Overall, then, Menem's partisan position in 1989–90 was fairly strong. His policies had the clear support of business. Organized labour, stronger in Argentina at that time than anywhere else in Latin America, did not support his policies but could not oppose them unconditionally. Menem was a Peronist and a man supported by many ordinary workers: he was also a supremely skilful negotiator. The military was divided, and the potential hostility of some military officers was a real threat. However, Menem could face down military rebellion when it came. The military were after all quite unpopular in

Argentina after the 1976–83 debacles, and Menem himself was by no means a creature of the military.

Mexico's Salinas also enjoyed partisan as well as institutional power. This is partly due to the fact that Mexican presidents always did, at any rate until the 'tequila crisis' of 1994–5. However, it is also because Salinas had been careful to build bridges to big business and to the United States before reaching the presidency, and was careful to be seen to negotiate with Fidel Velázquez, the long-standing head of the Mexican labour confederation (the CTM), and to avoid becoming completely isolated from the old-guard PRI. It did not hurt that his family had personal relationships with influential figures within the PRI. In addition Salinas negotiated a so-called governability pact with the main conservative opposition party, the PAN. Although the Mexican left was stronger than it had once been and was directly hostile to Salinas, it was not enough on its own to threaten the system. There were no serious partisan weaknesses in Salinas's position.

On the other side, there was Collor who stood for office with the discourse of a populist (Panizza 2000b), and who seems to have made few informal deals with other parties or political organizations. He had strong media support but no close political allies. The Brazilian political system, while allowing some scope for presidential decree power, is in many ways decentralized and lacking in organized focus. The ideas behind the 1988 constitution reflected a considerable distrust of centralized authority, largely in reaction against what was then seen as the over-centralization characteristic of post-1964 military rule. It is therefore hard for an individual politician, even a president, to dominate such a system without a wide range of political support. Collor did not have this and he suffered for it.

Venezuela's Pérez seemed to have significant partisan support by virtue of his leadership of Acción Democrática. However, as we have seen, AD was split between the supporters of the outgoing president Lusinchi and Pérez himself. It has been suggested that there is an institutional aspect here, in that the conflict for the nomination of the subsequent presidential candidate of the currently governing party will inevitably divide the president from other members of his party (Coppedge 1994). (In Mexico the system by which the outgoing president chose his successor effectively eliminated this source of conflict.) While this may well be true, there were other problems as well. For one thing the AD unions, who were previously politically moderate and generally loyal to leaders from within their own party, had to compete after 1989 with the more militant figures from Causa R (Murillo 2001). These, as we shall see in the next chapter, seem to have had some kind of connection with conspirators from within the military. It is also evident that Pérez did not act as though he needed as much partisan support as he (in retrospect) did and therefore alienated potential supporters. As with Collor, there seems to have been a mixture of unavoidable partisan weakness and faulty tactics that made the president weaker still.

In some important respects, Fujimori had even less partisan support than the other two. He was, in 1990, the beneficiary of a largely tactical vote. As late as February 1990 Fujimori's support was recorded at 0.5 per cent by opinion pollsters, and many observers believed that he was not seriously running for the presidency at all. Some people reckon that he only wanted to be a senator and that he allowed his name to go onto the presidential ballot in order to get the necessary name recognition. What moved popular preferences so rapidly were tactical considerations. Vargas Llosa had promised an economic and political liberal strategy that was widely unpopular, and his membership of the traditional white-skinned ruling elite was also a source of voter suspicion. For many of Vargas Llosa's opponents, Fujimori was the only conceivable alternative who could perhaps go into the second (runoff) round of the elections with some possibility of success. The Marxist left could not hope to elect a president. APRA, while still benefiting from a strong political machine, was unelectable due to the unpopularity of the Alan García government. There is a suggestion that Alan García himself, fearing that APRA would face an inevitable defeat and having private reservations about the APRA candidate, quietly started supporting Fujimori a few weeks before the first round (Crabtree 1992, p. 179). With a mixture of his own natural support and 'borrowed' help from others, Fujimori achieved 24 per cent of the vote in the first round of the 1990 presidential elections. This was enough to enter the second round, where the anti-Vargas Llosa vote concentrated behind him.

As a result of his initial anonymity, Fujimori was in a position of much greater weakness as president than any of the others considered here. The vast majority of Peruvians regarded him as a second-choice president. He had, moreover, little political experience, no majority in congress and no prospect of getting one. There was no system of mid-term elections in Peru. The trade unions were less important in Peru than in Bolivia or Argentina, but this was because of terrorism rather than because of any governmental credibility. In any case, Fujimori had no support there either.

Although Fujimori's position in civilian politics was weak in the aftermath of his election, this was evidently not the case *vis-à-vis* the military. Indeed, whereas Pérez ignored the military to his cost, and Paz Estensoro and Menem sought little more than its neutrality and political demobilization (despite Menem's earlier flirtation with the *carapintadas*), Fujimori sought its active support. This ultimately explains why his record in government proved very different from either of the others.

In political terms the alliance with the military was manifestly to Fujimori's partisan political advantage. This is clearly a case where incentive structures worked to destabilize democracy rather than deepen it. Ruling in alliance with the military was almost certainly a better option for Fujimori, so long as he could achieve it, than the other possibilities – governing alone or seeking coalition with either APRA or the right-wing coalition (Kenney 1996). However, the circumstances that permitted such a calculation of advantage were quite unusual. Most people who get elected to the presidency do have some hope of having sufficient political support to be able to govern without imme-diately having to seek an alliance with the military.

This discussion of partisan power does lend itself to a conclusion. This is that the politics of coping with economic crisis very much depends upon the initial political base with which the government starts out. The MNR and the alliance with Banzer helped Paz, Peronism helped Menem, and the Mexican state machine supported Salinas. However, this conclusion does not explain what happens when a president lacks sufficient partisan support. Failure is sometimes pos-sible in this situation, but it is not inevitable. Here we have something to learn from Fujimori.

Fujimori lacked partisan support and surely calculated that this was a problem. It is entirely likely that his lack of civilian backing induced him to look to the military. He did not face any constraint in the imme-diate sense of being prevented from carrying out economic policy – he probably exaggerated this point for political reasons. The problem was that he had no real security of tenure. He could be removed from office by a hostile congress as soon as the latter had the necessary motive and opportunity. Already in early 1992 Fujimori's wife started to make alle-gations of corruption against the president's relatives. These were fairly small-scale in comparison with what was being alleged against Collor in Brazil. Nevertheless Fujimori's lack of partisan support within civil society would surely have been an important factor in encouraging congress to consider impeaching him whenever this appeared to the advantage of the opposition parties.

Falling inflation and increasing returns to power

Partisan power will of course vary over time, depending on whether or not a government's policies succeed. Presidents typically increase their popularity, and therefore their partisan support, once they successfully bring down high rates of inflation and allow economic growth to resume. Fujimori certainly seems to have benefited from a tendency for presidents who successfully achieved a rapid fall in the rate of inflation to enjoy a honeymoon effect. This is a significant finding because it cuts against at least some arguments presented in the existing political economy literature. Przeworski described stabilization packages as 'necessary but costly' (Przeworski 1991, p. 47). Until the early 1990s, political economists tended to believe that effective anti-inflationary policies would reduce the popularity of the government of the day. Political practitioners also shared this belief – including in all probability Peruvian congressmen who thought that Fujimori's sharp economic adjustments would make the president less rather than more popular. This is, no doubt, a part of the explanation for why inflation in several countries was allowed to mount as it did during the 1980s. Incumbents calculated (possibly wrongly) that inflation would be less politically damaging than an effective counter-inflationary policy.

The idea that anti-inflationary policies are necessarily politically costly would have fitted some electoral facts as well. As we have seen, candidates for the presidency who advocated shock treatment tended to perform poorly in the polls. This was the case with Vargas Llosa in Peru and Eduardo Fernández in Venezuela, both of whom lost elections that they were expected to win largely because of their advocacy of orthodox policies. This is no doubt partly a matter of psychology. A person with a bad toothache may wish to avoid going to the dentist, but once the treatment is finally over she or he may be very glad to have been. However, it is also a matter of globalization. Shock treatment in Peru and Argentina at the beginning of the 1990s was still a matter of pain followed by gain, but there was less pain and more (and above all quicker) gain than had been the case a decade earlier.

In Peru and Bolivia there was an additional factor increasing the attractiveness of orthodox stabilization policies after the fact. Both of these countries, unlike most of the region, are classified as sufficiently poor to enjoy some loans from the IFIs on concessionary terms. The fact that Peru's Alan García had actually defaulted on the country's concessionary debt – an unusual step for Latin America even in the 1980s – increased the prize available to Peru from reinsertion into the world financial economy. There was the opportunity of resumed IFI lending on concessionary terms even before the tougher negotiations that would inevitably have preceded a 'Brady' deal.

The comparative evidence therefore shows that successful counter-inflationary policies in the 1990s fed through quite quickly to the popularity of those responsible for achieving them. Brazil's Cardoso, who served as finance minister in 1993–4 when the Real Plan was put in place, used its popularity to launch a successful candidacy for president in 1994. Paz Estensoro, who was eighty-one years old at the end of his term, did not seek to capitalize on his economic programme. However, his planning minister, Sánchez de Lozada, did launch himself as presidential candidate in 1989. Sánchez de Lozada got more votes than any other candidate and Banzer came second, but in the end the congress chose the third-placed candidate. Menem sought to use his popularity by negotiating a change in the country's constitution to permit him to run for re-election, and then running for re-election and being elected. Salinas, too, enjoyed enhanced popularity as the result of there being much lower inflation during his term of office than under his predecessor. As we have seen, Venezuela's Pérez did not enjoy a political counter-inflationary bonus, and this may have been important. If Venezuela had already been experiencing high inflation early in 1989 (as opposed to this being no more than an economists' prediction), then Pérez's stabilization measures might have been better received.

Another president who failed to enjoy any such bonus was Collor. Serious corruption allegations surfaced against Collor in May 1992 and he was impeached in December. This impeachment was a political process, but only partly so. The allegations made against Collor were extremely serious and apparently well founded. However, most observers agree that Collor was already losing popularity by early 1992 and that the allegations found him in a position of weakness due to isolation (Mainwaring 1997; Panizza 2000a, 2000b). It is possible that one factor explaining why Collor benefited less from declining inflation than the others was that, though a conservative politician trying to impose semi-market-oriented reforms, he did not win the support or confidence of business leaders. He clashed several times with the São Paulo business confederation FIESP.

However, only in the case of Peru did this counter-inflationary bonus facilitate constitutional breakdown by increasing Fujimori's partisan power to the point that this clearly exceeded constitutional power. His increased popularity was real enough. After he closed the national congress, Fujimori organized a fresh constituent assembly, successfully submitted the proposed new constitution to a referendum, and then successfully ran for presidential re-election in 1995. None of this could have happened as it did were it not for Fujimori's popularity. As we shall see, this cannot be ascribed just to economic conditions. Security factors were important as well. Even so an economic failure would assuredly have hurt his popularity significantly and increased his political vulnerability.

Conclusions: the role of economic crisis

Difficult economic conditions in Latin America have made democratic consolidation harder to achieve in the region, but they have certainly not made constitutional breakdown inevitable. The fact that national experiences of economic crisis have proved significantly different from each other suggests that purely economic interpretations of unconstitutional politics are insufficient. We need a political aspect as well. The conclusion here is that, while both partisan and formal institutional power are relevant to any such analysis, partisan power mostly matters more. Constitutional breakdowns occurred when partisan coalitions had both the desire and the ability to bring them about. There is nothing automatic about this process. Economic factors impact on the political process mainly by shifting the relative power of partisan groups, and the beneficiaries of this shift might then be emboldened to break the rules of the game from their newly strengthened position.

Economic factors were not, in the majority of cases, the prime concern of those who sought institutional rupture. The military/security dimension was important in both Venezuela and Peru, and will be discussed in a later chapter. Economic considerations were, though, of more importance in persuading the Mexican technocratic elite to ignore irregularities in the 1988 elections and, more remarkably still, to democratize Mexico thereafter. Salinas and his allies calculated that it would be possible to persuade most people to support an irregularly elected president if economic conditions improved – as indeed they did.

The positive aspect to this discussion is that even non-consolidated democratic institutions in most Latin American countries survived the hyperinflationary crises that struck at the end of the 1980s. It is too early to pronounce confidently on the likely long-term consequences of renewed economic setbacks since 1998. So far, their short-term effects have included some part in the fall of Fujimori in Peru, an abortive coup in Ecuador and the election of Hugo Chávez in Venezuela. They also precipitated a full-scale constitutional, though not yet democratic, crisis in Argentina. If the argument here is correct, then the longer-term effects will depend upon the political realignments that may be occurring in the face of a renewed need to reconsider the basics of economic strategy.

8

Chávez and the Crisis in the Punto Fijo System in Venezuela

In February 1992 Lieutenant-Colonel Hugo Chávez led an unsuccessful coup attempt against the elected Venezuelan government. He was then imprisoned. Amnestied by President Caldera at the beginning of 1994, Chávez organized a political movement with such success that he won the December 1998 presidential elections with 56 per cent of the vote. Rather than have to share power with a congress that was elected in November 1998, Chávez then organized a referendum on whether to call a constituent assembly. He won the referendum in April 1999, had a new constituent assembly elected and then put the old congress under pressure to dissolve itself. Chávez won a further referendum in December 1999 to have the new constitution approved, and he stood once again for election as president under the new constitution, winning by a substantial margin in July 2000. The new constitution, unlike the old, permits immediate presidential re-election. Chávez remained a polarizing influence thereafter, and in April 2002, in what seemed almost a mirror image of the February 1992 coup, he himself narrowly survived a coup attempt. This failed to overthrow the government but did leave the Chavista system apparently weakened.

It is too early to provide a full and balanced assessment of the Chávez presidency. What is already clear, though, is that it is personalist and plebiscitary. Chavismo represents a positive rejection of the civilian institutions – legislative, judicial and bureaucratic – that existed before 1998. To the extent that Chávez has relied on any branch of the state, this has been the military. Military officers have increasingly filled bureaucratic positions that were formerly occupied by civilians. While as of June 2001 some 176 officers held formal positions in the public sector, a further 29,000 ordinary troops become involved in 'Plan Bolivar 2000', which was a kind of military-led public works programme (Trinkunas 2002). It is also clear that state bias has continued and perhaps even intensified since 1998. Selectivity in the use of state resources, whether in the military, local government or trade unions, has operated to reward supporters and punish enemies. There is therefore a sense in which non-consolidated democracy based on a Bolivarian concept of presidentialism is something preferred by Chávez in principle. This represents a complete turnaround from the principles of the pre-1988 democratic system – the so-called Punto Fijo system.[1] The Punto Fijo system was designed around strong political parties and negotiated solutions to political problems. In practice, though, it suffered from the key problems identified in the first part of this work. The rule of law was weak, the bureaucracy was patrimonial and the state was biased.

Although the Punto Fijo system did not succeed in consolidating Venezuelan democratic institutions, it did help produce a genuine culture of democracy. However, when push came to shove, this democratic culture did not prevent – in fact it possibly facilitated – the overthrow of the national constitution. When campaigning for the presidency in 1998, Chávez was entirely clear about what he wanted to achieve, and his vision of Venezuela won popular support. The traditional parties, with their emphasis on negotiated solutions to problems, received a derisory share of the vote. The argument that Venezuela has a democratic culture but not a liberal or pluralist one seems plausible indeed.

This discussion focuses on some essentially limited aspects of what is inevitably a complex story. It is concerned mainly with the decline of the pre-1998 system. Economic issues were discussed in the last chapter, and this chapter attempts to address broader institutional issues.

The discussion highlights three aspects of vulnerability. One of them is the conflict that was forced underground but still existed between what we might call liberal and Bolivarian concepts of governance. In this context it is certainly significant that the Punto Fijo system generated enemies who considered it justifiable to try to overthrow an elected government by force. These enemies were not all either demonstrably anti-democratic or insane. If they had been either, then the repeated verdicts of the Venezuelan electorate during the years 1998–2000 could not be understood at all – as indeed they have not been by at least some of Chávez's opponents.

---

[1] The post-1958 democratic system in Venezuela was generally known as the Punto Fijo system, after the name of the house belonging to Rafael Caldera where the pact was negotiated.

At the risk of repetition, the central point is that any particular set of democratic institutions somehow relates to a set of values that are narrower than a preference for democracy per se. Venezuela's Punto Fijo institutions were based on a concept of pluralism and representation. They were incompatible in the end with the preference of Venezuelan voters for leadership and strong executive authority. While Chávez was particularly decisive in his rejection of the Punto Fijo system, earlier anti-Punto Fijo politicians such as Larrazabal and Uslar Pietri had once achieved some popular success. So indeed, for a time, did Pérez Jiménez. Rafael Caldera, one of the founders of the Punto Fijo system, also ran as an independent candidate for the presidency in 1993. Chávez's election victory in 1998 was, in this sense, surprising but not completely unprecedented.

The second aspect of vulnerability is that state patrimonialism under the Punto Fijo system reduced the ability of the system to defend itself when under attack. The fact that the military conspiracy before February 1992 got as far as it did without anybody in authority noticing was devastating for the prestige and indeed the survival of the system. This is partly because there was an almost textbook relationship between state bias and policy inefficiency. It is also because state bias itself can create resentment among those excluded, and therefore a desire to rebel. While it is not accurate to suggest that the Chávez movement was made up exclusively of people prepared to support the Punto Fijo system but repelled by its patrimonialism, some Chávez sympathizers did indeed think in this way.

This brings us to the third aspect. Venezuela's negotiated democracy in the end found it impossible to cope with a crisis of legitimacy. The system had participants and supporters, but when it came to it the supporters of the system were unwilling to come together and make sacrifices for the common interest. The fact that Acción Democrática's Alfaro Ucero was willing to pursue his absurd 1998 presidential candidacy almost to the finish rather symbolized the problem. Once confidence in a political system and its leaders was lost, then the pacted and negotiated characteristics that were once seen as a democratic strength were turned into a source of weakness. This is because they worked against the emergence of effective leadership from within the system.

There is, no doubt, much more that can be said. However, the Venezuelan experience does suggest that some conditions necessary for democratic consolidation can be regarded as analogous to features of a body's immune system. Democracies will not necessarily face severe challenges all the time, but when they do their ability to defend themselves is critical. Law enforcement and an effective bureaucracy are part of the defence mechanisms of any democracy. In their absence, problems that should normally be resolvable may turn into severe crises. There is a sense in which Venezuela's Punto Fijo system succumbed to an opportunistic infection because of its lack of effective defences.

Non-consolidated democracy and the Punto Fijo system

Venezuela's Punto Fijo system did enjoy some apparent strength. The system was based around very strongly organized, established parties that competed for office under electoral rules but also dealt with policy problems by negotiating deals behind the scenes. Venezuela's democratic system was certainly free of some of the most common weaknesses upon which pre-1980 democratic breakdown in Latin America were generally blamed. Those who ran the dominant parties were politically moderate. They routinely negotiated and co-operated with each other. There was little political exclusivity. The result was a significant degree of consensus within the political elite. There is no suggestion that any Venezuelan government, with the exception of that of Pérez during 1989–92, had policy objectives to which the majority of Venezuelans objected in principle. There was little ideological polarization. The kind of social conflict that led to crisis and tragedy in Spain in 1936 and Chile in 1973 was avoided. Indeed, according to most of the criteria accepted by 1990s political scientists as predictive of democratic stability, Venezuela scored high.

A longer-run historical perspective might have identified some problems that were not immediately apparent. Venezuela had a long history of authoritarian rule and a form of democratic transition that was less consensual than often claimed at the time. A brief democratic interlude from 1945 to 1948 saw very strong political partisanship, and the opposition to the elected Acción Democrática government soon resorted to the time-honoured practice of 'knocking at the doors of the barracks'. These importunings were successful, and the military overthrew Acción Democrática in 1948, staying in power until early 1958. The military regime of Pérez Jiménez (1948–58) was particularly corrupt and personalistic.

When Pérez Jiménez was finally overthrown, tensions quickly appeared among the victors. Those military officers who had taken personal risks to bring down the dictatorship wanted some political reward. So did the Communist Party which, after a period of ambivalence, finally committed itself against the dictatorship. So, of course, did the leadership of Acción Democrática, which had been persecuted by the dictatorship and which stood to win free and fair elections. However, there was some tension between the party activists who had remained in Venezuela and fought the dictatorship and the most established opposition leaders who were abroad, and who had 'learned' from the 1945–8 period that they would have to manage power cautiously if their chance came again.

The Punto Fijo agreement involved Acción Democrática, COPEI (the Christian Democratic Party), which had during 1945–8 been a semi-disloyal opposition, and some other political individuals and organizations. It was an agreement to establish the principles of liberal democracy such as free and fair elections, to limit any political disputes that might destabilize the democratic system, and to exclude the Communists, who were seen as potential enemies of democracy. Quite realistically, the Punto Fijo leaders believed that a democratic system which featured active Communist participation would risk the wrath of the United States and the early return of the military. Parallel to the party-political system, there was also set up a corporatist system of economic decision-making that gave considerable discretionary power to business and also involved organized labour, whose power was evidently less (Arroyo 1983; Crisp 2000). One might define the end result as a kind of liberal corporatism.

Punto Fijo democracy was essentially a marriage of convenience – a set of political arrangements made for pragmatic political purposes. It was the result of a classic 'pacted transition' rather than an institutional rupture. This is not to suggest that the leaders of post-1958 Venezuela were especially narrow or intolerant. Nor were they unpopular. Acción Democrática and COPEI enjoyed some conclusive election victories between 1968 and 1988. However, Punto Fijo institutions faced an element of rejection from the outset from those who believed that democratization did not change enough.

There were indeed several important respects in which the system did not change under democracy. As we saw in an earlier chapter, recruitment to the public bureaucracy remained patrimonial. The law remained the servant of executive power while executive power itself remained to some significant degree the servant of private interests. The government was certainly very sensitive to the wishes of business elites, which quickly accommodated to the new order. In order to neutralize any potential business opposition to democracy, the private sector was allowed to become heavily involved in policy-making. Meanwhile the business sector itself faced relatively little scrutiny, either in respect of its tax liabilities or as regards its general conduct of business affairs. It was, for example, an open secret well before the collapse of the Banco Latino at the beginning of 1994 that much of the banking system was politicized and corruptly run.

At the same time the party elites, especially that of Acción Democrática, actively sought to control the judiciary. At first there were honourable motives for this. The new democracy faced some military disaffection and was also opposed by the far left, which, encouraged by the Cuban Revolution, soon sought to overthrow the system by force. A judicial system controlled by party elites could make sure that no undue partiality was shown to critics of the system. Later on, however, the same judicial control was used to protect members of the political elite from full investigation of their illicit business dealings. This problem is discussed at greater length below, and it is fundamental.

Another continuing aspect was that Venezuela remained dependent on oil revenues. The pattern of the economy, established when large-scale oil revenue began to flow to the state from around the end of the Second World War, remained in place with few changes until the early 1990s. Taxes were low and government spending quite high. The budgetary system essentially involved the flow of oil money from industry to state (the ownership of the industry being largely irrelevant), and its allocation by the state via preferred contracts, employment opportunities, etc. (see Karl 1997). This economic structure, too, reinforced a kind of liberal corporatism.

The initial performance of the Punto Fijo system was not all bad. While it is hard to be precise on this point, there is some evidence that the quality of public spending did initially improve under democratic government (Aranda 1984). More money was spent in rural areas, and some genuine poverty alleviation – or at least disease eradication – did occur. The 1950s and 1960s also saw the development of import substituting industrialization (ISI). While ISI was always going to be problematic in Venezuela, given the country's lack of natural comparative advantage in manufacturing, the system did at least create jobs. However, it proved inadequate to deal with the problems that followed the 1970s oil boom, when large-scale corruption re-entered the system. Things turned increasingly sour at the beginning of the 1980s as capital flight, commodity price fluctuations and administrative corruption interacted in a series of downward cycles, and crisis was never far away.

Although lower oil prices were certainly a negative factor, they were compounded by economic mismanagement. Much of this mismanagement had an institutional basis. For example, the Venezuelan economy has been characterized for many years by capital flight. Although some Venezuelan economists at times seemed to welcome this as a means of cooling the economy (see the discussion in Mahon 1996), it is generally regarded as negative (Rodríguez 1991). Even when oil prices were low, a pattern was generally maintained according to which oil money flowed into the coffers of the Venezuelan government, was then transferred to Venezuelan citizens (not always honestly) and was finally shifted out of Venezuela (again, not always honestly). This pattern raises obvious policy problems. One is that wealthy and even middle-class Venezuelans face a permanent temptation to speculate against their own currency, especially if there is a fixed or managed exchange-rate system in operation (this is also true of the banks). When deteriorating economic conditions lead wealth holders to stampede for the exit, even large export surpluses are not enough to stabilize the currency. This was, of course, true of Mexico too (also then a major oil exporter) in 1982, and the general Latin American debt crisis struck Venezuela with similar severity in the spring of 1983. The only reliable antidotes would have been effective bank regulation, a proper system of taxation and a competent system of accounting for public spending. In other words, there was a necessary role for law enforcement and bureaucratic regulation, but what there actually was turned out to be partisan and generally ineffective.

Then there is the complex but unavoidable issue of oil psychology. Most Venezuelans believe, or at any rate used to believe, that theirs is a naturally rich country. This is certainly the case in commodity terms (Venezuela has access to cheap hydropower and other minerals than oil). However, commodity abundance does not necessarily turn into development, and during the period of low oil prices (essentially 1986–98) the value added from oil exports was rather low – certainly much too low to turn a country of 18 million people into a nation of millionaires. It has been claimed (Romero 1997) that the resulting gap between the expectation and the reality creates cognitive dissonance and a 'we were robbed' element in the political culture. Such an attitude makes people more likely to be corrupt but also more willing to blame their problems on corruption, and to object to corruption if it excludes them from the system.

Romero's argument is certainly interesting, but popular resentment at the Punto Fijo governments (and later support for Chávez) may have owed more to institutional failure than to the mere perception of corruption. The RECADI scandal of the 1980s (briefly discussed below) and the collapse of most of the banking system in 1994 did enormous damage to the Venezuelan economy. Both of these events were significantly the result of poor regulation and weak law enforcement. Institutional aspects of the decline of the Punto Fijo system may not be the entire explanation, but they are a necessary part of any other kind of explanation – even one based on arguments about commodity dependency.

Institutional weakness, Carlos Andrés Pérez, and the decline of the Punto Fijo system

There is already a growing literature on the Punto Fijo system that relates its collapse mainly to institutional problems. However, there are significant differences in the arguments presented. A recent work by Crisp (2000, p. 4) defines institutions (as public choice theorists generally do) as 'formal structures that have codified rules of behaviour.' Crisp argues that there were real shortcomings in Venezuelan formal rules because they 'failed to evolve to reflect new social and economic realities' (ibid.). Crisp then describes an essentially corporatist political system in which elites – business, labour and party-political – were able to block demands for change without themselves having any desire for change. This forced pressures for reform outside of constitutional channels and in the end brought down the system.

Buxton (2001) also considers institutions but puts much more emphasis on their informal characteristics. The essential problems were 'the patrimonial nature of the state and the clientelistic predisposition of the dominant parties' (2001, p. 218). Moreover 'the judiciary did not function on the basis of a rule of law' (ibid., p. 220). The result was a dangerously, and eventually unacceptably, wide gap between what elected party politicians said was happening and what most people believed was happening. In the long run, people simply lost confidence in their own political system.

Both arguments have merit, though the Buxton approach is closer to the one taken here and closer to the notion of democratic non-consolidation. It is of course possible that a different formal institutional design might have enabled, or perhaps forced, the political elite to reform the system sooner than it did. Crisp is right to state that the system of economic policy-making under Punto Fijo was rigid and oligarchic (Crisp 2000). Party, trade union and business leaderships were authoritarian figures within their own constituencies and essentially collaborationist *vis-à-vis* each other. The exclusiveness inherent in such a situation made it easier for radical opponents of the whole system to get a hearing. What made this more damaging was the fact that the Punto Fijo system was designed to be socially inclusive and to use oil money as a means of co-opting a whole range of social groups. This design worked adequately when the economy was progressing, but disastrously when (as happened from around 1981) the economy went into decline. At this point, distributional coalitions became negative-sum.

But how should the system have been different? In a consolidated democracy, there would have been an independent judiciary, a meritocratic bureaucracy and a system of congressional oversight with real teeth. These would have helped punish outright corruption and somewhat deterred the large-scale appropriation of the state by purely private interests. A tougher-minded system of this kind would have conferred economic benefits as well as legitimatory advantages, at least in comparison with what actually happened. A bureaucratically effective and law-enforcing corporatist system may well have its disadvantages, but it would have been a real improvement on what there was.

Punto Fijo democracy did not start out particularly corrupt. It is very hard to be sure but, to judge by the emphasis of both the media and the secondary literature, democratization seems at first to have led to some reduction in the level of corruption from that prevailing under the Pérez Jiménez dictatorship. Pérez Jiménez was for a time the incumbent holder of the *Guinness Book of Records* position of 'world's most corrupt dictator'. He even served a prison sentence for corruption at a time when this was virtually unheard of in the region. Most authors discussing Venezuelan politics in the 1960s referred to corruption much less than they did both earlier and later. This is possibly because the first democratic patriarchs of Venezuelan politics, Betancourt of AD and Caldera of COPEI, were much less tolerant of corruption than their later counterparts. It is also possibly because there was less public concern about corruption during periods of economic growth than during harder economic times. Certainly one discussion of the 1978 election cited persuasive evidence that 'administrative corruption may not have been as important an issue' as some politicians at that time supposed (O'Connor 1980, p. 67).

There is no doubt that popular concern about corruption was on the increase by the mid-1980s. Popular resentment grew as the economy declined. Some people believe that the amount of corruption started to increase under the first presidency of Carlos Andrés Pérez. This began in 1974, which was the peak year for the entire post-war Venezuelan economy. Following his departure from the presidency, Pérez only just avoided a move to strip him of his congressional immunity (ex-presidents are senators for life) so that he could face corruption charges. Questions of personal morality aside, the Pérez government's desire to recycle oil income somehow, and its belief that money would no longer really be a problem for an oil-exporting country, led to a change in the dominant culture of Venezuela. Thenceforth there was much more of a 'get rich quick' mentality among both political and economic elites.

This mentality did not change at all when the oil boom ended at the turn of the 1980s. For example, the RECADI programme was set up in 1983 to control the supply of foreign exchange. There was a differential exchange-rate system put in place by the government with the object of allocating preferential rates of exchange to economic activities of high social priority. The actual system was left open to corrupt arbitrage and capital flight. Estimates of illegal capital flight vary from $8 billion to $11 billion (see Crisp 2000 for the lower estimate; Little and Herrera 1996 for the higher one). In rough terms, at mid-1980s prices, this amounted to the loss of an entire year of total export income. Only one person suffered a criminal conviction in this case, a naturalized Chinese who – though probably guilty of something – was certainly not a major player.

It is certainly the case that administrative problems, in the organization of the police and prosecution services and in the RECADI programme itself, played a part in allowing capital flight to take place (Little and Herrera 1996). However, the failure of the system to do anything about these problems was political, cultural and above all inertial. The Punto Fijo state was simply not a law-enforcing body. Crisp seeks to equate the RECADI scandal with that of Watergate in the USA (Crisp 2000, p. 164). Yet the Watergate scandal led to the resignation of a president, prison sentences for most of his close advisors and a major change in the constitutional balance within the USA. The RECADI scandal led to the arrest of one Chinese restaurant owner. In the USA the effect of the Watergate scandal was cathartic, while the effect of the RECADI scandal in Venezuela was to build up popular frustration and resentment. It also considerably impoverished the average Venezuelan.

Corruption apart, it is far from clear that the political rules of the Venezuelan system were especially rigid. There was certainly no lack of things happening on the electoral front. After the defeat of the left-wing insurgency of the 1960s, the first Caldera government (1969–74) made a major attempt to integrate the formerly armed left into the constitutional process. The 1970s therefore saw the creation and development of the left-wing MAS. The 1980s saw agreement to introduce direct election for governorships (first held in 1989) and to press ahead with policies of decentralization that might have amounted to significant change. There were also efforts to reform the internal structure of the main parties, with various experiments with systems of presidential primary election (Coppedge 1994). These changes do suggest, as does the Chávez victory of 1998, that Venezuelan democratic culture has a certain adaptiveness. The problem was more with the culture of partisanship, selective law enforcement and patrimonialism than with the quality of political representation as such. It could be argued that the Venezuelan political system reflected the attitudes of local public opinion only too accurately.

The Chávez coup attempt

As we saw in the last chapter, in February 1989, shortly after winning presidential elections for the second time, Pérez surprised everybody by imposing some very tough economic stabilization policies. Public opinion had not been prepared for this – quite the contrary – and popular reaction was violent. There were major riots in Caracas that were brutally repressed by the police. Hundreds of people died. From a purely economic point of view, the stabilization measures that Pérez imposed were essentially successful, and the economy did start to recover in 1990. However, even though there was some subsequent alleviation of the worst economic conditions prevailing in 1989, public opinion was unwilling to forgive Pérez for the initial deception and subsequent brutality. In the eyes of many people, Pérez was a marked man. What made matters worse was the fact that Pérez began his second term with poor relations with the Lusinchi wing of Acción Democrática, which he made little attempt to repair even when himself unpopular. This left him completely exposed to attack from extra-constitutional sources, the potential threat from which he completely ignored. When Chávez attempted his coup against Pérez, in February 1992, some surveys put Pérez's approval rating as low as single figures.

While the February 1992 coup attempt certainly was directed against Pérez, it is important not to regard it as purely a reaction against the unpopularity of the government of the day. While there were opportunistic factors behind the coup, there were long-term issues involved as well. A key point is that the Punto Fijo system always had enemies. As we have seen, the Punto Fijo settlement was a product of democratizing politics under Cold War conditions. As such, it marginalized both the civilian Communists and some nationalist military officers. There was certainly some resentment both in the barracks and on the street from 1959 onwards that a team of middle-class politicians who had mostly spent the dictatorship in comfortable exile should enjoy almost the entire inheritance from its overthrow. The 'insider' quality of Venezuelan democracy was strengthened in the 1960s when Acción Democrática repeatedly purged dissidents from its ranks. The system was sufficiently closed for the military hierarchy to have considered a coup in 1969 to prevent the transfer of the presidency from Leoni of AD to Caldera of COPEI, although there were few policy disagreements between the two. The offer of a coup was, however, firmly declined.[2]

It is therefore clear that, although the majority of Venezuelans for some time regarded the Punto Fijo democratic system as a success, a small but influential minority felt excluded and angry. They had wanted a different kind of democracy. The military subsequently became an effective political focal point for a conspiracy of the disaffected. The relationship between the Punto Fijo system and the military was one of some subtlety, and one that involved ancestral political antagonisms. We need to consider it briefly here.

It is increasingly clear that the Chávez coup involved people who (or whose families) had been long-term enemies of the Punto Fijo system. They would certainly have considered themselves democrats but not as liberals, and many of them had Marxist pasts that they had by no means fully repudiated. Some others could almost be described as Fascists. The role played in the Chavista movement by those excluded by the Punto Fijo institutions (or who excluded themselves from them) can be seen from the first Chávez cabinet. This included Luis Miquilena as interior minister, Domingo Rangel as foreign minister, Ali Rodríguez as energy minister and Jorge Giordani as planning minister. All four had their roots in an essentially Marxist and not a liberal tradition.

According to Nelson Sánchez (Sánchez 2000) there was an undercurrent of military opposition to the Punto Fijo system from its earliest days. A number of officers, who had been involved in the 1958 overthrow of the Pérez Jiménez dictatorship and then found themselves politically marginalized, formed the so-called Front of Career Military Officers in 1977. This was intended to be one pillar of a tripartite system, the others being the radical church and 'the people', which aimed to re-create the popular battle against Pérez Jiménez in 1957 and 1958. Contacts were later made between this group and some former left-wing insurgents of the 1960s (on this, see Zago 1998; Blanco Muñoz 1998; Garrido 2000; Gott 2000).

The former guerrilla Douglas Bravo told Garrido that contacts between ex-Communists and sympathetic military officers date back to

---

[2] Information provided by David Myers in oral presentation at the LASA conference in Washington, September 2000.

the end of the 1960s. Some of the Marxist left had realized by then that an attempted left-wing insurgency in the 1960s had failed, and they believed that this was because the left had become too sectarian. They therefore started to look for allies as part of a movement of the nationalist left. It is incidentally worth noting that something similar was occurring in Peru at the end of the 1960s, when some former left-wing insurgents formed a ruling alliance with radical military officers under General Velasco Alvarado. Hugo Chávez seems to have been contacted by the Career Military Officers' movement through his brother, who was a civilian left-winger active in university circles. According to Medina (quoted in Buxton 2001, p. 159), Chávez was himself impressed by the Velasco government but criticized it for being too reliant on radicals within the military and insufficiently based on civilian popular support.

There were conversations between Nelson Sánchez (of the Career Military Officers), Douglas Bravo and Chávez from around 1982, just when the oil boom was beginning to turn sour. Soon afterwards, Chávez organized and led a small group of his own within the military – the Ejercito Bolivariano Revolucionario 200. Participants in these various groups did not intend an immediate uprising, because the political system still had too much support. However, they did intend to monitor the course of events and await a suitable opportunity to challenge the system. Meanwhile contacts between Chávez's military supporters and a small but growing left-wing political party, the Causa R, continued to develop. In 1986 Ali Rodríguez and Pablo Medina, both left-wing civilians, started to discuss the possibility of organizing a military-supported popular revolt.

By the end of the 1980s, the Causa R had started to develop as a serious electoral force. It won three deputy positions in congress in 1988 and the governorship of Bolivar state in 1989. As a result of hopes by some Causa R leaders that they could achieve power by electoral means, relations between Causa R and the military radicals became rather more difficult thereafter. Nevertheless, despite the fact that a number of people associated with Causa R were no longer prepared to back a coup, there were conversations between the anti-system left and some non-commissioned officers who were prepared to press on. A conflict of leadership had led Chávez to postpone the coup attempt from 16 December 1991 to 4 February 1992 (Zago 1998). There is, however, little doubt that some members of the Causa R party would have joined a post-coup government if the attempt had succeeded. In January 1992 Pablo Medina of Causa R met Chávez to discuss who would be in a post-coup cabinet (Buxton 2001, p. 162), but Causa R kept their heads down once it became clear that the coup attempt had failed.

Later on, much of the Causa R party followed Pablo Medina into the newly formed PPT and moved over to support Chávez when the latter launched his presidential candidacy in 1997.

Even at the beginning of 1992, the numbers of those involved in anti-system plotting was fairly small in proportion to the population as a whole, but their ability to operate within the military gave them an importance out of all proportion to their actual numbers. Economic trends had by then favoured the plotters, and the insensitivity and brutality with which the Caracas riots of February 1989 were put down proved a major embarrassment for the system. The coup attempt was therefore a combination of long-term conspiracy and short-term opportunity. It involved an inner core of Chavistas, who were clearly on the left of the political spectrum, and a number of military officers whose ideological orientation was quite different.

The failure of the Venezuelan state

It is therefore clear that the Punto Fijo system faced some determined and potentially powerful enemies. What is remarkable, though, is its failure to defend itself more effectively than it did. A few weeks after the coup, President Pérez was said by a close associate to be 'muy golpeado' (a play on words but meaning very shaken up) by what had happened. According to the same source, military intelligence 'failed completely' to discover what had been going on (interview with Miguel Rodríguez, March 1992). How is this failure of detection to be explained? In the immediate aftermath, the official government line was that the coup was the work of a few fanatics. Under such circumstances the overlooking of the coup attempt might have been lamentable but understandable. Not everybody found this explanation convincing at the time, but we now know it to be almost wholly false. Another interview source, a cabinet minister at the time of the coup attempt, seems to have stated much more accurately that civilian control of the military was weak due to the penetration of military intelligence units by the political parties, and their own involvement in corruption scandals (interview with Gerver Torres, March 1992; see also Trinkunas 2002). The government's failure to predict or understand the coup attempt was also very much commented upon by observers who sympathized with Chávez (Muller Rojas 1992). They saw this as yet another symptom of state incapacity and vulnerability.

In fact the military was almost routinely involved in corruption scandals during the whole Punto Fijo period (Arroyo 1983). For years the civilian political elite turned a blind eye to corruption in the military out of the belief that this would help to keep the generals out of politics. However, most opportunities for enrichment involved principally senior officers, and leadership of the coup attempt came from the middle ranks of the army. There was also significant support from within the air force. Chávez was a lieutenant-colonel at the time of the coup, while the other leaders were of similar or lower ranks. The attempt also encountered considerable support from non-commissioned officers, which is unusual in post-1945 South America. After it failed, no fewer than 273 sergeants were dishonourably discharged from the military. The sheer number of those involved is sufficient refutation on its own of the idea that the coup was the work of a small number of extremists.

We have already noted that military coup attempts in pre-1982 South America were often motivated, in part, by tension between the professional aspirations of the military hierarchy and the clientelistic forms of control sometimes preferred by elected civilians. In the Venezuelan army, recruitment and promotion of officers according to military criteria of meritocracy were in place up to the level of lieutenant-colonel. However, promotion to colonel or general had to be approved by congress – which is to say, by the leaders of the two major parties. Burggraaff and Millett may be right to say that there are only a few recorded instances of overt political interference in military promotions in Venezuela (Burggraaff and Millett 1995), but the overall perspective of more junior officers was that promotions procedures were heavily politicized. This was perceived as being contrary to the integrity and autonomy of the military. While these considerations did not greatly influence Chávez and the inner core of the coup leadership, who were already committed opponents of the system, they did influence many middle-ranking officers who were less ideologically motivated and more frustrated with the status quo.

In Venezuela, in a move to improve education levels within the military, middle-ranking officers were after 1970 required to attend postgraduate courses at university. Several of the 1992 coup leaders were, at the time that the coup was being organized, studying political science at the Simon Bolivar University. One academic responsible for teaching military officers at that university told the author that there was in 1992 overwhelming support within his class of army officers for Chávez and his coup attempt, and an almost total contempt for the generals. These were seen as having sold out to the politicians for personal advantage (interview with Luis Castro Leyva, March 1992). The middle-ranking officers saw many of their military seniors as poorly qualified political appointees (Gott 2000; Norden 1998; Trinkunas

2002). The senior officers had meanwhile lost touch with what was going on in the more junior ranks, since they interpreted their promotions (often correctly) as a reward for political rather than bureaucratic achievement.

Chávez himself stated that no colonel or general was involved in the February coup attempt (quoted in Blanco Muñoz 1998). This in itself is not so very surprising. What is surprising is that no colonel or general knew enough about what was being planned to bring it to the attention of the authorities. There is no possibility of any conspiracy of silence here. Senior officers would have had overwhelming reason to oppose a coup had they known that one was being planned, because a successful coup led by a lieutenant-colonel would have totally upset the military hierarchy. In such an eventuality, all of the senior officers would have been visibly humiliated by evidence that they had failed to control their juniors, and they would almost certainly have been forced to resign en masse.

The failure of party-based government to control the military was therefore due to a mixture of political failings and organizational military failings (Myers and O'Connor 1998). The political aspect should certainly not be ignored. Scholarly discussion of organizational problems within the military is definitely valuable and useful, but it is important that civil–military relations are not seen as a specific topic – a kind of separate, rather technical aspect of democratic politics. The crisis in civil–military relations was intimately bound up with problems affecting the system as a whole.

The crisis facing the patrimonial state by the early 1990s was evident across most of the Venezuelan public sector. There is a considerable amount of research tending to suggest that ineptitude or worse had by the early 1990s come to characterize much of the Venezuelan state. For example, research on the behaviour of the Federal Electoral Council in the early 1990s concluded that this was controlled by the dominant parties, and there was corruption, manipulation of the laws, incompetence and, on occasion, downright falsification of election results (Buxton 2001). The failure of the state to operate in a professional way in many areas of social policy was also evident (Angell and Graham 1995). The same point in respect of the judicial system was discussed in chapter 3.

The conclusion must be that the failure of the political elite to control and manage such core state institutions as the military reflected deep-rooted problems of state institutionalization. The failure of the state to control the military was, in fact, entirely typical of relations prevailing at that time between Venezuelan politicians and the state. Civilian control over the military broke down in the place where Venezuela's political institutions were at their most vulnerable – at the point of contact between the clientelistic practices of party politicians and the bureaucratic norms of a professionally run junior officer corps.

It cannot be denied either that Chávez enjoyed a great deal of luck, as well as the benefit of his opponents' mistakes. Possibly the worst thing that could have happened in February 1992 from his own point of view would have been for his coup attempt to succeed. In such an eventuality, strong opposition from the United States, the domestic business community and the political class as a whole would surely have made a military government unviable. Although Chávez later declared that he would have asked Rafael Caldera to take office as a provisional president, it is entirely likely that Caldera would have refused.

The failure of politics: Venezuela, 1992–3

What helped Chávez was not only the dignified way in which he accepted failure and imprisonment when the attempted coup was finally suppressed. It was also the utterly hopeless way in which the AD/COPEI party elites – particularly AD – responded to a difficult but not necessarily doomed political outlook after 1992. Chávez's opponents did indeed accuse him of being a potential dictator, but there were very few people listening. A good reason for their refusal to listen was the inability of Venezuela's political leaders to note the warning signs and make a real effort to reform the system.

Former president and independent presidential candidate Rafael Caldera made a speech in the immediate aftermath of the February coup, publicly declaring his support for some of the aims (though not the methods) of the coup leaders and promising them an amnesty should he be elected. This speech dramatically improved Caldera's position in the opinion polls ahead of the December 1993 elections. He moved from the position of an also-ran to that of clear front runner – a position he maintained up to the election itself. The fourth-placed candidate in the presidential election, with some 21 per cent of the national vote, was Velásquez of Causa R, which party (as we have seen) had clearly sympathized with the Chávez coup. There is compelling evidence that there was some electoral malpractice directed against the Causa R candidacy, though it is unlikely that this would have been enough to change the identity of the victor in the presidential election.

A fresh coup attempt occurred in November 1992 and serious military unrest persisted during 1993 and thereafter. Continuing tensions within the military were a major factor behind the November coup attempt. This was led by Admiral Gruber with support from the air force. According to Gruber's own account (quoted in Gott 2000), he met the defence minister in March 1992 and complained strongly that promotions procedures within the military had become over-politicized. When these complaints were ignored, he starting planning his own coup in August and launched it in November. The failure of this coup was partly the result of operational difficulties and partly because civilian support was less than expected.

Chávez himself suggests that the lack of support for Gruber had to do with the popular backing given to Caldera (Blanco Muñoz 1998). It is certainly true that Caldera was a man respected by many Chávez supporters as someone who had left COPEI (a party which he had for a long time led) and broken away from the two-party system. Arias Cárdenas and some other officers involved in the February 1992 coup attempt had by November signalled their support for Rafael Caldera's presidential candidacy.

It also seems as though some members of the business elite, desperately needing military intervention in order to (as they thought) protect their economic interests, embarked on a deliberate policy of further democratic destabilization. A bomb was set off in Venezuela's Central Park in August 1993. In the same month, Ramón J. Velásquez, who had replaced the impeached President Pérez for the remainder of his term, told a group of European and US diplomats in August that he feared that the Banco Latino was conspiring with the navy to overthrow him (confidential interview with a British diplomat). The British embassy alerted the US ambassador to what had been said. The US government, with European support, then made it very clear to the Venezuelan military that a coup would not be accepted. At around this time, a group of officers visited the Pentagon to try to discover whether Washington would support a coup against Velásquez. The potential leaders of this coup were identified as right-wing anti-Chavistas who sought to defend their proposed move by saying that Velásquez of the Causa R would probably win the December 1993 elections and that this could not be tolerated. The US administration secretly taped the conversations and passed them on to the Venezuelan defence minister during his visit to Washington in August 1993 (confidential interview). The officers concerned were quietly moved on. However, when the Banco Latino went into liquidation in February 1994, its books indicated that one senior officer may have received a payment of $300 million from the bank (Buxton 2001, p. 163).

Although these events were very disturbing, the traditional party politicians probably had one last chance to restore lost credibility to the system. In the spring of 1992 many Venezuelans regarded Chávez more as a 'whistleblower' than a potential president. This gave the government some chance to make a new start but also put them in a dilemma. How should they respond to the coup? Should they pardon everybody or punish everybody? If the authorities insisted on punishing the coup leaders but nobody else, they risked creating resentments which would prove destabilizing. Keeping Chávez in prison left the government open to a charge of hypocrisy to the extent that it was willing to discipline popular rebels while the courts routinely let obviously corrupt politicians alone. Civilian supporters of Chávez were ready and able to take to the streets to protest his gaoling. However, if the government tried to purge the political system as a whole, then they could not avoid some high-profile casualties.

It seemed at first as though the party elites would attempt reform. Following the coup attempt, President Pérez immediately sought to negotiate an understanding with Eduardo Fernández, the leader of COPEI. The immediate reaction of both was that the two dominant parties needed to coalesce and negotiate a programme of reform that might restore some credibility to the system. This was an understandable first move. Neither of the major parties wanted a coup, and Fernández was close to business elites who did not want a coup either. Many business leaders, however, were not so much pro-democracy as opposed to Chávez and his left-wing supporters, who were seen as dangerous (interview with Anibal Romero, 3 April 1992). Ominously, leading Venezuelan businessmen were no longer unconditionally supportive of the country's party-political system.

It seemed to outside observers, at first, as though a deal had been struck. The political elite would seek to restore some credibility by calling for law and order and arresting some notoriously corrupt political insiders. Political leaders and business elites would agree to give up their own 'black sheep' if the others did so as well. Pérez then brought independent AD leader Pinerua Ordáz into the cabinet with a mandate to crack down on corruption and the previous abuse of power. The rhetoric against political figures perceived as corrupt was then stepped up. Readers of the Venezuelan press were led to believe that there would be a number of spectacular arrests designed to restore some moral credibility to the system. At the end of March 1992 Fernández publicly called on Pinerua to start such a crackdown (*El Universal*, 1 April 1992).

However, there were cynics. Luis Matos Azocar, a dissident member of AD, from which he was in March 1992 in the process of being expelled, gave a press conference to mark his departure from the party. He stated that the congressional AD, by that time thoroughly alienated from Pérez, would press for the president's resignation if Pinerua brought any prominent supporters of ex-President Lusinchi to justice (*El Universal*, 1 April 1992). (Lusinchi had been president at the time of the RECADI scandal.) A major problem here was that Pérez himself was by no means immune to suspicions of corruption. His critics asked why Pérez should be protected and Lusinchi sacrificed. If Lusinchi and Pérez were both protected, of course, no other party faction would agree to have its own members arrested. In the end Matos proved correct. Anti-corruption measures against individuals were lost in the judicial system and no purge of corrupt individuals took place. There can be no doubt that this failure was the result of the party establishments looking after their own. Senior judges were thoroughly controlled by the party system and could be relied upon to follow the lead of the main party bosses.

Some well-informed observers claim that corruption had by the 1990s penetrated so deeply within the dominant parties that reform from within had become impossible. For example, Jorge Giordani told the author that party leaders at times actively encouraged lawbreaking among their subordinates as a kind of initiation into serious politics and as a means of guaranteeing their own untouchability if the political climate changed (interview, 25 November 1998). On the rare occasion where an individual was actually punished for corruption (as eventually happened to Pérez himself), this was more of a sanction for a lack of conformity to the system, or for other kinds of difference, than for corruption itself.

It is certainly significant that the party leaders, while blocking an anti-corruption drive, were willing to sacrifice Pérez's market-oriented economics programme. They were also willing to sacrifice Pérez himself, who was impeached for corruption by congress and later gaoled. There is little doubt that Pérez was guilty of corruption, but also little doubt that his removal involved political considerations. Even more to the point, the Pérez impeachment was intended to mark the end of the house-cleaning and not the beginning. In the end the party politicians based in congress were not prepared to sacrifice any of their own. While this might have been understandable in personal terms, it did nothing to reconcile disaffected military officers (who were perfectly capable of reading newspapers) to the democratic system. A kind of high-water mark of political insensitivity was reached in July 1993 when a measure was introduced into congress (though not passed) that would have decriminalized corruption and reduced it to the status of a civil misdemeanour.

The fundamental problem here is that the Venezuelan state was based on a set of negotiated understandings. These could not quickly be revised at a time of crisis. Conflicts within and between the major parties made it impossible for them to adjust quickly to new circumstances. In any case it is difficult to see how a corrupted judiciary and bureaucracy could have regained public trust without a major purge, and that would have undermined the entire basis of the pacted political system.

Caldera, non-consolidated democracy and the military, 1994–9

The election of Caldera to the presidency in December 1993 did change the political landscape. For the first time since the Punto Fijo system was set up, Venezuela had a president who was not a member of either of the main political parties. Although himself one of the main authors of the Punto Fijo system, Caldera owed his victory very significantly to his publicly expressed sympathy with the aims (not the methods) of the coup leaders. Somewhat in the manner of De Gaulle in May 1958, Caldera, while being careful to act constitutionally himself, won the election as a result of some kind of perceived association with those who had acted unconstitutionally. There is an important sense in which the pacted party-political system was defeated when this happened. Even so, Caldera was ultimately a man of the system, although he did at least understand the need for change.

Caldera was, both by temperament and by intellect, a conciliator. In office, his policy towards the military rebels was co-optative. Chávez and the coup leaders were amnestied, and a proportion of those purged after the 1992 coup attempts (around 250 out of 500 originally forced out) were reintegrated into the army. The coup leaders themselves took advantage of their freedom to enter democratic politics. One of them, Arias Cárdenas, accepted a senior position in the Caldera administration and then in 1995 was elected to the governorship of Zulia. With the election of Caldera, therefore, any notion that the February 1992 coup leaders had done something morally wrong and deserving of punishment was no longer accepted either by the government or by the majority of public opinion.

Nevertheless this did not end the crisis in civil–military relations. Caldera's treatment of the military was very much constrained by the threat of a new coup attempt. According to two close associates of Caldera, the incoming government regarded a renewed coup as a real possibility (interviews with Luis Castro Leyva, 20 April 1997, and Teodoro Petkoff, 7 April 1997; see also Trinkunas 2002). So, indeed, did the US government, which – during an incident in July 1994 – sent the defence secretary, William Perry, to Caracas. Perry invited a number of Venezuelan generals to a meeting at the US embassy in Caracas and simply told them that the USA would not tolerate a coup.

Caldera's treatment of the military was pragmatic and managerial rather than reforming. There was no real attempt to reprofessionalize the army. Upon taking office in February 1994, Caldera sacked the entire military establishment and promoted his son-in-law Rojas Pérez to a key position. When asked why he did this, he replied 'so I can sleep at night' (interview with Luis Castro Leyva, 20 April 1997). The incoming government also felt constrained in some of its policies due to fear of military opposition. This was notably the case in its handling of the 1994 banking collapse. The government agreed to indemnify depositors when the banks failed and then imposed exchange controls rather than risk capital flight and hyperinflation. Refusing to indemnify depositors in the failed banks was legally possible but politically unthinkable at a time of social unrest and questionable military loyalty. Luis Castro told the author that the government feared an 'Albanian situation' (in which rioters briefly took control of the country) if unrest developed. The government believed that the military could not be relied upon in the event of a renewed political crisis, and economic policy was constrained as a result.

The Caldera government was later accused by its critics of inertia in respect of other kinds of state reform. However, if Caldera could afford neither civil nor military unrest (civil unrest might have brought in the military), the result was enormously to empower veto groups – especially in congress, where the government lacked a majority. It is true that Caldera did have policy options that he did not use, such as calling the military into government and closing congress altogether. In a moment of crisis in July 1994 some senior political figures publicly called on Caldera to send the army in to close down congress, and there was a widespread perception that he did give the option serious thought (interview with Rodríguez Iturbe, 30 November 1998). If he had finally chosen this option, the military would probably have backed him in the short term while thereafter reducing him to a figurehead presidency. Had this happened of course, the Punto Fijo political system would have ended even sooner than it did.

The alternative was the acceptance of continuing state weakness. Between February 1992 and the inauguration of Chávez in February 1999 – and even thereafter – no Venezuelan government could be con-

fident that it genuinely monopolized force. Caldera did keep the military out of government, but the price for this was the existence of a
semi-permanent crisis of vulnerability. All that Caldera could do was
hold the line and hope that the economy would improve sufficiently
for the government's credibility to recover. Due to the collapse of the
Banco Latino and most of the rest of the Venezuelan banking system
in 1994, and continued problems in the international oil market thereafter, this did not happen. Meanwhile the former coup leaders were
energetically building up their own political party and planning
Chávez's electoral campaign for 1998. Overall, a mixture of military
unrest, a powerful but politically unfocused congress and a generally
fragmented political scene made it almost impossible for Caldera to
carry out the kind of institutional reform that most Venezuelans evidently wanted.

The dangers of Caldera's co-optative strategy could be seen in late
1998. On 19 October, by which time Hugo Chávez had established a
clear lead in the race for the presidency, General Rojas Pérez made
some intemperate comments to the effect that the military might not
accept a Chávez electoral victory. These remarks nearly provoked a
crisis because Chávez still had many supporters within the military.
According to Bernardo Álvarez, a member of the Polo Patriotico (interview, 30 November 1998), some of Chávez's supporters sought a
meeting with General Salazar, then Venezuela's military attaché in
Washington, in October. Salazar had earlier shown some support for
Chávez upon the latter's release from imprisonment, and he was
widely known to be personally hostile to General Rojas Pérez. According to Álvarez, Salazar responded to the overture from the Polo
Patriotico by talking to some US generals and warning them of a
coup attempt. At the same time, he gave the Chavistas some significant
information on the identity and disposition of the so-called Clan de Los
Llanos (i.e., Rojas Pérez supporters) within the military. Upon receipt
of this information, Chávez publicly accused some people in the military of plotting against him. Caldera responded by calling the generals together and telling them that he would totally oppose any military
intervention in the electoral process.

It is not clear whether this incident really deserves to be described
as a 'near miss'. The US military attaché, interviewed confidentially,
was privately sceptical that a genuine coup attempt was imminent,
though without ruling out some form of military unrest short of overthrowing the government (confidential interview). However, the incident does highlight the fact that civilian control over the military and
therefore the state after February 1992 remained tenuous. What kept
the peace, more than anything else, is the fact that the original coup

leaders and the traditional parties both had reasons for not wanting a coup to happen. In other words, it was factions and political calculations rather than secure democratic legitimation that kept democracy in place after February 1992. This does not bear out the view, still expressed in places in the academic literature after 1993, that Venezuela was at that time a stable democracy.

The Caldera period shows, yet again, how difficult it is to reform a patrimonial state when confidence in it has collapsed. There was a risk attached to doing little and hoping that confidence would gradually recover, but this may indeed have been the most plausible option. Caldera could not have foreseen that the established parties would compound their unpopularity by some disastrously counter-productive electoral manoeuvres during 1998 while Chávez proved a brilliant campaigner. However, an attempt at drastic reform from a position of weakness would have risked bringing down the entire system. It may well be that Caldera played the best cards that were available to him, but in the end Chávez could not be stopped.

The state and non-consolidated democracy in Venezuela: conclusions and a postscript on Chávez

One could see the evolution of post-1958 democracy as a kind of 'decline and fall'. No democracy can be completely inclusionary since all institutional structures are likely to privilege some forms of political organization over others. There also, inevitably, had to be certain exclusionary features in any democratic system set up in Latin America during the Cold War in any country with a potentially powerful Communist Party. However, while the Punto Fijo system did have its partisan and exclusionary aspects, it had inclusionary and flexible aspects as well. Indeed the system was reformed after 1969 and again after 1989 (when local elections for governor were established) in ways that do not suggest any determined strategy of political exclusion. The Chavista state is much more openly partisan, with a much more evident willingness to use the state for political advantage.

The key point about the Punto Fijo system in this context is its political vulnerability. This problem went far beyond the corruption, unpopularity or policy failures of particular governments. Patrimonialism and weak law enforcement amounted to a kind of immune deficiency, allowing the Punto Fijo system to succumb to what was in essence an opportunistic attack. The lack of respected 'focal point' institutions subsequently deprived Venezuelan elite politicians of a necessary means of self-defence when the system as a whole came under threat. Because the political order was based on a set of mutually accommodating organizational arrangements underpinned by partisanship, organizational and often personal self-interest undermined every step that the political authorities sought to take in defence of the system. There was no institutional underpinning that could permit the self-reinforcement of the system when it came under pressure.

It is of course true that very poor policy performance aggravated this problem. Surveys showed quite a high level of support among Venezuelans for democracy until around 1980 and a fall off thereafter. In the mid-1990s, Templeton noted that 'discontent and disillusion is most critical among those segments of the population that gave support to the democratic regime in its early years and that appear to have benefited least from it' (Templeton 1995, p. 102). To some extent, though, very poor policy performance itself was the consequence of institutional problems. Some authors have suggested that this disillusionment was due to the collapse of the oil price and popular willingness to blame corruption for the difficult but unavoidable circumstances that resulted. However, many electorates in the world might be expected to blame corruption if they found that illegal capital flight within the space of a few years amounted to the value of a full year's export income – and that only a Chinese restaurant owner was prosecuted as a result.

A democratic state needs to keep its politicians reasonably honest or else it will lose credibility. Bargaining and negotiation within the political class will not necessarily do the job because of the well-known limitations on self-regulation. Some people may suppose that Venezuelan politicians were likely to be particularly corrupt, perhaps on account of the influence of oil or the tradition of corruption handed down from authoritarianism, or perhaps because of flaws in the Punto Fijo arrangements themselves. However, the ability of people in power to resist everything except temptation is human, not especially Venezuelan. Democratic political life does need a degree of discipline, and this has to be imposed by autonomous state institutions.

As far as post-1998 Venezuela is concerned, the relevant conclusion would therefore have to be about continuity as much as about change. One form of non-consolidated democracy has replaced another. A non-consolidated democracy is inherently a more provisional and flexible form of government than consolidated democracy because it does not necessarily break down when the constitution is broken. This may make it look as though it is permanently on the borderline of radical change. However, seemingly radical changes in the political process need not have any positive (or for that matter negative) effect on the building of political institutions for the long term. There may be instead a dreary succession of personalists who have on offer more of the same – a state that is biased towards incumbents and whose partisan attitudes inhibit democratic consolidation and damage economic performance.

9

Non-Consolidation and Semi-Authoritarianism: Fujimori's Peru

This chapter is largely about Fujimori's Peru. Fujimori was elected to the presidency in 1990 as an independent candidate, quite legitimately although to the surprise of most observers. As late as February 1990 his standing in the polls was no more than 0.5 per cent. In April 1992 he called in the military to close congress. This was obviously an illegal move, but it was also a popular one. Not only did constitutional governance not self-reinforce in 1992, but in fact the constitution was broken with enthusiastic popular support. The rest of Fujimori's government was eventful, with the high points being the approval of a new constitution by plebiscite in 1993 and Fujimori's re-election by a large popular majority in 1995. In 2000 a further attempt at re-election appeared successful if controversial, but opinion soon turned against the president and forced his resignation in November of that year. For students of democratic non-consolidation, Peru in the 1990s offers a very rich field of observation.

In retrospect, there can be little doubt that Peruvian representative institutions were very vulnerable in April 1992. The obvious point is that both Fujimori and his military supporters had everything to gain by closing congress and ruling through the executive because there was every likelihood that the move would be popular – as indeed it turned out to be. International responses were actually adverse, but they could be negotiated as long as Fujimori retained popular support at home (Costa 1993). Foreign governments could not easily maintain their opposition against plebiscitary evidence in Fujimori's favour from Peru itself. Moreover the international community needed Peruvian co-operation on other matters, including – as it appeared at least – on the drugs issue.

The popularity of the Peruvian coup is evidence that people will not necessarily support a constitutional order merely because it is one. The circumstances, though, were much more extreme than in Venezuela, and popular rejection of politicians was of no real surprise given the magnitude of the policy failures of democratically elected rulers in the 1980s. One might regard Peru at the beginning of the 1990s as forming an extreme example of non-consolidated democracy. However, while specific aspects of the local situation are always interesting, the general lessons to be drawn – that a democracy is vulnerable if it performs badly enough and if there is a strong enough partisan coalition ready to overthrow it – are rather straightforward.

The more interesting comparative questions have to do with the end of the Fujimori government. This is partly because the Fujimori story does have a clear ending, which is not so far the case with Chávez. It is also because democracy survived despite the existence of a number of negative indicators. The decisive dynamic was the unravelling of the partisan coalition behind Fujimori, as manifested in the breach with Vladimir Montesinos and the resulting defection of a decisive number of congresspeople to the opposition. The key underlying factor, as so often, was probably the role of public opinion.

The Fujimori government also showed something that is relevant to Mexico as well and will be discussed further in the next chapter. Non-consolidated democracy, as we have seen, tends to produce partisan rather than constitutional politics. The state is likely to be biased and politics may be very corrupt. However, partisan governments are not necessarily ineffective. Semi-authoritarian systems are sometimes capable of achieving spectacular policy triumphs in the short run. The arrest of Abimael Guzmán in September 1992 and Mexico's entry into the NAFTA in 1994 (something discussed in the next chapter) form two items in a rather short list of major Latin American policy triumphs in the 1990s. The problem is that partisan governments tend both to inherit and to pass on partisanship, and there are some things that partisan governments cannot easily do – such as professionalize the bureaucracy (except perhaps in some narrow aspects) or establish powerful independent law enforcement.

The military and counter-insurgency in Peru

One important factor specific to Peru at that time was the role of its military. Although Peru has had long periods of military rule, none of its military governments was so obviously intolerable that a return was virtually unthinkable. (This is true of Ecuador and perhaps Venezuela as well.) Moreover the military was involved during the 1980s in a 'dirty war' against the Sendero Luminoso insurgency. Inevitably this kind of operation runs the risk of bringing the military back into politics. The combination of a recent history of reasonably popular military rule and military involvement in counter-insurgency was an ominous one for constitutional stability. The fact that Peru was a major participant in the illegal drugs trade complicated matters further.

There is a lot that we still do not know about civil–military relations in Peru in the 1990s. What is quite clear, though, is that the 1992 autogolpe was only the tip of a very large iceberg of military-political intervention. This intervention had much to do with the role of Sendero Luminoso, on which there is a significant literature (Palmer 1992, McClintock 1998). It now appears that this was a disciplined insurgency that had long been planned and organized by its leader, Abimael Guzmán. Unlike previous insurgencies in Peru, which had generally suffered severe problems due to lack of money, Sendero was able to raise 'taxes' from coca growers and smugglers. By the mid-1980s Sendero was able to pay its volunteers significantly more than the state paid to schoolteachers (Kay 1999).

It was probably unavoidable that the failure of either of Peru's elected presidents Belaúnde (1980–85) or García (1985–90) to deal effectively with Sendero Luminoso and the MRTA – or indeed the drugs trade – would create political tensions. One of the reasons for these tensions was that the civilian presidents were worried about the political implications of setting the military loose against Sendero. Belaúnde had been the elected president overthrown by the military in 1968, and he did not want to bring them back. Meanwhile military officers were not willing to take illegal measures against suspected Senderistas without the assurance of political backing. They did not want to risk defeating Sendero and then being tried for human-rights abuses committed during the conflict. Furthermore conflicts within the military remained, not least over how to deal with Sendero. Some officers, like some civilian politicians, tended to believe that it was ultimately a political organization that could best be defeated with a 'hearts and minds' policy rather than crude force. Others, though, were crude repressives.

As a result of these factors, the Peruvian state in the 1980s faced a whole series of policy dilemmas – dilemmas that were too much for the government of Alan García, who had long run out of ideas by 1990. There were problems in civil–military relations and problems in deciding both how to confront Sendero and how to deal with Peru's illegal drugs trade. On the whole the military was unwilling to confront the coca traffickers for fear of forcing them into the hands of the guerrillas. There is no serious doubt that the insurgents were enjoying significant amounts of income from 'taxing' the drug trade. Both anti-drugs and anti-guerrilla efforts in any case involved considerable abuses of human rights by the Peruvian security forces, which was a factor increasingly taken into account by the US congress when considering aid to Peru.

By the end of the 1980s, a section of the military was sufficiently unhappy with the government and the course of events to contemplate a coup. Some observers put the date at 1988, others at 1989, but there is little doubt that something was planned at around that time with the involvement of civilians as well as military officers (Rospigliosi 2000). The would-be leaders of the coup were unabashed right-wingers.

However, the political outlook was complex and militated against an immediate coup. Alan García had military supporters as well as opponents, and people whom he controlled in other ways (US Embassy 1993). García also had the reluctant backing of the US government, which did not greatly like the president but did oppose a military coup. Meanwhile Vargas Llosa, who was by the late 1980s the undisputed leader of the civilian right, wanted nothing to do with military inter-vention: he expected to win the elections on his own. However, some officers disliked Vargas Llosa, not because of his policy proposals, but because he had when a relatively young man written a satire on military life based on his own unhappy educational experiences at a military college.

The coup could not go ahead under these conditions, but there was an activist set of military officers who certainly were prepared to inter-vene in the political process. At some point after the election of Fujimori, these interventionists and the Fujimori government came to an understanding. Fujimori had been elected, but he had few congres-sional allies and no organized source of support. He faced hyperinfla-tion and other severe economic problems. He was clearly receptive to the idea of an alliance with the military.

It is generally accepted that the active architect of this alliance was Vladimiro Montesinos (Rospigliosi 2000). Montesinos, a cashiered former officer who was by then a civilian, was firmly aligned with the right-wing repressive forces within the military who believed that a 'no holds barred' counter-insurgency was the only way to defeat Sendero. Montesinos had worked in intelligence for many years, and continued to be close to the military when active as a lawyer in the 1980s. He is said not to have been a part of the team working on the 1989 plan, but he knew of its existence and agreed with its conclusions. At the time of Fujimori's election, then, there existed plans for a coup in Peru and a group of officers prepared to try to carry it out. The role of Vladimiro Montesinos was to act as a kind of broker between the potential coup leaders and Fujimori himself, then after the coup he had to make sure that the military was purged of those opposed to it. The role of Fujimori was to authorize the coup and to use his popularity and legitimacy as elected president to win the subsequent battle for public opinion. The coup, therefore, involved a mutual accommodation between Fujimori and the military. Each had reasons for wanting the support of the other.

The political positioning that took place between 1990 and 1992 certainly left the military in no doubt that Fujimori was prepared to put counter-insurgency at the top of his list of priorities. Meanwhile the leaders of Peru's main non-presidential institutions (judicial as well as congressional and party-political) were not. During 1991 the Peruvian congress and judiciary repeatedly obstructed Fujimori's national security policies. In the first twenty months of his government, the courts released over 200 terrorist suspects for lack of evidence.

The story of the 1992 coup is not very different in principle from the story of many pre-1980 military coups in the region as a whole. It involved a civil–military coalition – not all civilians or every military officer, but enough to make the intervention work. It came at a time of national crisis. Supporters of the coup had good subjective reasons for taking the view that they did. Opponents of the coup were tarnished, in some cases by their association with the policy failures of 1980–90 and in others by their lack of enthusiasm for all-out war against Sendero. There is really no doubt that Sendero itself was very unpopular with the broader Peruvian public.

The success of the coup reinforced the position of authoritarian figures who were now in positions of power. One of the consequences of a successful coup is that it rewards active participants. These figures can then promote allies to key military positions and thereby marginalize those who were not active participants or credible supporters. The state can be reorganized on a friends/enemies basis. The coup was clearly a triumph for both Fujimori and Montesinos, who were able to reorganize the state to their own satisfaction. Montesinos was already head of military intelligence, but his powers within the military at that time were relative rather than absolute. Following the coup, he was able to move his allies into position. From then on, the army became less of an autonomous body and more of a political machine run by Montesinos, Fujimori and – though to a lesser degree – army commander Hermoza.

Once the coup had proved successful, the cause of opposition to Fujimori and Montesinos became much more difficult. International reaction was at first hostile and then grudgingly accepting once it became clear that Fujimori retained popular approval. Fujimori's popularity also reduced the leverage available to Peruvian opponents of the government. Any anti-Fujimoristas left in the military would either have to plan to impose a dictatorship without American or domestic support – an almost impossible project – or else keep their heads down. There is evidence of anti-Fujimori organizing in the army, based on a group of middle-ranking officers under the name Comaca, but this did not immediately lead to political action (US Embassy 1993).

There is little doubt that Fujimori, Montesinos and the supporters of the April 1992 coup were prepared to launch a full-scale 'dirty war' against Sendero Luminoso. However, in September 1992 the head of Sendero, Abimael Guzmán, was arrested in Lima – by the Peruvian police and not by Montesinos or his allies. The Fujimori government quickly took credit for this, and did follow up Guzmán's capture intelligently. The military sought to 'turn' Sendero supporters by offering leniency in return for what the government called 'repentance'. In the end Sendero and the MRTA were both defeated relatively quickly and with fewer abuses of human rights than occurred in other countries where insurgencies were effectively defeated – or, indeed, in pre-1992 Peru.

Domestic, international and business responses to the autogolpe

Under these circumstances, the most interesting question is not so much why the coup succeeded in the short run, but why it did not lead to a complete democratic breakdown. It seems clear that influential Peruvians – including both elites and public opinion as a whole – were willing to accept some kind of strong-arm 'state of emergency' in the short term but that they did not want an overt dictatorship. This was also somewhat true of international influences.

The coup provided an immediate boost to Fujimori's popularity. The opinion polls unanimously showed both that the closure of congress was popular and that Fujimori himself became more popular as a result of it. Fujimori used the post-coup situation to call for a whole series of votes: for a constituent assembly, for approval of the new constitution, for his own re-election and finally – though in the end fatally for his reputation – for a further re-election in 2000. This is something worth explaining. After the capture of Guzmán in September 1992 and the economic improvement of the following year, Fujimori's higher popularity could be explained in performance terms. However, this was not so evidently the case in April 1992, when more weight has to be given to the discontent felt by ordinary Peruvians towards their political system.

There is survey evidence, electoral evidence and impressionistic evidence, all of which suggest a swing in popular orientation against established political institutions dating from around 1988, when the policies of the once-popular García government were starting to fail visibly. It does seem that both Belaúnde of Acción Popular (in 1980) and García of APRA (in 1985) were genuinely popular when first elected to the presidency and for a period thereafter (Graham 1992; Crabtree 1992). This was also a period in which the United Left (IU) appeared likely to mount a serious electoral challenge – its candidate won the mayoralty of Lima in 1983. It had serious supporters as well. By the 1990s the challenge to Fujimori from the established parties of left or right had become feeble. APRA, IU and the moderate conservative parties (Acción Popular and the Christian Democratic parties) cumulatively failed to achieve a double-digit share of the vote either in the presidential elections of 1995 or in the local elections of 1998. Limited corroboration that voter attitudes changed decisively in the late 1980s is provided by one poll which showed an increase from 35 per cent to 63 per cent between April 1986 and February 1993 in the numbers of people who stated that they were not interested in politics (Rospigliosi 1994).

Vargas Llosa's political testimony bears further witness to the sharp decline in public respect for the political parties during the 1980s. The victory of Belmont as independent candidate for the mayoralty of Lima in 1989 was initial evidence of this, Fujimori's presidential victory of 1990 was further corroboration and popular support for the 1992 coup was cumulative proof. Vargas Llosa convincingly attributes his own defeat by Fujimori, at least in part, to his excessive closeness to the traditional parties. He recounts that he was advised by his private pollster to distance himself from the conservative parties who were backing his candidacy, that he failed to take this advice, and that he paid the price (Vargas Llosa 1994). Cotler, too, noted that the return of Peru to democracy in 1980 raised hopes that 'traditional structures and the accompanying behaviour would change' and then growing disillusionment when voters concluded that it would not (Cotler 1995).

There is also a longer story of military personalism in Peru. The left-wing General Juan Velasco (1968–75) enjoyed some popular support during his presidency, and is still mentioned by many Peruvians as their most effective president of recent years. Before that the conservative General Manuel Odría (1948–56), with whom Fujimori has sometimes been compared (Vargas Llosa 1994; Crabtree 2001), also started as a pure military man and later acquired a significant popular following. This was strong enough to save him from humiliation in national elections in 1962 and 1963, though not enough to win the presidency.

Nevertheless the polls throughout the 1990s continued to show a general electoral preference for democracy, and it is clear that most voters did not want an overt dictatorship. Rospigliosi is right to suggest that the polls indicated a support for what he calls 'plebiscitary democracy' rather than liberal democracy (Rospigliosi 1994; see also Carrion 1996). The reason for this seems to have been both conjunctural (in other words, the consequence of bad experiences with parties in the past) and cultural, in the sense of being based on a traditional distrust of the law and the state. Civilian politicians were not much trusted either. While congress and the traditional parties have consistently faced a high level of popular rejection during the 1990s, this was far from the case with the church, the independent press and human-rights organizations – all of which were consistently viewed with strong popular approval (Conaghan 1996).

In the Peruvian case, there may have been an ethnic factor as well. Peru has always had a small white-skinned elite that has generally dominated the political process under democracy and dictatorship alike. When a political leader has attempted to be 'of the people' in Peru, he has tended to emphasize his non-white physical characteristics. In the 1970s General Velasco allowed himself to be nicknamed 'El Chino', though, physically speaking, it is hard to see why. Fujimori's Japanese origin was clearly an advantageous characteristic when faced with white-skinned elite opponents such as Vargas Llosa (in 1990) and Perez de Cuellar (in 1995). It is noteworthy that Fujimori's eventual elected successor, Toledo, allowed himself to be referred to as 'El Cholo' in his own campaign slogan.

Given the state of Peruvian public opinion at the time, the problem that international opponents of the coup faced was the lack of a plausible alternative to Fujimori from their own viewpoint. Bankers and foreign investors certainly did not want Peru to fall into complete anarchy or Sendero Luminoso to take power. Fujimori's predecessor as president had defaulted on Peru's foreign debts and allowed hyperinflation to develop. Fujimori, though, had shown every sign of wanting to reintegrate Peru into the international community. By the end of 1991 there had been some considerable negotiations with the IFIs, and relationships were starting to improve (Teivainen 2000). The US government tended to reflect a multiplicity of viewpoints but was on the whole less friendly. Relations with the US State Department improved somewhat when the Peruvian government signed an anti-drugs agreement in May 1991, though the State Department continued to be concerned about human rights abuses committed by the Peruvian military. Fujimori visited Washington in September 1991 in order to try to get aid flowing again, but at this point the US congress again raised issues of human rights abuses. However, the CIA was much more concerned with Sendero.

Some international official bodies, such as the Organization of American States and the European Union, did oppose the coup strongly. However, they lacked real teeth in the absence of stronger domestic opposition to it. The Peruvian government actively sought to win over the private sector by promising that the process of market-oriented reform would be accelerated. Carlos Bologna, the finance minister, defended the coup because this 'gave greater judicial security to the reforms' (quoted in Teivainen 2000, p. 122). This is an interesting comment on how much judicial security there had previously been. In domestic terms, this strategy worked. The major business organizations did support the coup. In the end, the international pressure on Peru dissipated once Fujimori promised to call fresh elections for a new constituent assembly. When on 22 September 1992 Fujimori gave a detailed timetable for the resumption of electoral politics in Peru, the IDB called off the lending embargo that it had informally put in place in April (Costa 1993).

Peru's semi-authoritarian state

As far as economic policy was concerned, the main 'Washington consensus' policies were capably, and sometimes imaginatively, pursued. State assets were privatized, trade was liberalized and the macro-economic situation stabilized. There were important areas, such as tax collection and the development of private pension schemes, in which there was evidence of greater organizational commitment (Durandt and Thorp 1998). Economic growth resumed after 1993. Indeed, from 1993 until the end of the decade Peru enjoyed an economic record that was much better than those of its neighbours. There were some problems after 1997, but there was a genuine and marked increase in economic performance during the first part of the 1990s (Kay 1996). This provided considerable additional resources to the Peruvian state that the administration could use for public works and other popularity-boosting measures. Fujimori also improved relations with the country's neighbours, taking real political risks in Peru in order to settle a long-standing border dispute with Ecuador in 1998. In addition there was progress on the security front. Undoubtedly there were human-rights violations, but there was far less indiscriminate killing by the security forces under Fujimori than there had been during the 1980–90 period.

One thing that made all of this possible was the support that Fujimori continued to receive from the majority of Peruvians. Polls did not show any real fall in his popularity until the last year of his presidency. By the time that the new constitution was subject to referendum, in October 1993, Peru's semi-authoritarianism was starting to record some genuine policy achievements. Inflation had fallen, Sendero Luminoso had declined and economic growth was resuming. When Fujimori stood for re-election in April 1995, Peru was undergoing a genuine economic boom. Fujimori ran a triumphal campaign and carried all before him. Facing what was in many ways an attractive opposing candidate (Perez de Cuellar had been secretary-general of the UN), Fujimori won on the first ballot with nearly 65 per cent of the vote.

Along with business and popular support, Fujimori's government also enjoyed the support of the military. Here, though, there lie some complex and ambiguous considerations, and there are almost certainly some important factors that we do not know. One thing that is clear is that Fujimori and Montesinos ran the military much more like a personal machine than a bureaucratic hierarchy. This machine had a decidedly shady quality.

We have already noted that Peru during the 1980s had a significant illegal drugs trade. This continued to be the case during the 1990s. The illegal drugs trade poses particular problems for academic analysis. It is important not to make unsubstantiated allegations about anybody's complicity, but it is also important not to be naïve. It is entirely clear that drugs money has penetrated very senior political levels in most countries involved with exporting drugs. There is evidence that the successful 1994 presidential campaign of Samper in Colombia was significantly funded by drugs money – though it is not clear how much Samper himself knew (Dugas 2001). There is also little doubt that drugs money penetrated earlier presidential campaigns in Colombia. In 1982 the Colombian gangster Pablo Escobar was elected to that country's senate. Drugs money penetrated Mexican politics to the point that in 1995 the brother of former president Salinas was publicly named as being involved in the trade. In 1997 the senior Mexican drugs czar was dramatically arrested for involvement in drug trafficking. In Bolivia, too, some very senior politicians were mentioned as recipients of payoffs from coca interests. The famous Montesinos videotapes, which seem to record Vladimir Montesinos in the act of physically bribing politicians and military officers to support the 1992 coup, may represent another example of the political uses to which drugs money can be put. It may well be the case that the post-coup Fujimori government was to some extent propped up by illegal drugs money (Simpson 1994).

Fujimori's fall

The issue of presidential re-election was a key element in the process that led to the ultimate defeat of Fujimori. In the case of Peru, this related to a second presidential re-election. Once the 1993 constitution had been approved, nobody very seriously doubted that Fujimori would run for re-election in 1995 and that he would win. However, the 1993 constitution allowed only one consecutive presidential re-election, and Fujimori's presidency should therefore have ended in 2000. After 1996, however, some of Fujimori's supporters put forward the preposterous-sounding argument that the 1993 constitution was not retroactive and that the 1990–95 term did not therefore count as such. (The fact was that the 1990–95 term started under the 1979 constitution, which did not allow re-election at all.) Given this very tendentious legal position, it is not difficult to see that the Peruvian re-election issue could not easily be resolved by compromise. Instead it clearly polarized the political situation.

Fujimori's supporters started publicly advocating his re-election in 1996. The case for re-election was taken to the constitutional tribunal, and when three judges declared their opposition to the move they were impeached by the Fujimori-controlled congress and sacked. In the end the courts were intimidated into allowing his candidacy. Meanwhile Fujimori's popularity, while a bit lower than it had been at the 1995 high point, held up reasonably well. When elections were finally held in 2000 with Fujimori as a candidate, it is clear that his base of support was enough to give him a chance of victory. Independent polls mostly put his vote at above 40 per cent. However, there was evidence, too, that the state – which was clearly biased in Fujimori's favour – may have overstepped the line from non-consolidated democracy to outright falsification of the vote (thereby implying non-democracy), though admittedly to a limited extent only. According to official results, Fujimori won the first round of elections on 7 April with only just under 50 per cent of the vote, and prepared to enter the runoff round. When Toledo, the principal opposition candidate, announced that he would not participate in the second round on the grounds that fraud had been committed in the first round, Fujimori was duly inaugurated for a third term in July 2000.

In the subsequent few months, the Fujimori presidency disintegrated. The downfall of the regime was precipitated on the military/security side. On 21 August there were public revelations to the effect that Vladimir Montesinos had been involved in arms trafficking to the Colombian FARC. This certainly caused serious annoyance to the CIA and to Washington in general. The next decisive problem came when an independent Peruvian television station showed a video featuring Montesinos in the act of bribing an opposition congressman to join the government party. Faced with this revelation, Fujimori turned against Montesinos and ordered his resignation. A power struggle then developed between the two. On 16 September Fujimori declared that fresh presidential elections would be held in 2001 and that he would not be a candidate, thereby implicitly undermining the validity of his own 2000 election victory.

Montesinos then left Peru, while Fujimori evidently tried to shore up his government by selectively purging the security forces of Montesinos supporters. The National Intelligence Service, which Montesinos had directed, was abolished. Fujimori proposed an amnesty, which would have covered his military supporters as well as his opponents, but this was unacceptable to the opposition and to the public at large. By late October, when the amnesty bill was being discussed in congress, opinion polls were starting to show a decisive shift in the public mood against Fujimori.

On 23 October 2000 Montesinos returned to Peru and was somehow allowed to go to ground. Fujimori announced that he was searching for Montesinos but did not find him. However, the government did find a number of Montesinos's videos, and the suspicion is that some of the most incriminating ones were destroyed. Almost immediately afterwards, the Swiss authorities revealed that Montesinos had illegal bank accounts in that country worth at least $48 million. On 29 October there was the first open sign of military unrest, with a small but significant formal act of insubordination in Arequipa.

All of these scandals had the effect of inducing a number of congresspeople to defect from the Fujimori coalition and move over to the opposition. The opposition was now in a position to take the view that the Fujimori government was illegitimate and had the votes to make this opinion tell. On 16 November 2000, aided by defectors from the government, Fujimori's opponents won a decisive vote in congress. At this point there arose a situation that was in some ways similar to that of April 1992, when Fujimori used troops to resolve the issue in his favour. In November 2000, however, Fujimori was no longer as popular as he had once been, and it was clear that public opinion would not support the president in any confrontation. International opinion was also clearly against Fujimori at this point. The military, too, seemed unwilling to support the president, given his loss of prestige due to the conflict with, and the disappearance of, Montesinos.

Rather than fight, Fujimori took advantage of a state visit to Asia to fly to Japan, resign the presidency and emigrate. It is far from clear that Fujimori's cause was completely lost at the point when he decided to depart – he still had genuine supporters in both congress and the military – but the act of flying to Japan certainly ended his political career in Peru. Congress quickly declared him to have resigned (it later impeached him), and on 22 November a new government took office.

There are many things about this dramatic and confusing story that are still not clear. However, it is clear that the political process had been only temporarily suppressed by the autogolpe and by Fujimori's big election victory in 1995. The autonomy of the state, which increased considerably during 1992, started to decline again towards the end of the decade. There was a good deal of evidence to show that Fujimori after around 1997 was becoming less of a reforming modernizer and more of a traditional, if authoritarian, politician. For example, a pro-posed civil-service reform was cancelled by the government in 1997 for fear of creating problems. The pace of market-oriented reform also slowed notably, and there were signs of growing politicization in the tax-collecting agency (SUNAT) as the government increasingly tended to give an easy ride to its supporters (on SUNAT, see Durandt and Thorp 1998). There was every sign that Fujimori's support base was not enough for him to consolidate a reforming semi-authoritarian state. The state which he controlled was instead as biased as that of any of his predecessors.

It seems reasonable to suggest that the fundamental conflict within the pro-Fujimori camp in the last years can be regarded as being between a liberal-conservative pro-business elite and a military/secu-rity elite. Many business interests were willing to support Fujimori for a time (Teivainen 2000, p. 132). They admired his reformism and effi-ciency, but they did not want to pay the price of living in an authori-tarian regime forever. In economic terms, the attitude of the US government was important to business figures. This was not because of any admiration for the USA but because Washington could influence the political risk analyses that determined Peru's external economic environment. By the end of the 1990s many leading businessmen were willing to say privately that Fujimori had been a good president but that he should now leave and allow the normal political process to start again.

However, Fujimori had military supporters with connections to the drugs trade and blood on their hands. These people enjoyed considerable latitude to run the security state under Fujimori and had run it in a highly authoritarian manner (OAS 2000). The judiciary was either cowed or ignored and the press was subject to major restriction. The hard-liners evidently feared that a new government would ask too many questions about corruption and the abuse of human rights. Fujimori eventually tried to resolve the problem by remaining at the head of a softer, less authoritarian state – hence his dismissal of Montesinos – but eventually he lost support on all sides. It is likely that he would not have done so, at least to the same extent, had it not been for the conflict over his second re-election.

Conclusion

The political rise and fall of Fujimori, particularly the latter, bring out further some of the themes discussed in the first part of this work. The military certainly provided alternative political leadership for those who did not want constitutional democracy. It offered a plausible alternative because the military was itself generally well regarded in Peru. It is also, crucially, because the continuing activities of Sendero and the MRTA gave the military a motive for intervening. However, the military would not have been able to act on its own. The cover provided by Fujimori's popularity muted international and domestic civilian reaction to the coup. This popularity, in turn, had much to do with the institutional and policy failings of previous governments. These factors were essentially temporary. The sharp reduction in insurgency activity from the mid-1990s made it much less likely that the military would support Fujimori as a united body in 2000. The moment of extreme crisis had gone.

Moving from causes to consequences, it is clear that Fujimori's semi-authoritarian form of government can prove both popular and successful for quite long periods of time. We really should not ignore the fact that the average Peruvian was financially better off, physically more secure and less threatened by inflation in 2000 than in 1990. Similar change for the better could not so easily be detected in respect of the 1980–90 period. Moreover Peru is the only Andean republic, with the possible exception of Bolivia, to have enjoyed significant material progress during the 1990s.

The main reasons why Fujimori could not, in the end, sustain an overt authoritarianism have to do with some of the issues discussed in the first part of this work. There was a real sense in Peru that a second re-election was not acceptable. This did not stop Fujimori declaring himself the winner and taking office, but it did mean that his support was much weaker than before and willing to defect much more easily. International pressures mattered to some extent, although the US government's efforts to express strong disapproval of Fujimori were in 2000 watered down by the response of other Latin American countries, including Brazil. Perhaps most important of all, when public opinion started to swing decisively against Fujimori in late 2000, the decisive organs of the Peruvian state – congress and the military – followed the polls rather than the president.

It is an interesting question whether the switch of public opinion away from Fujimori could be described as an incidence of democratic self-reinforcement. Certainly there are people prepared to argue that the coup of 1992 violated the letter but not the spirit of democracy, because emergency measures are sometimes necessary in a crisis. To try to maintain the same kind of semi-authoritarianism in 2000 once the crisis was clearly over was a violation of both spirit and letter of democracy. However, an argument of this kind might exaggerate the sophistication of more than a limited segment of Peruvian public opinion. An alternative hypothesis – also partially valid – is that Fujimori was simply not as popular in 2000 as he had been in 1992. People were more secure about insurgency and less impressed with Fujimori's economic management. Peru had been caught up in a period of recession, following on from the downturn in the Asian markets starting in 1997, and some of the gloss had been taken off the government's economic record. A cynical view, which may also fit some other Latin American countries, is that, in the absence of strong institutions, the economic cycle is democracy's best friend.

It is too early to discuss the Toledo presidency with any assurance. However, it already seems clear that the dramatic political and economic developments that Peru underwent between the return of civilian government in 1980 and the early part of the following century were not matched by institutional consolidation. Politics has continued to be characterized by extreme forms of partisanship, state bias and a lack of secure political balance. As was the case in Venezuela, the experience of regular elections and the opportunity to learn from the past do not seem to have translated into the successful consolidation of democracy.

10

Mexico: Technocratic Governance and Democratization

Until very recently at least, Mexico has possessed several characteristics typical of biased states in Latin America. The most important of these are the fact that the public administration is based on presidential appointment and the relatively weak system of law enforcement. There have been attempts to strengthen and reform the legal system during the process of democratization, but it is not yet clear that these have had very much success. There are also considerable disagreements about the proper role of the presidency in Mexico's democratic political system. However, there are a number of respects in which Mexico is different from the other countries considered in this work. The most important differences have to do with the characteristics of pre-democratic Mexico and the path of democratization subsequently taken. In economic terms, too, there are real differences between Mexico and the South American republics.

This discussion relates mainly to the pattern of democratization in Mexico. Democratization invariably changes the pattern of political contestation and the nature of political partisanship. The same question can be posed for Mexico as for other Latin American countries: has democratization helped with the consolidation of institutions? As noted, the best case for an affirmative answer would have to be based on the transformation of economic institutions. Mexico, unlike other countries in the region, is now predominantly an exporter of manufactured goods and a member of the NAFTA. Even this process of economic transformation was prolonged and characterized by a number of major crises. There were economic crises in 1982, 1986 and 1994 and a political crisis in 1988. It could be argued that these crises ultimately facilitated democratic transition rather than proving an obstacle to it.

Mexico's dominant party and presidential system

Before returning to these themes, a little bit of background information is necessary. Following the revolution (1910–17) and subsequent political upheavals, Mexico created a very stable political system around two fixed points. One was the official party – known as the PRI since 1946 – which established a virtually complete dominance of the electoral system. Elections were routinely held for the presidency, governorships, congress and municipalities, but the PRI almost always won them. The other was the presidency, which was all-powerful within the political system.

What permitted Mexican politics to take on an authoritarian aspect before 1982 was the election-winning role of the PRI, whose corporatist control of organized labour was strong and its rural machine stronger still. Given this apparatus of control, built up on the basis of social reforms carried out in the 1930s, the PRI could generally deliver election victories to order. There certainly were electoral malpractices involving the PRI, but survey and other evidence indicates that the party enjoyed a bedrock of support as well. Many, probably most, PRI victories in Mexico during the years 1940–82 were genuine in so far as Mexico could be said to have a genuine public opinion at that time. When opinion polling started in the country on a significant scale in the early 1980s, observers were genuinely surprised at the extent of support for the PRI (Basáñez 1987). No doubt popular preferences were shaped during the long period of PRI hegemony. Nevertheless democratization did not lead to the immediate collapse of the PRI, which, even after its defeat in the elections of 2000, continues to be an influential force in Mexican politics. The fact that its share of the popular vote declined only slowly after 1982 gave subsequent Mexican governments a much greater range of strategic political options than they would have had if their support were in danger of collapse – as was often the case with South American military regimes. In this respect the contrast between the process of democratization in Mexico and that in most South American countries is evident.

Mexico's was unusual among dominant party systems in that the key locus of power was the presidency and not the party. During the 1930s President Cárdenas (1934–40) used his office to defeat Plutarco Elías Calles, who was then boss of the official party. On subsequent occasions, notably in 1965 and again in 1975, conflicts between the party president and the national president were decided in favour of the national president. The national president served for six years. He could never be re-elected, but he did choose his successor. This intense presidentialism was designed to limit pluralism within the PRI, as indeed it did, and to maintain political unity above all things. The nature of the presidential institution generally persuaded scholars that Mexico was politically authoritarian until the late 1980s, despite the holding of regular elections.

What eventually changed the system was an increase in electoral contestation. This might be said to date from as far back as the 1977 political reform (Alvarado 1987; Gentleman 1987), but the process was extremely gradual. In 1989 an opposition candidate was for the first time declared the winner in a state governorship election. In 1997 the PRI for the first time lost absolute control of the Mexican congress. In 2000 an opposition candidate, Vicente Fox, finally won presidential elections in Mexico. Opposition electoral victories gradually forced the system to change in other ways as well.

The other, very important, respect in which Mexico changed substantially after 1982 was economic. In 1982 Mexico, like many other Latin American countries, was principally an exporter of commodities (notably oil) and had tried to industrialize behind tariff walls. At the end of 1982, though, relations between the Mexican government and its economic elite were seriously negative, and those between the Mexican government and Washington were only somewhat less so. However, in 2002 Mexico was a member of the NAFTA, a close ally of the USA and a large-scale exporter of manufactured goods to the United States. It is worth at least considering the hypothesis that institutional consolidation might occur in Mexico as a result of adaptation to changed international conditions, though it is too soon to be sure that this is indeed happening.

If this does prove to be the case, then such institutional consolidation as may be taking place in Mexico may be only tangentially related to the process of democratization. It may instead have everything to do with the preferences of a small technocratic elite that governed the country (through the system of presidential appointment) during 1982–2000. This elite was able to use the partisan support brought in by the PRI as a political base to shape the pattern of Mexico's future in ways that the majority of Mexicans would have rejected if they had been asked. Mexico just might turn out to be a (comparatively rare) case of consolidation via globalization.

Bureaucratic politics and the technocratic state

In this context two key aspects of non-consolidation considered here – semi-patrimonialism and weak law enforcement – have had a double role in Mexico. By allowing a process of change from above that would otherwise have been difficult or even impossible, they played an important part in facilitating the kind of economic transformation that took place. Given that democratization, as it occurred, was closely linked to this economic transformation, then these aspects of politics may actually have helped. However, if Mexican democracy is now to consolidate, then a deeper institutionalization will be necessary. Yet powerful political interests within Mexico now have every incentive to maintain the status quo.

The Mexican state has been based almost entirely on patronage since the days of the revolution. Presidential power to appoint has covered central government, local government and the PRI. Added to the role of the PRI in producing routine election victories at every level of government, this power of appointment was crucial to the way in which the system worked. It gave overwhelming advantages to the presidency and led to a fairly strongly centralized regime, even though political competition was not completely absent. Political competition, whether taking the form of 'court politics' or constrained mobilization politics, was intended mainly to win the presidential ear and get presidential support. Informal groups, so-called *camarillas*, tended to act as teams in pursuit of advancement via presidential preferment. *Camarillas* often involved extended families covering more than one generation, with the result that the core political elite was formed to a significant degree by informal family linkages as well as formal procedural norms (Camp 1984). The core political system became a self-perpetuating oligarchy, although one that was never completely closed to outsiders. The Mexican state therefore became a very powerful instrument of control while to some extent maintaining the appearance of government by consent.

There is a significant academic literature on public administration in Mexico during the 1940–82 period, including works by Vernon (1963), Smith (1979), Basáñez (1981), Grindle (1977) and Hansen (1971). They describe a system that had two key characteristics. One is that formal and informal rules were quite separate. Informal rules generally reflected the power of the presidency, while formal rules were routinely ignored. The other is that different parts of the central government behaved quite differently from each other.

Formal rules contained a significant façade element, since it was considered important to maintain the appearance of regular elections, respected procedures and established hierarchies. Informal rules determined how power was exercised and were taken more seriously. Political discipline was maintained from the top, via the presidency. However, discipline was less rigid further down the scale, and a certain amount of political disorder was tolerated (at the discretion of the president) in order to keep alive the revolutionary myth. Corruption was also tolerated, although kept within limits. General Obregon, a revolutionary general who became president of Mexico in the 1920s, was once asked how he maintained stability within the army and replied, 'I know of no general who can withstand a bombardment with 50,000 pesos.' Indeed much of the post-revolutionary Mexican bourgeoisie was composed of former revolutionary fighters who were encouraged to move into the private sector and take advantage of government contracts. The taxman rarely called unless to punish a case of political (not financial) indiscipline.

However, there were islands of administration in which the Weberian spirit was not entirely absent. The economic part of the state was significantly autonomous of day-to-day politics. Professionals who were to some degree insulated from the political process largely staffed the finance ministry, the central bank and the development banks (Santín Queroz 2001). Meanwhile the 'political' part of the state bureaucracy was run on a mixture of corporatist and clientelistic criteria, with some deliberate overlapping to allow for political competition. Turnover was generally high, particularly in the more political positions. These included some national ministries, local and regional government and positions in the ruling PRI itself.

There were some tensions within the system. Vernon (1963) was the first to draw attention to conflict between the 'technocrats', mainly economists, whose job it was to keep the economy going, and the 'politicians', whose job it was to maintain the political system. For many years, this tension was largely resolved by a policy of separate spheres. Until the mid-1970s it was an unwritten rule that no finance minister would succeed to the presidency. Nevertheless economics ministers were, in effect, chief executives over the economic area of public life. Antonio Ortíz Mena, finance minister from 1958 to 1970, essentially ran the economy, though (despite being the most outstanding cabinet minister of the period) he was never seriously considered a presidential nominee. The system also required a political discipline which was accepted during the 1940s and 1950s but visibly resented by the Mexican student movement of 1968.

The first major change to this system of public administration occurred during the 1970s. What precipitated it was the fact that Mexico's political authorities, especially under President Echeverría (1970–76), chose to regard student protests at the end of the 1960s as representing a challenge to the system's economic policies rather than to its political authoritarianism. There was quite a marked change of economic direction thereafter towards greater state intervention (Enríquez 1988). The new macro-economic orientation seemed underpinned during the 1970s by Mexico's increased levels of oil production and the rising international price of oil. However, the 1970–82 period also saw a very large build-up of foreign debt, which tended to weaken the economy and make it crisis-prone.

The rise of the 'technocrats' can best be seen as involving two separate steps. At first the increased amount of state intervention in the economy led the government to look for technically qualified Mexicans to take on the additional responsibilities. Although the *camarilla* system remained in place, the qualities looked for in aspirants to office changed somewhat. Formal educational qualifications gradually mattered more, with economists coming into demand. Qualifications from privately run Mexican universities or foreign universities were particularly valued. Only after 1982 did the second step take place – namely the capture of the state by a neo-liberal technocracy.

Between 1970 and 1982 Mexico developed into a state increasingly run by technocrats but not really a technocratic state. The principle of presidentialism limited the emergence of any genuine bureaucratic autonomy and the system was still more patrimonial than Weberian (Torres Espinosa 1999). This was less of a problem before 1970 because of an implicit 'separate spheres' arrangement and a semi-Weberian economic state. However, efforts to make the state more technocratic after 1970 and even more so after 1976 tended to politicize the technocracy. State agencies associated with such seemingly technocratic functions as economic planning tended to convert themselves into political instruments of intra-bureaucratic contestation. Meanwhile the judicial system remained largely subservient to presidential direction (Marvin Laborde 1997). There was, therefore, no real antidote to arbitrary presidential rule from within the state itself.

Changing course: the 1982 crisis and its consequences

This is not the place for a full discussion of the 1976 or 1982 economic crises (see, for example, Bailey 1988; Teichman 1988). A few points do, however, need to be made by way of background for the later period. The first is that the deteriorating financial climate of the 1980–82 period hit the living standards of ordinary Mexicans only from around the middle of 1982. While inflation was a growing problem during the 1970s, there had been no general interruption in a trend towards rising living standards. There was therefore no reason to expect the crisis, at least in its early stages, to result in a popular rejection of the PRI. Moreover the government's response to financial crisis, to announce the nationalization of the banks on 1 September 1982 with no prior notice at all, met with mixed reactions. Some middle-class Mexicans, notably those whose dollar deposits held (quite legally) in Mexican accounts were forcibly exchanged back into pesos at an unfavourable rate, were outraged. The bank nationalization was, however, initially popular with the public as a whole because it tended to follow the government's lead and blame the crisis on speculators (Basáñez, 1991).

Earlier, the 1981–2 presidential succession, considered purely as a political phenomenon, had taken place without major incident. The economic crisis occurred after the 1982 elections had already been held. In 1981 López Portillo had nominated Miguel de la Madrid as his political successor. De la Madrid was an orthodox economist and a political conservative. However, he was also a pragmatic figure who had been able to win the trust of economic nationalists within the government without sharing their economic views (Torres Espinosa 1999; Castañeda 1999). There was no real likelihood that de la Madrid, once inaugurated as president, would have taken the enormously risky step of breaking with the international economic order. Instead, he initiated a change of economic direction by moving towards free trade and free-market economics.

De la Madrid's task of altering the course of Mexican economic policy in the direction of market-oriented reform was only possible by making full use of his power of appointment within the bureaucracy. There was no popular demand for market-oriented reform. In the short run, the political strength possessed by Mexican business remained limited. This was partly because of the bank nationalization itself and partly because many businesses faced financial problems as a result of the economic crisis. Some of the biggest Mexican conglomerates had shown scarcely more fiscal discipline during 1980–82 than had the Mexican government. As a result, big business needed government help too badly to want to attack the system openly, even though it manifested unhappiness behind the scenes. Meanwhile most of the PRI, while normally loyal and deferential to the government of the day, certainly did not want a decisive market-oriented economic transition. The right-wing opposition did pick up some middle-class support after 1982, but it was not strong enough to mount a genuine confrontation with any hope of success.

In political terms, the results of de la Madrid's market-oriented economics were rather ironic. The PRI machine on which the state was based relied most for support on those who had least to gain from the government's post-1982 policies. The rural vote remained rock-solid for the PRI, and the trade unions – despite some grumbling – remained generally loyal as well. Meanwhile business, particularly big business, was still very unhappy about the bank nationalization. Some urban voters, particularly in the north of the country, shifted their electoral support to the PAN, which until then had been quite a marginal party. The PAN remained a minority party, but it did strengthen.

In economic terms President de la Madrid's decision to abandon López Portillo's economic nationalism and adopt market-oriented reforms, no matter how reluctantly taken or gradually adopted, increased Mexico's vulnerability to international influences. Essentially there was a decisive loss of policy autonomy *vis-à-vis* the international community and in particular the United States. However, it was quite some time before the Mexican business community and lenders to Mexico realized how decisive the change in policy direction would eventually be. During 1983 and 1984 there were some limited moves in the direction of market-oriented reform, but these did not go very far. Some people in the Mexican government, probably including de la Madrid, hoped that a traditional macro-economic stabilization programme together with a limited change of emphasis would be enough (Chislett 1985). Economic growth could then resume as before. In the long run, nothing much would have changed.

This calculation turned out to be wrong. In mid-1985 there was a renewed crisis. The international oil price fell, and Mexico's economic problems worsened. On 19 September 1985 an earthquake hit Mexico City. The authorities handled things poorly and popular discontent increased. Meanwhile the Mexican public was also becoming increasingly alienated and disillusioned with the national economic performance. From 1983 onwards, a somewhat larger number of Mexicans (though by no means a majority) were willing to vote for the opposition parties. The government responded with a policy of ballot-rigging but this, in turn, created both domestic and international scandal. Although it was far from clear at the beginning of 1986 that Mexico was about to go down the globalization/democratization route, it was becoming evident that the status quo might prove untenable.

Pressures on the system at this time were much more economic than political. The Mexican state's ability to control domestic politics was impressive, due to its long record in government, its ideological eclecticism and its well-developed political machinery. Even under the adverse economic circumstances of the mid-1980s, the PRI would have faced no more than isolated election defeats even under conditions of open electoral competition. Under the actual conditions of ballot-rigging, things could be arranged so that the opposition parties won virtually nothing at all. The opposition parties were in no position to mount a national challenge because it was the government that determined the election results. Its response to ballot-rigging, to threaten public order, was not a plausible tactic because the means of coercion were securely in government hands. The only short-term political threat to the state came from internal disunity, and this could develop only if the political discipline governing the whole system were somehow relaxed.

The state could handle the 1982 crisis and the subsequent need for macro-economic stabilzation, but more complex issues arose as it became clear in Mexico (as it did in the other countries of the region) that radical market-oriented reform could not be avoided. In 1985, when the international oil price turned down decisively, Mexico still did not have enough of a non-oil economy, in either fiscal or export terms, to offset the negative consequences. Moreover government–business relations were far from ideal. Further, possibly severe, economic decline therefore seemed unavoidable. There was also a danger that an economic shock would precipitate both political unrest and capital flight – which might, in the worst case, have been a mutually reinforcing combination. Bluntly put, the Mexican authorities were stuck and they needed help from the USA.

By this time, sections of opinion in the USA – particularly conservatives within the US Republican Party – were starting to become very critical of Mexico. They drew attention to its continuing political authoritarianism at a time when countries such as Brazil and Argentina were becoming democracies. They were still concerned that economic nationalists might return to power, and they were dissatisfied with residual aspects of Mexican nationalism – such as the country's unwillingness to break absolutely with the Sandinistas in Nicaragua. They disliked the fact that drugs money was starting to penetrate Mexican politics. They were afraid that a complete economic crisis might lead to a complete social breakdown (Sanders 1986). Yet the USA had good reasons for wanting to negotiate a deal with Mexico. The alternative, possible default in Mexico and continued debt deflation in Latin America, was clearly not in the best interest of the US economy. We have no clear evidence of overt pressure on Mexico to change its political system as the price of winning necessary economic support; however, according to one source interviewed by the author at the time (who requested confidentiality), the Mexican government during 1986 increasingly realized that it had to take US public opinion seriously if the US government was to be persuaded to help the Mexican economy recover.

It will be some years yet before the documents that indicate how closely the US government tied its eventual offer of economic help to political change in Mexico become available. It is clear that the USA was, by 1986, pressing for democratization across Latin America. It is also clear that the Mexican government agreed an electoral reform in October 1986. This enormously strengthened the minority parties who were guaranteed a share of the seats in all state assemblies. This put the opposition parties in a much stronger position if it came to serious competition with the PRI. The partisan power of the PRI, by the same token, was significantly weakened.

It is not especially new to point out that political liberalization can have unintended consequences. This, certainly, happened in Mexico. What is notable, however, is that Mexico's slow transformation involved two stories. One is the story anticipated by the Mexican authorities. This was that the PRI would remain in office for quite a lot longer while the project of market-oriented reform would be brought to a successful conclusion. They did not anticipate the other story at all. This was that the left, strengthened by a split in the PRI itself, would become a direct challenger to the government's entire socio-economic programme.

The emergence of Salinas and the 1988 elections

In October 1987 Miguel de la Madrid 'unveiled' Carlos Salinas de Gortari, who had been his planning minister and an economic liberal, as his presidential successor. Following the nomination of Salinas a serious split developed within the PRI. The defection of the left-wing Democratic Current and its eventual transformation into a full-scale electoral challenge to the PRI in 1988 has been well discussed elsewhere (Bruhn 1997; Castañeda 1999; Garrido 1993). Although in the end the challenge failed, it tells us a very great deal about what the regime was intending to do. The background facts are as follows.

The 1985–8 period saw a continuation and deepening of the government's market-oriented policies. In 1986 Mexico entered the GATT and started a major trade reform. There was rather more in the way of privatization after 1986 than there had been before. Furthermore in 1987 the government started direct negotiations on economic policy with business and labour representatives. All significant business organizations were invited, including some that had been quite critical of government policy in the past, while only relatively tame labour organizations were involved. Although (apart from the GATT) the list of market-oriented reforms was not particularly long even at the end of 1988, the political atmosphere had changed decisively. Mexican business was largely reassured, while the political left was now unhappy.

The nomination of Salinas was highly significant in such a context because it implied that continuation and further deepening of the market-oriented reforms was on the agenda for the next *sexenio*. In the past, incoming presidents often shifted their policy line to mark a clean break from that of their predecessors (the so-called pendulum effect), but Salinas had been much too involved in de la Madrid's government for this to be likely on this occasion. Salinas had by October 1987 become as identified with market-oriented reform as de la Madrid himself. However, most Mexicans did not want market-oriented reform. Most PRIistas did not want market-oriented reform either. Nor did most small and medium-sized businesses (who made up the vast majority of all business organizations) want enhanced international competition – although there were a few big-business interests that wanted deeper integration into the international economy (Salas Porras 1998).

Among all the leading candidates for the PRI presidential nomination, there was an acceptance that Mexico would have to make the necessary compromises to run a capitalist economy that was deep in debt and dependent on the USA. However, only Salinas had a genuinely economic liberal project (which he himself called 'social liberal') that was the product of choice rather than necessity. It would be impossible to imagine either of Salinas's main rivals within the PRI, Bartlett or Del Mazo, taking Mexico into the NAFTA, even on the doubtful premise that the US government would have accepted Mexico under this leadership. Yet such was the organization of the Mexican state that Salinas could be nominated for the presidency while being clearly identified with a line of policy that (whatever its merits or otherwise) was supported by very few Mexicans.

However, by the mid-1980s a more populist challenge to the government's economic orientation was starting to manifest itself. A small group calling itself the Democratic Current formed in January 1986 with the aim of lobbying within the PRI against Mexico's market-oriented reform programme. When they found themselves marginalized within the PRI, the leaders of the Democratic Current sought to take advantage of the slowly opening electoral scene to challenge the PRI in the 1988 elections. Shortly after the nomination of Salinas, one of the PRI's satellite parties, which had recently gained some organizational independence once proportional representation had been introduced into state legislatures, decided to nominate Cárdenas for the presidency.

The Cárdenas candidacy did very much better than most observers initially expected. De la Madrid admitted later that he had underestimated Cárdenas (Castañeda 1999, p. 211). Indeed Cárdenas may have actually won the 1988 elections had the votes been honestly counted. Even as it was, Salinas was comprehensively defeated by Cárdenas in the Mexico City conurbation and lost to the conservative opposition party, the PAN, in the second city, Guadalajara. Polls also showed that the majority of Mexicans believed that the election had been stolen by the PRI. Many scholars agree with them (Castañeda 1999; Bruhn 1997).

By 1988 the Mexican electorate was mainly urban, but there was still a significant rural constituency. In rural areas, the PRI could generally be relied upon to produce votes to order – sometimes of people who were bribed, sometimes of apathetic people who were transported to polling stations and offered a free meal, sometimes of people who had not voted at all or who did not even exist. The legacy of the 1930s land reform had given the PRI an apparatus of rural control that it had not relinquished, but it was far less entrenched in urban areas, where it had to face what in other countries would be considered normal political competition. Urban voters in Mexico generally make up their minds between candidates much as voters do everywhere. The PRI's corporate control of organized labour was advantageous, but not decisively so. In presidential elections up to and including 1982, the vast majority of urban voters preferred the PRI because they were reasonably contented with the country's economic performance and because there was no realistic alternative. A secular and mildly nationalist party such as the PRI also held out more popular appeal than parties associated with the Catholic right or the Marxist left. Some city dwellers, mainly in the north, did vote for the PAN – but not enough to make a big difference to the outcome. However, in 1988, if only big-city votes had been counted, then the PRI would have lost.

President Salinas and reform from above

The relatively poor showing of the PRI in 1988 was attributed to two different factors. One, stressed particularly by the opposition, was that the government's policy stance was unpopular. Between 1982 and 1988 living standards fell, public investment was cut and inflation increased. Given the depth of the 1982 crisis and the subsequent problems in the oil market, economists have not generally blamed the de la Madrid government too harshly for these poor economic results. But many ordinary Mexicans did. A long period of economic growth had come to an end, and popular resentment at this turnabout remained strong.

However, the view of de la Madrid and Salinas was that the PRI machine had become torpid and complacent due to a lack of competition. The party had become, essentially, a patronage network for loyalists who could not find work in the government. When the system liberalized sufficiently to allow a real electoral challenge, the PRI did not know how to cope. Such an interpretation was not entirely fanciful, and the PRI machine certainly was strengthened under Salinas. This, though, occurred in the context of what remained a decidedly top-down view of Mexican politics.

No matter how one interprets the 1988 elections, they could scarcely be said to constitute a vote of support for market-oriented reforms or a demand for their continuation. Under Salinas, though, the market-oriented direction of policy was not merely continued, but intensified. Furthermore, although the strong electoral showing by the left was not completely ignored, the Mexican state under Salinas made every possible effort to ensure that the left failed to prosper in subsequent local and regional elections (Bruhn 1997). By way of contrast, the government's relationship with the PAN improved considerably, and the latter party was able to gain a number of state governorships. Critics described the government's electoral policy as 'selective democracy' – friendly to the PAN and hostile to Cárdenas's new party, the PRD. On the whole, the policy succeeded.

Meanwhile the continuing market-oriented transformation of the Mexican economy led to the decisive weakening of those social forces most opposed to market-oriented reforms – notably organized labour and small businesses. In Mexico, much more than in the Far East, the manufacturing export sector was highly concentrated in a small number of dynamic big businesses, some of which were foreign-owned but others of which were Mexican. By the mid-1990s the strongest and best-run Mexican companies were fully capable of competing with US-owned companies in North American markets (Salas Porras 1998). The damage done to the smaller business sector was, however, considerable. The Salinas period therefore saw a significant increase in the concentration of wealth and power in Mexico.

It is evident that the policy of continuing with liberal capitalism required an alliance with the USA if it was to succeed. The only sector of the Mexican economy with a potential for dynamism was manufacturing exports, and these could prosper only if the US market was made available. Even in the short run, Mexico needed the USA if it was to make headway in dealing with its debt problem. Until something was done here, significant economic recovery would be impossible. According to Salinas's own account of his presidency (Salinas 2000), his government was informed by two priorities. The first was to resolve the continued problem of Mexico's foreign debt. This had been largely secured against the promise of oil revenues, and then the international oil price had fallen drastically during 1985–6. The figures no longer added up. Rapid non-oil export growth did not help much here because the problem was a shortage of tax revenue rather than export receipts.

The Bush administration in Washington was sympathetic to Salinas's argument. After all, the US administration did not want Salinas to fail and to have Mexico return to a path of left-wing nationalism. Accordingly arrangements were put in place for what eventually became the Brady Plan. This traded the writing-off of some of Mexico's debts against a Mexican promise to continue with policies of macro-economic stabilization and 'Washington consensus' reform.

The longer-term priority was to develop a stronger trade relationship with the USA. According to Salinas, the US president had already raised the possibility of Mexico joining the existing US–Canadian free-trade agreement. Salinas refused to move until there was some progress on the debt, but once this had been achieved he was willing to take up the US offer (Salinas 2000). Between 1990 and 1992 there were detailed and complex US–Mexican negotiations on the NAFTA. Clinton's election as US president in 1992 required some changes to be made, but in the end the agreement was ratified by the US congress in 1993.

The NAFTA project was enormously significant in a whole range of different ways. For one thing the Mexican government did not negotiate it alone but also brought in a range of business interests who were explicitly asked to help. These negotiations further improved relations between government and Mexican big business. Subsequently the effect of NAFTA membership constrained the government's economic powers through a series of internationally accepted rules. There can be no doubt that these limited the power of the Mexican state *vis-à-vis* Mexican business as well as *vis-à-vis* the international market. The GATT, which Mexico had joined in 1986, had done this to some extent but not nearly so much.

Finally there was a directly political aspect to the NAFTA: it required the visible democratization of Mexico, otherwise the US congress would not have approved it. The ballot-rigging therefore had to stop. As an indicator of change, the Salinas government twice in its term of office demanded the resignation of the governor of Yucatán. On the first occasion, in 1990, this was as punishment for losing the city of Merida to the opposition. On the second occasion (with a different governor), in 1993, it was as punishment for winning back the city through excessively strong-arm tactics. On the latter occasion, the political opposition threatened to take its concerns to the USA if something was not done – and something was done (Amezcua and Pardinas 1997).

Democratization, privatization and the 'tequila crisis'

At the end of 1993, the Salinas presidency looked very successful. Because the political system was still highly presidentialized, the Salinas government continued to enjoy all of the incumbency advantages of Mexico's biased state while allowing the opposition to make slow and limited headway as democratization proceeded. Salinas used the powers of the presidency as intensively as any incumbent since the 1940s. It was his policy to allow Mexico to democratize, but to use the intervening period to close down any possibility that a democratic Mexico would return to politics of economic nationalism or fiscal populism.

Salinas also managed the economy with political considerations in mind. In 1988, despite the negative effect of low international oil prices, the Mexican current account was in near balance – having been vastly in deficit in 1982. The peso was cheap and imports were expensive. This is an unpopular situation and contributed to the impression held by most Mexicans that they had become worse off since 1982. After 1989, however, the real (inflation-adjusted) value of the peso was allowed to increase. The current-account deficit rose from $2.7 billion in 1988 to $24.4 billion in 1992 and $19.6 billion in 1993. Exports grew quite rapidly during this period, but imports grew even faster. The ability to increase imports at a rapid rate contributed to a 'feel-good' effect. This growing deficit was financed in part by what turned out in retrospect to be a privatization programme that was at least partially corrupt and in some ways irresponsible. The Mexican banks, in particular, were sold to financial groups, some of whom the Mexican authorities knew – or should have known – were not fit to run them.

Of greater importance in the short term than the privatizations themselves was the ability of the government to provide a view of Mexico that was attractive to financial investors. Democratization, the NAFTA and the privatizations all helped here. Most economists agree in hindsight that the emerging deficit was excessive, or at least that it was allowed to run on for too long. However, there was no such agreement at the time.

In 1994 the logic of electoral competition for the first time started to come into conflict with the logic of good economic management. The PRI faced a serious electoral challenge in national elections in 1994 and, given the events of 1988, badly wanted to be seen to win honestly. By and large, it did so. However, there were some respects in which the economy was deliberately managed for political advantage. For example, while the current-account deficit was largely a private-sector deficit, some of it could be attributed to a boom in the lending of the state development banks, whose activities were quietly taken off-budget in 1991 (*Proceso* [Mexico City], 31 December 1994). Lending by the state development banks was particularly heavy in politically contested areas that the PRI badly wanted to win. One example was the district of Chalco in the Estado de Mexico, which the opposition won in 1988 but the PRI recovered in 1994.

By the beginning of 1994 Salinas seemed to have re-created the electoral ascendancy that the PRI had come close to losing during 1986–8. There was no need to continue to rig the ballot. The system had liberalized sufficiently to satisfy the United States. The PRI now enjoyed business support and did not face any kind of problem in financing its campaigns. As a fail-safe device, the PAN had been allowed to emerge as a loyal opposition whose economic policies did not differ markedly from those of Salinas himself.

Yet the year 1994 proved to be a disaster for Mexico. There were a series of political shocks. The Zapatista movement had started an armed rebellion on 1 January, and gained worldwide attention. Then there was the murder of Luis Donaldo Colosio, who had been the PRI's presidential candidate for 1994, and the subsequent murder of José Francisco Ruiz Massieu, who was secretary-general of the PRI and a brother-in-law of the president himself. Finally, the incoming Zedillo government attempted a limited devaluation of the peso in December. This was mishandled and resulted in a currency crisis followed by an economic slump.

Salinas has continued to deny responsibility for the 'tequila crisis', claiming that this was principally the consequence of technical errors made by the incoming Zedillo administration (Salinas 2000). From a technical economic standpoint Salinas's argument has some merit, even though it cannot be denied that the incoming administration had to deal with a large current-account deficit that was bound to become harder to finance as US interest rates rose. However, it is also the case that investor confidence in Mexico was cumulatively lost during 1994 largely because of the various shocks and scandals of that year. Some of the events that led to the loss of confidence could not be blamed on the political elite, but others clearly could. Moreover political corruption, some of which was associated with drug trafficking, also contributed to a general structural weakness in the Mexican banking system and indeed elsewhere.

A good deal of capital flight that put increasing pressure on the peso during the course of 1994 involved Mexicans, and much of it amounted to the proceeds of law-breaking. In the past, the sixth year of a presidential term was known as a time when there would be more corruption than usual as office-holders took their rewards before leaving. In Mexican slang, the sixth year was known as the 'Año de Hidalgo' – with the Hidalgo denoting a face on a banknote. This is part of the explanation for the capital flight that had already caused problems in 1976 and 1982, and came close to derailing the entire market-oriented project in 1994–5.

There were also many linkages between the owners of some of the privatized banks, the heavy financial support given to the PRI ahead of the 1994 elections, and the laundering of the proceeds of drug trafficking (Oppenheimer 1996). Some of those who bought the privatized banks subsequently looted them while contributing heavily to the 1994 election finances of the PRI in order to try to buy political protection. Some $35 million was given to the PRI nationally by the BancoUnion/Aeromexico group, whose leaders were later arrested for fraud. There are many other examples of disreputable relationships in which the Mexican state helped particular economic groups, including some presumed connected to the illegal drugs trade, who showed their gratitude by financing the PRI.

Even more dramatically Raul Salinas, the president's brother, was later found to be the owner of a bank account in Switzerland which contained over $100 million. The Swiss authorities initially attempted to confiscate the money because they presumed that it came from the proceeds of drug trafficking. Raul Salinas, in the course of denying that this was the case, claimed that he had borrowed the money 'on a friendly basis' from some leading Mexican businessmen. His story was corroborated in part by one businessman, who admitted lending him $50 million. His company, Iusacell, was granted an important telecommunications contract by the Salinas government. (This contract, if those responsible were to be believed, had nothing to do with the original loan.) Iusacell was able to use its government contract to add value to the company, which was floated on the New York stock exchange in June 1994 (a few months before the end of the Salinas presidency) with a value of $2.5 billion. Most of this money was later lost in the 'tequila crisis' and the change of government (Philip 1998).

In September 1994, when investors were just starting to worry about the size of the Mexican current-account deficit and the continuing reduction in the government's dollar reserves, José Francisco Ruiz Massieu was shot dead in Mexico City. It was obviously a contract killing. The brother of the murdered man, Mario Ruiz Massieu, was appointed to investigate the killing at his own request and with the support of all the main parties in Mexico. During his investigation, Mario made some very dramatic public allegations that the murder was the responsibility of senior figures within the PRI who were opposed to democracy. He then, equally dramatically, resigned his office. This, too, was very destabilizing from the viewpoint of the peso.

Many people believed the story that Mario told, but a rather different story emerged when Mario was himself arrested in the USA in February 1995 and charged with illegally transferring dollars into the country. He later died in a US prison while awaiting trial on charges of money laundering and drug trafficking. Raul Salinas was later convicted of the killing of José Francisco Ruiz Massieu – it was said to have been a drastic way of resolving a custody battle with Raul's sister – and Mario had significantly destabilized the Mexican currency as a means of distracting attention from this.

In the end, both aspects of the Salinas presidency were essentially revealed. On the one hand, the economic reforms were genuine, and some had positive and durable effects. They were, admittedly, bought at a considerable social cost, but it is hard to see how else Mexico could have transcended the complex economic crisis of the mid-1980s. Mexico entered the NAFTA in 1994, and the ensuing six years saw very large increases in the export of manufactured goods. Millions of industrial jobs were created in the 1994–2000 period. This, though, was a strategy that could probably only have worked with the protection given to the policy-making elite by the PRI's political machine.

On the other hand, there were financial abuses on a scale that dwarfed the imagination even of those who were most suspicious of the Salinas government. These, too, had their roots in the patronage-driven character of the Mexican state, the weakness of autonomous law enforcement, and the arbitrary nature of the presidentialism that lay at the heart of the system. The financial abuses, admittedly added to some misjudgements in policy-making, were significantly responsible for the 'tequila crisis'. This did enormous damage to the Mexican economy and, had it not been for prompt and large-scale financial support offered by the US government, might have threatened the entire global financial system. It certainly exported recession to several other countries in Latin America.

Mexican politics after the 'tequila crisis'

The political impact of the 'tequila' shock in the end proved containable. This was partly due to the fact that elections had been held in 1994 and the presidency had changed hands. It was helpful to Zedillo that he could blame the problem on his predecessor. The scandalous behaviour of the Salinas family made this a plausible case, and the arrest of Raul Salinas made a real impact on the Mexican public. However, the main point is that the Zedillo government was still able to rely on the PRI machine, and this, in turn, could continue to rely on the rural vote. The financing and day-to-day behaviour of the PRI continued to be characterized by significant illegality, and depended upon the biased character of the state and the weakness of independent law enforcement. Partly as a result of historical tradition but also on account of its access to illegal resources, the PRI continued to be able to gather a reasonable number of votes even under the most negative economic conditions. These gave the party a 'bedrock' level of support of around 30 per cent nationally – more in certain regions of the country. This was not proof against defeat, but it was proof against electoral destruction.

In economic terms the 'tequila crisis' strengthened rather than weakened Mexico's outward-looking economic orientation. The US government found it necessary to help the country financially, and conditioned a very large loan against the continuance of market reforms. Even with US support, 1995 proved to be a wretched economic year for Mexico, with 35 per cent inflation and a 6.2 per cent economic contraction (Inter-American Development Bank 1997). Without US support, these results would have been far worse. The crisis therefore did not persuade the government's technocrats that there would be any merit in an underlying change of economic orientation. On the contrary, Mexico was more deeply integrated into the North American economy in 2000 than it had been in 1994.

The de facto alliance between market-liberal technocrats and traditional politicians taking advantage of the biased character of the Mexican state had never been without strain, and it weakened further after 1994. The Salinas administration held it together by methods already discussed, but Zedillo allowed a growing separation to occur between the technocracy and the PRI. Zedillo's technocrats tended to believe that the so-called dinosaur politicians were a drag on progress and modernization. They were also a potential source of macro-economic destabilization. The 'dinosaurs' themselves argued that they would not have to resort to disreputable political tactics if the government whose loyalty they took for granted occasionally did something popular. Meanwhile there were ordinary PRIistas who wanted to support a modern, social-democratic party that was distinct from the political Catholicism of the PAN and the collectivist orientation of the left-wing PRD. However, the Zedillo period did not see the kind of rupture that took place in 1986. Instead the PRI became significantly more independent of government. The gradual, and it must be said limited, bifurcation between ruling party and state played an important part in the defeat of the PRI candidate in 2000. Even so, it later became clear that a significant part of the PRI's campaign spending in that year was provided by money from the state oil monopoly.

The Zedillo administration continued the project of integrating the Mexican economy with that of the USA. Today it would be enormously costly for Mexico to leave the NAFTA, to the point that such a step seems inconceivable. While the word 'irreversible' should be used sparingly in human affairs, it is genuinely hard to see how Mexico's 'North American' economic orientation can now be changed decisively – unless completely unexpected developments should take place within the USA itself. Whereas critics of the political system could write a decade ago that Mexico had a 'presidential economy' (Zaid 1987), it now has a genuinely capitalist economy which is integrating with the rest of North America.

It now seems that there has emerged a consensus on Mexico's development strategy and ruling economic principles. This consensus did not involve the PRD, but parties representing some 80 per cent of the electoral vote in the 2000 elections had essentially signed up to it. This was a rather similar strategy to that proposed by Salinas in 1988, which would have been overwhelmingly rejected then if there had been occasion for an honest vote either within the PRI or among the general public. There is a sense in which the Mexican political elite, having lost the 1988 elections, subsequently elected a new people. More prosaically, it appears that the post-democratic transition in Mexico is closer to that of Chile, where the incoming opposition broadly accepted the existing direction of economic policy, than in Peru or Brazil, where democratic politicians tried to do quite different things and generally failed.

Towards democratic consolidation in Mexico?

It seems that Mexico has evolved into a kind of duality based on the different strengths of the two forces making for consolidation. The country appears to be in the process of acquiring a genuinely consolidated 'economic state' without necessarily acquiring a professional bureaucracy or an effective system of law enforcement. The existence of an economic state does not just mean that the top economics ministries are run by technocrats – true though this is – but also that there is a broad consensus on economic strategy. However, further away from the 'Naftonian project' there is plenty of evidence of non-consolidation – in the sense of weak law enforcement, patrimonialism and the exercise of arbitrary executive power at local and state level.

There remains a good deal of corruption in politics. For example, in 1995 Roberto Madrazo, the governor of Tabasco, made it clear that he would not resign his office despite publicly admitted evidence that his campaign broke the electoral rules. Official information provided to the press by the Zedillo government showed that Madrazo had spent $70 million on his governorship campaign for the state – in contrast to a legal limit on campaign spending of some $1.5 million. Since Tabasco is a poor state with a total population of only 1.5 million, the 1994 election was a significant economic as well as political event. However, Madrazo refused to resign when the overspending became public and established in court that he could not be removed from office as a result of this. The government minister most clearly associated with pressing Madrazo to resign had himself to resign instead. In 1999 Madrazo became a major contender for the PRI nomination for the presidency, and in 2002 he was elected to the presidency of the PRI. There is little doubt that Madrazo's campaign spending was not an isolated occurrence. According to one insider (who would know), election overspending has been so common in state elections during the 1990s that the process is considered virtually normal (interview with Manuel Camacho, April 1999). Madrazo survived disclosure because his behaviour was not seen as particularly unusual. Again, we have the point that a reputation for illegal behaviour is not necessarily damaging to the political career of a person thus detected.

It is obvious that overspending of this kind during election campaigns is effectively exclusionary. What is worse is that big-spending candidates tend to re-create precisely those preferential relationships with the state that were common under Mexico's previous authoritarianism. Voters who were once told how to vote by the PRI now sometimes accept instructions from well-financed and open-handed political bosses of other parties as well. Many of these are sustained, directly or indirectly, from the proceeds of drugs money, and it is not hard to see what drug traffickers want from the state in return.

It is not suggested that elections are routinely bought across the whole of Mexico. The big urban centres have seen contested elections fought on genuine policy issues. However, democracy in the poorer and more backward parts of the country has certainly been devalued to a significant degree by a lack of legal control. This situation is evidently capable of influencing closely fought national elections. Moreover, even if democratic contestation is not significantly undermined by illegalities of various kinds, then democratic consolidation surely is.

A similar picture of weak law enforcement emerges when we consider issues of human rights in Mexico. It may well be, indeed, that publicity reveals only the small tip of a large iceberg. Examples of comparatively recent cases of the abuse of power can be given. In 1995 the governor of Guerrero was eventually forced to resign after television coverage exposed as false his denial that a group of peasants was killed in cold blood by security forces when on their way to a demonstration. Human-rights abuses were also evident in the state of Morelos where, early in 1998, the head of the anti-kidnapping unit, the state attorney-general and other senior law-enforcement agents were arrested following the death under interrogation of a seventeen-year-old suspect. In Chiapas, the state governor and the interior minister were forced to resign following the massacre, on 22 December 1997, of forty-five peasants associated with the Zapatistas.

Nobody seriously supposes that democratization is a kind of magic wand which immediately solves all of a country's problems. Unpunished corruption and general lawlessness certainly existed in authoritarian Mexico. The problem is that, when the key transition took place, both domestic elites and the global community (which wanted democracy mainly in the sense of voting) were quite happy with a political system which was formally democratic but in many respects utterly partisan. The nature of the system permitted a transition to 'Naftonian' capitalism as well as democracy.

The political system has evidently inherited two important characteristics of non-consolidated democracy from the past. The judicial system is weak, and the state bureaucracy is full of presidential appointees. However, it may well be in the process of changing from hyper-presidentialism to a system in which the presidential role is much weaker but not yet fully defined. In the past, Mexico's extraordinarily powerful presidentialism was a key distinguishing feature – along with the PRI, the most important single feature – of the entire political system. It could to some extent mitigate the consequences of judicial and administrative weakness, albeit in a top-down and arbitrary way. It remains to be seen whether judicial and administrative problems will prove more damaging than they have been now that the role of the presidency has weakened, or whether democratization will eventually strengthen these institutions instead.

Mexico in comparative perspective

What distinguishes Mexico from most of the rest of the region is the strength of the pro-market and pro-democracy partisan coalition that controlled the state during 1982–2000. This coalition was strong enough to survive some major challenges such as the bailout of 1982, the Baker Plan of 1986, the Brady Plan of 1989, NAFTA membership from the beginning of 1994, and the second bailout in 1995. It is also important that the transition to democracy, which might have upset the partisan coalition, did not in the end do so until the new pattern of international economic integration was fully established. As it happened, democratization and neo-liberal reform could be rendered compatible by the method of democratization chosen by de la Madrid and – more so – by Salinas. Some potential alternative paths not taken would not have allowed the same degree of congruence.

The countries of South America have not generally had the same option of 'North Americanization'. While Mexico's political institutions bear many hallmarks of non-consolidated democracy as it exists in other parts of the region, its economic structure is now quite different. A key question is therefore whether 'Naftonian' consolidation will start to impact on a broader set of social and political institutions or whether the non-consolidation of other political institutions might impact upon the economic future of the country. It is possible that there may develop a kind of 'separate spheres' arrangement involving a professionally run economy and significant patrimonialism elsewhere.

So far the evidence is ambiguous, but the 'separate spheres' arrangement seems more likely than the others. While Mexico does not really have a Weberian civil service, the technocratization of the state since the 1970s has distanced the Mexican pattern somewhat from a pure patronage model of bureaucracy. It is notable that the victory of Vicente Fox in the presidential elections of 2000 has not seen a wholesale shift in the identity of the country's economics ministers or in the autonomy of the central bank. Fox's first government contained such key technocrats as Gil Díaz as finance minister and Guillermo Ortíz (who had been finance minister and head of the central bank under Zedillo) as head of the central bank.

What is clear, though, is that the self-reinforcing aspect of institutionalization in Mexico – the aspect that enables us at least to ask whether the word 'consolidated' can be justified – is fundamentally economic. It involves Mexico's international affiliations, the possibly non-partisan 'technification' of its economics ministries and the existence of an economic project (convergence with the rest of North

America) to which virtually the entire private sector can sign up. The economic rules of the NAFTA are, under current and foreseeable circumstances, the only rules in town. Democracy is necessary because members of the club must be democrats. No government could hope to prosper if it openly broke the rules of club membership. While not what Madison or Montesquieu had in mind, this might well in Mexico's case be the only feasible way of consolidating institutions.

Conclusion: Democracy, Development and Partisan Conflict in Latin America

One of the most basic questions about democracy – second only to 'what is democracy?' – is why it sustains itself over time. Why should those who win elections and control the government permit their subsequent defeat? The extreme example of democratic non-sustainability is 'one person, one vote, once'. There are indeed examples, in Europe as elsewhere, of anti-democrats coming to power by democratic means. We have noted that the concept of democratic consolidation, as expressed by Przeworski (1991) and others, does deal with this question. However, if the 'consolidationist' literature is correct, then democracies are secure only when backed up by a considerable number of other favourable factors.

This is not generally the picture in Latin America. Here we have seen long-established patterns of political behaviour, of which the most important are a lack of respect for law and a semi-patrimonial system of public appointment, working against democratic consolidation. Biased states, as we have come across them in the Latin American context, do not make it impossible for democracy to survive after a fashion, but they do make it much harder to legitimate the rules of the democratic process.

This book has sought to understand how biased states operate in practice. Naturally they do not work identically in all countries. Nor is state bias an inherently unchangeable condition, though it does in practice tend to reproduce itself over time unless positively prevented from doing so. Alternative institutional paths are possible, and some have been created. For example, presidentialism does seem to work much better in Chile, Costa Rica and Uruguay than in other parts of the region. However, this book has tried to show that it is possible to produce an interpretation of state bias in Latin America that gives some sense of its key characteristics without the assumption that these are either unchanging or identical across the entire region.

State bias, democracy and politics

Three fairly strong conclusions have emerged. One is that state bias reduces the quality of democracy but does not necessarily make democracy unsustainable. Not even in Fujimori's Peru or Chávez's Venezuela was there a full-scale democratic breakdown. Secondly it does not seem to over-empower the presidency in all cases, even though this is what one might have expected from the incumbency advantages of biased states. At the level of caricature, there are two extreme patterns of presidential politics in Latin America's non-consolidated democracies: the rule-breaker with strong partisan backing and the weak figure facing intractable partisan opposition. The former is not effectively restrained by the law, and the latter cannot enjoy the use of even such legal powers as he has. There is sometimes an alternation between the two. In Argentina, Menem gave way to de la Rúa. In Peru, Fujimori gave way to Toledo. In Venezuela, Caldera was replaced by Chávez.

Thirdly, biased states do not generally perform well in policy terms, especially in today's global conditions, and this is indeed a problem. If today's non-consolidated democracies are at risk in the region this will be primarily because of policy failure. It is possible that a prolonged period of development failure plus recurring crises may turn a significant proportion of public opinion away from the idea of democracy altogether.

This is a relatively new problem in the region. After all, it could be argued that the breakdown of democracy in Latin American countries before 1980 had mainly to do with the strength of anti-democratic elites. Precarious democracies were certainly vulnerable when they failed in policy terms, but in general they were not given much of a chance. Democracy failed mainly because it had not been sufficiently accepted. This is not an argument that can be put today. Democracy has been tried but it has not unambiguously succeeded. While outside observers can quite plausibly blame difficult structural problems for this lack of success, domestic public opinion may not always be so accommodating. For this reason, it really cannot be said that the danger of democratic breakdown has gone away.

This author would emphasize the view that the most serious risk to democracy in Latin America comes from prolonged development failure. This is despite the fact that, as pointed out in chapter 7, most non-consolidated democracies did prove able to deal with the hyper-inflationary crises of the 1980s. However, crisis resolution is one thing, and dealing with cumulative development failure over a period is

another. Whereas pessimistic viewpoints about the region's commitment to democratic values have mostly been proved wrong, pessimistic
viewpoints about its ability to achieve economic progress have mostly
been proved right. Living standards in Latin America are in general no
more than slightly higher than they were two decades ago, while the
relative and absolute numbers of people living in poverty have both
increased.

While these findings seem reasonably robust, there is a lot more to
be said about the role of financial and political globalization, about
political culture and about institutional analyses of non-consolidated
democracy. Here the conclusions have to be rather tentative, but they
are presented below.

Non-consolidated democracy and globalization

The region's development problems are indeed partly the fault of
financial globalization. Admittedly globalization is a complex process
whose effects on governance have been many and varied. However,
the globalized economy that has further developed since 1982 has facilitated capital movement and given a lot of responsibility to local
regulatory institutions. To put it mildly, this combination has not been
advantageous to the region, since its regulatory institutions are widely
distrusted and capital flight has been a problem for many years.
'Globalization' should not be regarded as an all-purpose explanation
of everything, but it has created policy problems that Latin American
governments have found difficulty in resolving. One really cannot
ignore the fact that most Latin American economies performed much
better before 1980 than they have since.

The development of international institutions, to the extent that this
has happened, has had more positive political effects. International
preferences for democracy have been influential in keeping democracy
afloat in the region, although they should not be regarded as decisive.
The strengthening of international law and good governance institutions has generally been positive, though it is not entirely clear that the
trend towards greater internationalism will survive the outrages of
11 September 2001. Moreover, while there is no real doubt that the US
government and other influential international actors prefer democracy in some sense, they have often reacted rather opportunistically
to particular events in the light of specific circumstances. This was true
when the Mexican elections were essentially rigged in 1988, and it was
still true in 2002 when the USA and the UK appeared for a time to be

supportive of the Carmona coup attempt in Venezuela. Even when there was a genuine international preference for constitutional democracy, this was not always effective. The US government did not prevent the Fujimori coup in 1992 and was unable to bring down Fujimori in 2000 in any simple-minded sense. While the USA clearly disapproved of Fujimori's further re-election, most authors regard the main factors in the Peruvian situation at that time as domestic in character (Crabtree 2001).

Financial globalization might have had a rather paradoxical effect on democracy as distinct from its effect on economic performance. As already argued, its economic consequences have been mixed but on the whole negative. On the face of it, poor policy performance by democratic governments should be bad for democracy. The actual policy requirements of global capitalism could be negative as well, on the assumption that there is likely to be an unavoidable and significant difference between what Latin American electorates want and what international markets want. This difference has sometimes seemed most effectively bridgeable under semi-authoritarian figures such as Salinas and Fujimori, though we have already noted that more conventionally democratic presidents had some success against hyper-inflation as well.

Yet any general hypothesis that financial globalization has been bad for democracy as such, while seemingly plausible in particular circumstances, has not so far been confirmed in the region as a whole. Economic austerity has probably inhibited democratic consolidation by making it harder for existing institutions to win popular support. However, it has also made it harder for the strong leader figures who might, in earlier generations, have successfully established personalist authoritarianisms. Globally imported financial problems certainly played a major part in the fall of Fujimori, and put major constraints on the non-democratic impulses of some leading figures in the Mexican PRI. While highly authoritarian governments can and do survive recession – Chile and Mexico both did in the 1980s – sustained authoritarianism probably requires deep political foundations (as in 1980s Mexico and indeed Cuba) or else a profoundly polarized civil society (as in 1970s Chile). The shallower roots put down by semi-authoritarian figures who were ultimately dependent upon popularity proved insufficient when economic circumstances deteriorated.

It is not completely straightforward to argue that globalization is bad for semi-authoritarianism as well as for democratic consolidation. Short- and long-term contexts need to be separated out here, as do regional and nationally specific factors. The early 1990s did see the emergence of a number of ambitious attempts to carry out economic stabilization and market reform in a highly presidentialist way. The successful reduction of high levels of inflation, and a temporary boost to public revenues from privatization, enabled some top-down strategies to appear successful. Not every personalist politician succeeded, but some did. It seemed for a time as though market reforms were capable of producing increasing returns to power, and this undoubtedly provides a large part of the explanation for the temporary success of some forms of 'neo-populism'. However, the recurrence of economic shocks and problems in the second half of the 1990s generally put this logic into reverse. While conditions of crisis might sometimes produce a demand for strong leadership, conditions of long-term adversity are more likely to be addressed effectively by a broad coalition. For this reason, globalization has not generally rewarded 'delegative democracies' – at least not yet. However, one cannot at all discount the possibility that quite subtle changes in global economic context may significantly influence the incentive structures facing particular Latin American systems in the future.

Political learning, presidentialism and political culture

A further explanation for the durability of non-consolidated democracy stems from the ability of Latin American political actors to adapt to the political problems posed by state bias through coping mechanisms of one kind or another. One of the most interesting of these has been presidential term limits. The literature on presidentialism has thus far paid less attention to term limits and the politics of re-election than to other important institutional aspects. However, an effective term-limit rule clearly does check the power of the executive in important ways, and allows for some pluralism within strong partisan organizations. The result is to make the system more flexible.

The change in the Mexican government from Salinas to Zedillo provides an excellent example of how a change in the presidency can reduce the general partisan advantage of incumbency. It also bears out an old saying in British politics to the effect that 'the other party makes up the opposition. A politician's real enemies are on his own side.' The same could be said of relations between Argentina's feuding Peronists, notably Menem and Duhalde.

It does seem also that limits on presidential re-election have often been supported by public opinion. Where presidents seek additional terms of office in Latin America, they often face a general presumption that this is not desirable. One cannot understand the fall of Fujimori without the observation that his pursuit of a second re-election was a controversial and risky step. Argentina's Menem also looked at the possibility of a second re-election, but in the end drew back. Conversely, the trend towards allowing consecutive presidential re-election may have negative consequences in countries such as Venezuela where such a change has been made.

The development since 1990 of the use of impeachment or other congressional ways of removing the president from office has been significant as well. It seems to have helped prevent the emergence of semi-authoritarianism, though possibly at the price of making some policy problems harder to resolve. It has done this by denying some incumbent presidents the autonomy that they sometimes need to tackle serious policy problems. Whether the threat of presidential impeachment or removal will ultimately move Latin American systems in the direction of parliamentary government is hard to say. However, those Latin American systems that have found ways of establishing two-way patterns of influence between president and congress have on the whole performed better than those that have not.

The role of public opinion is also important in keeping democracy alive even if non-consolidated. There are some puzzles here as well. One is the question of why public opinion should be important in preventing democratic breakdown. Why should the authoritarians not just move in notwithstanding? This tended to happen before 1980. Not all pre-1980 authoritarian governments were unpopular and repressive, but some assuredly were. Public opinion most certainly matters today, but it is not entirely clear why it *should* do so.

This book will not be the last word on this subject. However, it makes three suggestions as to how public opinion might be shaping the working of non-consolidated democracy. One is that the opinion polls can act as a focal point around which the military, street demonstrations, the media and other participants in direct-action politics can rally. As we have seen, basic legitimatory ideas about Latin America's democratic institutions do not always offer such a focal point and therefore leave a vacuum. It may well be that popularity legitimates governments in the region among political actors who are much less likely to be impressed by the theoretical virtues of constitutional procedures. The military, which is in some cases the decisive political arbiter, often look at what the polls say before deciding what to do. Meanwhile other political actors, who might hope to overthrow a weakly held constitutional order by turning the coercive forces of the state against the government or by bringing about a state of ungovernability, may look at the polls before deciding to polarize the situation. Where opposition forces try to polarize the situation without strong enough support from the polls, they risk defeat, as happened in Venezuela in April 2002.

A second point is that the volatility of public opinion itself limits the development of increasing returns to power. This reflects the 'Schumpeterian' argument that the value of electorates lies precisely in their unpredictability. One could conceive of a model in which public opinion followed the economic cycle, and the economic cycle was significantly beyond political control. In such a case no government would be secure for very long, no matter what it did. If every Latin American country experiences a crisis every decade or so, then incumbents will not generally be able to establish themselves in government for long enough to create and stabilize an authoritarian system. Once such governments fail, then democratization (or redemocratization) is likely to become the new focal point.

The third suggestion is that public opinion may actually bound non-consolidated democracy in a more definite way. Local public opinion does not always insist on full compliance with institutions, but it does want a looser form of compliance with democracy. Latin America is by no means full of authoritarian voters who respect only power. Public opinion is indeed capable of swinging decisively against a corrupt 'politics as usual' (such as Punto Fijo Venezuela) but also against once-popular figures who come to be seen as over-mighty *caudillos* (eventually Fujimori and perhaps one day Chávez). The fact that such swings in public opinion are to a degree unpredictable does not make them unimportant.

Understanding non-consolidated democracy

However we may try to explain the fact, it is appropriate to conclude that non-consolidated democracy has shown itself to be reasonably durable. We therefore need to find ways of analysing these systems without making the assumption that they are either in the process of consolidating or in immediate danger of breaking down. The conclusion here is that non-consolidated democracy leads inevitably to a kind of politics characterized by significant indeterminacy. This indeterminacy will be greater than that generally to be found in consolidated systems.

This conclusion has implications for how we study political institutions in Latin America. It does not amount to a radical critique of rational-choice institutionalism – i.e., it is not at all being suggested that this kind of approach is pointless. However, there is a suggestion that any work based purely on analysing the operation of formal institutions may be incomplete in principle – no matter how thorough and meticulous it may be. For example, Crisp and Escobar-Lemmon (2001, p. 176) state that 'taking a rational choice institutionalist perspective means recognizing that formalized structures and rules form a strategic context within which political actors make decisions.' While this claim is not false, we need to remember that informalized structures and the possibility of rule-breaking also form part of the strategic context of decision-making within non-consolidated democracy. An inescapable aspect of democratic non-consolidation is that politicians who base their strategy according to the formalized rules of the system alone are in danger of ending up on the losing side. Rules matter, but the potential for successful rule-breaking matters too.

Most Peruvian congressmen at the beginning of April 1992 did not take into account the possibility that their institution was about to be closed by force: Fujimori gambled and won. Most Venezuelan politicians (to say nothing of Venezuelan military intelligence) were entirely in the dark about military conspiracy before February 1992 and were also taken by surprise at the ability of Chávez to survive the April 2002 coup attempt. These events could be (and have been) rationalized after the fact, but anybody who saw the Venezuelan political elite at close quarters in March and April 1992 or in April 2002 would have been aware of how surprised it was. In Ecuador in January 2000 the overthrow of the president and his replacement by the vice-president did not take place according to any formal rule or institution, even though polls showed that the majority of the population supported it.

Two precepts explain quite a lot about the behaviour of political actors in non-consolidated democracy: one would say, 'when in opposition, wait until the government is truly unpopular and then strike at its heart', the other, 'when in government, seek popularity above all things and then use it as a political weapon against the opposition.' These are rational-choice rules in the sense that Machiavelli was a rational-choice philosopher. While the problem is that they are outcome-related rules and not process-related rules, they do suggest that we need to pay relatively more attention to polls and other indicators of the public mood than to the formal rules of the political process.

References

Abente-Brun, D. (1999) 'People power' in Paraguay, *Journal of Democracy*, 10 (3), 93–101.

Acha, E. (2001) The Peruvian state and the nature of the police forces. Unpubd PhD diss., University of London.

Adams, F. (2000) *Dollar Diplomacy: United States Economic Assistance to Latin America*. Aldershot: Ashgate.

Alesina, A., Hausmann, R., Hommes, R., and Stein, E. (1999) Budget institutions and fiscal adjustment in Latin America, *Journal of Development Economics*, 59 (2), 253–73.

Alvarado, A. (ed.) (1987) *Electoral Patterns and Perspectives in Mexico*. San Diego: Center for US–Mexican Studies.

Amezcua, A., and Pardinas, J. (1997) *Todos los gobernadores del presidente: cuando el dedo de uno aplasta al voto popular*. Mexico City: Grijalbo.

Anderson, C. (1967) *Politics and Economic Change in Latin America*. Princeton, NJ: Princeton University Press.

Angell, A., and Graham, C. (1995) Can social sector reform make adjustment stable and equitable? Lessons from Chile and Venezuela, *Journal of Latin American Studies*, 27 (1), 189–219.

Angell, A., and Pollack, B. (1990) The Chilean elections of 1989, *Bulletin of Latin American Research*, 9 (1), 1–24.

Aranda, S. (1984) *La economía venezolana: una interpretación de su modo de funcionamiento con una resumen del periodo 1975–86*. Caracas: Pomairs.

Arellano Gault, D., and Guerrero Amparán, J. P. (2000) Administrative reform of the Mexican state: a managerialist reform? A case study of the civil service project. Mexico City, CIDE, unpubd.

Arroyo, E. (1983) Elections and negotiations: democracy in Venezuela. Unpubd PhD diss., University of London.

Ayres, R. (1998) *Crime and Violence as Development Issues in Latin America*. Washington, DC: World Bank.

Bailey, J. (1988) *Governing Mexico: The Statecraft of Crisis Management*. London: Macmillan.

Baldez, L., and Carey, J. (2001) Budget procedures and fiscal restraint in post-transition Chile, in S. Haggard and M. McCubbins (eds), *Presidents, Parliaments and Policy*. Cambridge: Cambridge University Press, 105–49.

Basáñez, M. (1981) *La lucha por la hegemonia en Mexico*. Mexico City: Siglo XXI.

Basáñez, M. (1987) Elections and political culture in Mexico, in J. Gentleman (ed.), *Mexican Politics in Transition*. Boulder, CO: Westview Press, 181–201.

Basáñez, M. (1991) *El pulso de los sexenios: 20 años de crisis en México*. México City: Siglo XX1.

Beltrán, P. (1977) *La verdadera realidad Peruana*. Madrid: San Martín.

Blanco Muñoz, A. (ed.) (1998) *Habla el comandante: testimonios violentos*. Caracas: Pablo Neruda.

Brinkley, A. (1998) *Liberalism and its Discontents*. Cambridge, MA: Harvard University Press.

Bruhn, K. (1997) *Taking on Goliath: The Emergence of a New Left Party and the Struggle for Democracy*. University Park: Pennsylvania University Press.

Bulmer Thomas, V. (1994) *The Economic History of Latin America since Independence*. Cambridge: Cambridge University Press.

Burggraaff, W., and Millett, R. (1995) More than failed coups: the crisis in Venezuelan civil–military relations, in L. Goodman et al. (eds), *Lessons of the Venezuelan Experience*. Baltimore: Johns Hopkins University Press, 54–79.

Burki, J., and Edwards, S. (1996) World Bank, Latin American and Caribbean studies: viewpoints. Washington, DC, unpubd paper.

Buxton, J. (2001) *The Failure of Political Reform in Venezuela*. Basingstoke: Ashgate.

Caiden, G. (1991) *Administrative Reform Comes of Age*. Berlin and New York: Walter de Gruyter.

Camp, R. (1984) *The Making of a Government: Political Leaders in Modern Mexico*. Tucson: Arizona University Press.

Carrion, J. (1996) La opinión pública bajo el primer gobierno de Fujimori, in F. Tuesta Soldevilla (ed.), *Los enigmas del poder: Fujimori 1990–96*. Lima: Friedrich Ebert, 277–302.

Castañeda, J. (1999) *La herencia: arqueología de la sucesión presidencial en México*. México City: Aguilar.

Centeno, M. (1994) *Democracy within Reason: Technocratic Revolution in Mexico*. University Park: Pennsylvania University Press.

Chislett, W. (1985) The causes of México's financial crisis and the lessons to be learned, in G. Philip (ed.), *Politics in México*. Beckenham: Croom Helm, 1–16.

Ciurlizza, J. (2000) Judicial reform and international legal technical assistance in Latin America, *Democratization*, 7 (2), 211–30.

Cleaves, P., and Pease García, H. (1983) State autonomy and military policy making, in C. McClintock and A. Lowenthal (eds), *The Peruvian Experiment Reconsidered*. Princeton, NJ: Princeton University Press, 209–44.

Conaghan, C. (1996) Vida publica en los tiempos de Alberto Fujimori, in F. Tuesta Soldevilla (ed.), *Los enigmas del poder: Fujimori 1990–96*. Lima: Friedrich Ebert, 303–30.

Congdon, T. (1985) The rise and fall of the Chilean economic miracle, in E. Duran (ed.), *Latin America and the World Recession*. London: RIIA, 98–119.

Coppedge, M. (1994) *Strong Parties and Lame Ducks: Presidential Partyarchy and Factionalism in Venezuela*. Stanford, CA: Stanford University Press.

Costa, F. (1993) Peru's presidential coup, *Journal of Democracy*, 4 (1), 28–40.

Cotler, J. (1995) Political parties and the problems of democratic consolidation in Peru, in S. Mainwaring and T. Scully (ed.), *Building Democratic Institutions: Party Systems in Latin America*. Stanford, CA: Stanford University Press, 323–53.

Cox, G., and Morgenstern, S. (2001) Latin America's reactive assemblies and proactive presidents, *Comparative Politics*, 33 (2), 172–88.

Crabtree, J. (1992) *Peru and García: An Opportunity Lost*. Basingstoke, Macmillan.

Crabtree, J. (2001) The collapse of Fujimorismo: authoritarianism and its limits, *Bulletin of Latin American Research*, 20 (3), 287–303.

Crisp, B. (2000) *Democratic Institutional Design: The Powers and Incentives of Venezuelan Politicians and Interest Groups*. Stanford, CA: Stanford University Press.

Crisp, B., and Escobar-Lemmon, M. (2001) Democracy in Latin America: individuals in institutional contexts, *Latin American Research Review*, 36 (2), 175–92.

De Souza, A. (1999) Cardoso and the struggle for reform in Brazil, *Journal of Democracy*, 10 (3), 49–63.

Diamond, L. (ed.) (1999) *Developing Democracy: Towards Consolidation*. Baltimore: Johns Hopkins University Press.

Diamond, L., Plattner, M., Chu, Y., and Tien, H. (eds) (1997) *Consolidating the Third Wave Democracies: Regional Challenges*. Baltimore: Johns Hopkins University Press.

Dornbusch, R., and Edwards, S. (1991) *Macroeconomic Populism in Latin America*. Chicago: University of Chicago Press.

Dugas, G. (2001) Drugs, lies and audiotape: the Samper crisis in Colombia, *Latin American Research Review*, 36 (2), 157–74.

Dunkerley, J. (1979) The politics of the Bolivian army: institutional development 1879–1935. Unpubd DPhil. diss., University of Oxford.

Durandt, F., and Thorp, R. (1998) Tax reform: the SUNAT experience, in J. Crabtree and J. Thomas (eds), *Fujimori's Peru: the Political Economy*. London: ILAS, 209–28.

ECLAC (Economic Commission for Latin America and the Caribbean) (2001) *Social Panorama of Latin America 2000–2001*. Santiago, ECLAC.

Edwards, S. (1995) *Crisis and Reform in Latin America: From Despair to Hope*. Washington DC: Oxford University Press.

Enríquez, R. (1988) The rise and collapse of stabilising development, in G. Philip (ed.), *The Mexican Economy*. London: Routledge, 8–40.

Evans, P. (1979) *Dependent Development: An Alliance of Multinational, State and Local Capital in Brazil*. Princeton, NJ: Princeton University Press.

Evans, P., and Rauch, J. (1999) Bureaucracy and growth: a cross national analysis of the effects of 'Weberian' state structures on economic growth, *American Sociological Review*, 64, 748–65.

Ferraro, A. (2002) Politische Institutionen und Regierbarkeit in Lateinamerika:

empirische Untersuchung zur Politisierung der Verwaltung am Beispiel der argentinischen Staatsbürokratie. Hamburg, Institut für Iberoamerika-Kunde, unpubd.

Finer, S. E. (1962) *The Man on Horseback*. London: Pall Mall.

Fitch, J. S. (1998) *The Armed Forces and Democracy in Latin America*. Baltimore: Johns Hopkins University Press.

Fitch, J. S. (2001) Military attitudes toward democracy in Latin America: how do we know if anything has changed?, in D. Pion Berlin (ed.), *Civil–Military Relations in Latin America: New Analytical Perspectives*. Chapel Hill: University of North Carolina Press.

Fitch/Ibca (1999) Sovereign report. Peru, unpubd.

Foweraker, J. (1998) Institutional design, party systems and governability: differentiating the presidential regimes of Latin America, *British Journal of Political Science*, 28 (4), 651–76.

Freedom House (2001) Annual Survey of Freedom Country Ratings 1972–3 to 1999–2000. Washington, DC: Freedom House.

Garrido, A. (ed.) (2000) *La historia secreta de la Revolución Bolivariana*. Mérida: Editorial Venezolana.

Garrido, L. (1993) *La ruptura: la correinte democrática del PRI*. Mexico City: Grijalbo.

Gavin, M., and Hausmann, R. (1998) Fiscal performance in Latin America: what needs to be explained?, in K. Fukasaku and R. Hausmann (eds), *Democracy, Decentralisation and Deficits in Latin America*. Washington, DC: IDB, 33–64.

Geddes, B. (1994) *Politician's Dilemma: Building State Capacity in Latin America*. Berkeley: University of California Press.

Gentleman, J. (ed.) (1987) *Mexican Politics in Transition*. Boulder, CO: Westview Press.

Gilbert, D. (1977) The oligarchy and the old regime in Peru. Unpubd PhD diss., Cornell University.

Gott, R. (2000) *In the Shadow of the Liberator: Hugo Chávez and the Transformation of Venezuela*. London: Verso.

Graham, C. (1992) *Peru's APRA: Parties, Politics and the Elusive Quest for Democracy*. Boulder, CO: Lynne Rienner.

Grindle, M. (1996) *Challenging the State: Crisis and Innovation in Latin America and Africa*. Cambridge: Cambridge University Press.

Grindle, M. (1997) Patron and clients in the bureaucracy: career networks in Mexico, *Latin American Research Review*, 12 (1), 37–66.

Grindle, M. (2000) *Audacious Reforms: Institutional Invention and Democracy in Latin America*. Baltimore: Johns Hopkins University Press.

Haggard, S., and McCubbins, M. (eds) (2001) *Presidents, Parliaments and Policy*. Cambridge: Cambridge University Press.

Hagopian, F. (1996) *Traditional Politics and Regime Change in Brazil*. Cambridge: Cambridge University Press.

Hammergren, L. A. (1983) *Development and the Politics of Administative Reform: Lessons from Latin America*. Boulder, CO: Westview Press.

Hansen, R. (1971) *The Politics of Mexican Development*. Baltimore: Johns Hopkins University Press.

Haynes, J. (2001) Sustainable democracy in the third world, in J. Haynes (ed.), *Toward Sustainable Democracy in the Third World*. Basingstoke: Palgrave, 32–5.

Held, D., McGrew, A., Golblatt, D., and Perraton, J. (1999) *Global Transformations: Politics, Economics and Culture*. Cambridge: Polity.

Huntington, S. P. (1968) *Political Order in Changing Societies*. New Haven, CT: Yale University Press.

Ibáñez Rojo, I. (2000) The Unión Democrática y Popular: government and the crisis of the Bolivian left, *Journal of Latin American Studies*, 32, 175–206.

Imaz, J. de (1964) *Los Que Mandan*. Buenos Aires: Eudeba.

Inter-American Development Bank (1997) *Latin America after a Decade of Reforms*. Washington, DC: Inter-American Development Bank.

Inter-American Development Bank (2000) *Economic and Social Progress in Latin America: Annual Report 2000*. Washington, DC: Inter-American Development Bank.

Jones, G. (1999) Resistance and the role of law in Mexico, *Development and Change*, 29, 499–523.

Jones, M. (1997) Evaluating Argentina's presidential democracy, in S. Mainwaring and M. Shugart (eds), *Presidentialism and Democracy in Latin America*. Cambridge: Cambridge University Press, 499–523.

Karl, T. (1997) *The Paradox of Plenty: Oil Booms and Petro-States*. Berkeley: University of California Press.

Kay, B. (1996) Fujipopulismo and the liberal state in Peru, *Journal of Interamerican Studies and World Affairs*, 38 (4), 55–98.

Kay, B. (1999) Violent opportunities: the rise and fall of 'King Coca' and Shining Path, *Journal of Interamerican Studies and World Affairs*, 41 (3), 99–127.

Kenney, C. (1996) ¿Por qué el autogolpe? Fujimori y el congreso 1990–92, in F. Tuesta Soldevilla (ed.), *Los enigmas del poder: Fujimori 1990–96*. Lima: Friedrich Ebert, 75–104.

Kuczynski, P. (1977) *Peruvian Democracy under Economic Stress: An Account of the Belaunde Administration*. Princeton, NJ: Princeton University Press.

Lagos, M. (1997) Latin America's smiling mask, *Journal of Democracy*, 8, 125–38.

Lanusse, A. (1977) *Mi testimonio*. Buenos Aires: Lasserre, 125–39.

Lanzaro, J. (ed.) (2001) *Tipos de presidencialismo y coaliciones politicas en America Latina*. Buenos Aires: CLACSO.

Latinobarómetro (2000) Data 1996–2000. Unpubd paper presented to Carter Center, Atlanta.

Leftwich, A. (2000) *States of Development: On the Primacy of Politics in Development*. Cambridge: Polity.

Lijphart, A. (1993) Constitutional choices for new democracies, in L. Diamond and M. Plattner (eds), *The Global Resurgence of Democracy*. Baltimore: Johns Hopkins University Press, 162–74.

Linz, J. (1994) Presidential or parliamentary democracy: does it make a difference?, in J. Linz and A. Valenzuela (eds), *The Failure of Presidential Democracy: The Case of Latin America*. Baltimore: Johns Hopkins University Press, 3–90.

Linz, J., and Stepan, A. (1996) *Problems of Democratic Transition and Consolidation*. Baltimore: Johns Hopkins University Press.

Little, W., and Herrera, A. (1996) Political corruption in Venezuela, in W. Little and E. Posada-Carbo (eds), *Political Corruption in Europe and Latin America.* Basingstoke: Macmillan, 267–86.

Lowenthal, A. (ed.) (1976) *Armies and Politics in Latin America.* New York: Holmes Meier.

McGuire, J. (1997) *Peronism without Peron: Unions, Parties and Democracy in Argentina.* Stanford, CA: Stanford University Press.

McClintock, C. (1998) *Revolutionary Movements in Latin America: El Salvador's FMLN and Peru's Shinning Path.* Washington, DC: US Institute for Peace Press.

Mahon, J. (1996) *Mobile Capital and Latin American Development.* University Park: Pennsylvania State University Press.

Mainwaring, S. (1997) Multipartism in Brazil, in S. Mainwaring and M. Shugart (eds), *Presidentialism and Democracy in Latin America.* Cambridge: Cambridge University Press, 55–109.

Mainwaring, S., and Scully, T. (1995) Party systems in Latin America, in S. Mainwaring and T. Scully (eds), *Building Democratic Institutions: Party Systems in Latin America.* Stanford, CA: Stanford University Press, 1–36.

Mainwaring, S., and Shugart, M. (eds) (1997) *Presidentialism and Democracy in Latin America.* Cambridge: Cambridge University Press.

Mann, M. (1986) *The Sources of Social Power,* vol. 1. Cambridge: Cambridge University Press.

Mann, M. (1993) *The Sources of Social Power,* vol. 2. Cambridge: Cambridge University Press.

Martino, M. (2000) 'It's politics stupid!' Economic populism and pragmatism during the first Brazilian presidential re-election. Unpubd MSc diss., LSE.

Marvin Laborde, I. (1997) *Y ¿Después del presidencialismo?* Mexico City: Oceano.

Mayorga, A. (1997) Bolivia's silent revolution, *Journal of Democracy,* 8, 142–56.

Méndez, J. (1997) In defence of transitional justice, in A. J. McAdams (ed.), *Transitional Justice and the Rule of Law in New Democracies.* Notre Dame, IN: University of Notre Dame Press, 1–26.

Méndez, J., O'Donnell, G., and Pinheiro, P. (eds) (1999) *The (Un)Rule of Law and the Underprivileged in Latin America.* Notre Dame, IN: University of Notre Dame Press.

Miller, R. (1996) Foreign capital, the state and political corruption in Latin America between independence and the Depression, in W. Little and E. Posada-Carbo (eds), *Political Corruption in Europe and Latin America.* Basingstoke: Macmillan, 65–96.

Moctezuma Barragán, E., and Roemer, A. (2001) *A New Public Management in Mexico: Toward a Government that Produces Results.* Basingstoke: Ashgate.

Mouzelis, N. (1986) *Politics in the Semi-Periphery: Early Parliamentarianism and Late Industrialization in the Balkans and Latin America.* Basingstoke: Macmillan.

Muller Rojas, A. (1992) *Relaciones peligrosas: militares, política y estado.* Caracas: UCV.

Muñoz, J. (2001) Rural poverty and development, in J. Crabtree and L. Whitehead (eds), *Towards Democratic Viability: the Bolivian Experience.* Basingstoke: Palgrave, 83–99.

Murillo, M. (2001) *Labor Unions, Partisan Coalitions and Market Reforms in Latin America*. Cambridge: Cambridge University Press.

Myers, D. J. and O'Connor, R. (1998) Support for coups in democratic political culture: a Venezuelan exploration, *Comparative Politics*, 30 (2), 193–212.

Norden, D. (1996) *Military Rebellion in Argentina: Between Coups and Consolidation*. Lincoln: University of Nebraska Press.

Norden, D. (1998) Democracy and military control in Venezuela: from subordination to insurrection, *Latin American Research Review*, 33 (2), 143–465.

North, D. (1990) *Institutional Change and Economic Performance*. Cambridge: Cambridge University Press.

Nunberg, B., and Nellis, J. (1995) Civil service reform and the World Bank. World Bank Discussion Paper no. 161, Washington, DC, unpubd.

OAS (Organization of American States, Inter-American Commission on Human Rights) (2000) *Second Report on the Situation of Human Rights in Peru*, ⟨http//:www.cidh.org.oas⟩.

Ocampo, J. (1998) Beyond the Washington consensus: an ECLAC perspective, *CEPAL Review*, 66, 7–28.

O'Connor, R. (1980) The media and the campaign, in H. Penniman (ed.), *Venezuela at the Polls: The National Elections of 1978*. Washington, DC: American Enterprise Institute.

O'Donnell, G. (1988) State and alliances in Argentina 1956–1976, in R. Bates (ed.), *Toward a Political Economy of Development: A Rational Choice Perspective*. Berkeley: University of California Press, 176–205.

O'Donnell, G. (1994) Delegative democracy, *Journal of Democracy*, 5 (1), 55–69.

O'Donnell, G. (1999) Polyarchies and the (un)rule of law: a partial conclusion, in J. Mendez, G. O'Donnell and P. Pinheiro (eds), *The (Un)Rule of Law and the Underprivileged in Latin America*. Notre Dame, IN: University of Notre Dame Press, 303–30.

Oppenheimer, A. (1996) *México en la frontera del caos: la crisis de los noventa y la esperanza del nuevo milenio*. Mexico City: Javier Vergara.

Palmer, D. (ed.) (1992) *The Shining Path of Peru*. London: Hurst.

Panizza, F. (2000a) Neopopulism and its limits in Collor's Brazil, *Bulletin of Latin American Research*, 19 (2), 177–92.

Panizza, F. (2000b) Is Brazil becoming a 'boring' country?, *Bulletin of Latin American Research*, 19 (4), 501–25.

Panizza, F. (2000c) Beyond 'delegative democracy': 'old politics' and 'new economics' in Latin America. *Journal of Latin American Studies*, 32, 737–63.

Panizza, F. (2001) The primacy of politics: the symbolic economy of civil service reform in Uruguay. LSE, unpubd paper.

Panizza, F., and de Brito, A. (1998) The politics of human rights in democratic Brazil: 'A lei nao pega', *Democratization*, 5 (4), 20–51.

Parker, C. (2001) The political economy of emerging market investment: US private creditor influence in the Mexican financial crises of 1982 and 1995. Unpubd PhD diss., LSE.

Peters, B. G. (1989) *Comparative Public Administration*. Mobile: University of Alabama Press.

Philip, G. (1998) The lawless presidency, *Democratization*, 5 (1), 23–41.

Phillips, N. (1998) Globalization and state power: political and economic reform in Argentina. Unpubd PhD diss., University of London.

Potash, R. (1982) *The Army and Politics in Argentina 1945–62*. Stanford, CA: Stanford University Press.

Potash, R. (1996) *The Army and Politics in Argentina 1962–1973: From Frondizi's Fall to the Peronist Restoration*. Stanford, CA: Stanford University Press.

Prillaman, W. (2000) *The Judiciary and Political Decay in Latin America: Declining Confidence in the Rule of Law*. Westport, CT: Praeger.

Przeworski, A. (1991) *Democracy and the Market: Political and Economic Reforms in Eastern Europe and Latin America*. Cambridge: Cambridge University Press.

Przeworski, A., Alvares, M., Cheitub, J., and Limongi, F. (1997) What makes democracies endure?, in L. Diamond et al., (eds), *Consolidating the Third Wave Democracies: Regional Challenges*. Baltimore: Johns Hopkins University Press, 295–311.

Rauch, J., and Evans, P. (2000) Bureaucratic structure and bureaucratic performance in less developed countries, *Journal of Public Economics*, 75, 49–71.

Remmer, K. (1989) *Military Rule in Latin America*. Boston: Unwin Hyman.

Robertson, G. (2000) *Crimes against Humanity: The Struggle for Global Justice*. Harmondsworth: Penguin.

Rodríguez, M. (1991) Public sector behaviour in Venezuela, in F. Larrain and M. Selowsky (eds), *The Public Sector and the Latin American Crisis*. San Francisco: International Center for Economic Growth.

Rodríguez Veltzé, E. (2001) Legal security in Bolivia, in J. Crabtree and L. Whitehead (eds), *Towards Democratic Viability: the Bolivian Experience*, 179–94. Basingstoke: Palgrave.

Romero, A. (1997) Rearranging the deckchairs on the Titanic. *Latin American Research Review*, 32, 7–36.

Rospigliosi, F. (1994) Democracy's bleak prospects, in J. Tulchin and G. Bland (eds), *Peru in Crisis: Dictatorship or Democracy*. Washington, DC: Woodrow Wilson Center, 35–63.

Rospigliosi, F. (2000) *Montesinos y las fuerzas armadas: como controlar durante una decada las institutionces militares*. Lima: Institute de Estudios Peruanos.

Rueschemeyer, D., Stephens, J. D., and Huber, E. (1992) *Capitalist Development and Democracy*. Cambridge: Polity.

Sagasti, F. (2001) *Development Strategies for the 21st Century: The Case of Peru*. Lima: Agenda Peru.

Salas Porras, A. (1998) The Mexican business class and the process of democratisation: trends and counter-trends. Unpubd PhD diss., University of London.

Salinas, C. (2000) *México: un paso difícil a la modernidad*. Mexico City: Plaza y Janes.

Sánchez, N. (2000) Interview, in A. Garrido (ed.), *La historia secreta de la Revolución Bolivariana*. Mérida: Editorial Venezolana.

Sanders, S. (1986) *Chaos on our Doorstep*. Lanham MD: Madison Books.

Santín Queroz, O. (2001) *The Political Economy of Mexico's Financial Reforms*. Basingstoke: Ashgate.

Schedler, A. (1998) What is democratic consolidation?, *Journal of Democracy*, 9 (2).

Schmitter, P., O'Donnell, G., and Whitehead, L. (eds) (1986) *Transitions from Authoritarian Rule: Comparative Perspectives*. Baltimore: Johns Hopkins University Press.

Schumpeter, J. (1943) *Capitalism, Socialism and Democracy*. London: Allen Unwin.

Shepherd, G. (1999) The challenge of public administrative reform in Latin America, *Revista del CLAD, Reforma y Democrácia*, 13 February.

Shugart, M., and Haggard, S. (2001) Institutions and public policy in presidential systems, in S. Haggard and M. McCubbins (eds), *Presidents, Parliaments and Policy*. Cambridge: Cambridge University Press, 64–114.

Simpson, J. (1994) *In the Forests of the Night: Encounters in Peru with Terrorism, Drug-Running and Military Oppression*. New York: Random House.

Smith, P. (1979) *Labyrinths of Power: Political Recruitment in Twentieth Century Mexico*. Princeton, NJ: Princeton University Press.

Spink, P. (1999) Possibilities and political imperatives: seventy years of administrative reform in Latin America, in L. C. Bresser Pereira and P. Spink (eds), *Reforming the State: Managerial Public Administration in Latin America*. Boulder, CO: Lynne Reinner, 91–114.

Starr, P. (1997) Government coalitions and the viability of currency boards: Argentina under the Carvallo plan, *Journal of Inter-American Studies*, 30 (2).

Stepan, A. (1971) *The Military in Politics: Changing Patterns in Brazil*. Princeton, NJ: Princeton University Press.

Stepan, A. (1977) *The State and Society: Peru in Comparative Perspective*. Princeton, NJ: Princeton University Press.

Stepan, A., and Skatch, C. (1993) Constitutional frameworks and democratic consolidation: parliamentarianism vs presidentialism, *World Politics*, 46 (1).

Stokes, S. (2001) *Mandates and Democracy: Neoliberalism by Surprise in Latin America*. Cambridge: Cambridge University Press, 1–22.

Teichman, B. (1988) *Policy Making in Mexico: From Boom to Crisis*. Boston: Allen & Unwin.

Teivainen, T. (2000) Enter economy, exit politics: transnational politics of economism and the limits to democracy in Peru. Unpubd PhD diss., University of Helsinki.

Templeton, A. (1995) The evolution of popular opinion, in L. Goodman et al. (eds), *Lessons of the Venezuelan Experience*. Baltimore: Johns Hopkins University Press, 19–114.

Thorp, R. (1998) *Progress, Poverty and Exclusion: An Economic History of Latin America in the 20th Century*. Washington, DC: IDB.

Torres Espinosa, E. (1999) *Bureaucracy and Politics in Mexico: The Case of the Secretariat of Programming and Budget*. Basingstoke: Ashgate.

Trinkunas, H. (2002) The crisis in Venezuelan civil–military relations: from Punto Fijo to the fifth republic, *Latin American Research Review*, 37 (1), 41–76.

Tuesta Soldevilla, F. (ed.) (1996) *Los enigmas del poder: Fujimori 1990–96*. Lima: Friedrich Ebert.

US Embassy (1993) Retired general on plotting in the army and La Cantuta investigación. Lima: US Embassy cable, document no. 1993LIMA05862, 22 May.

Vargas Llosa, M. (1994) *A Fish in the Water*. London: Faber & Faber.

Vernon, R. (1963) *The Dilemmas of Mexico's Development*. Cambridge, MA: Harvard University Press.

Villalba, D. (1987) The incorporation of the lower classes in Venezuela. Unpubd PhD diss., University of London.

Villareal, R., and Villareal, R. (2000) Financial globalization: lessons from financial crises in Latin America since 1980, in A. Lamfulussy et al. (eds), *Fragility of the International System*. Brussels: Peter Lang, 89–135.

Weldon, J. (1997) Political sources of presidencialismo in Mexico, in S. Mainwaring and M. Shugart (eds), *Presidentialism and Democracy in Latin America*. Cambridge: Cambridge University Press, 225–58.

Weyland, K. (1997) The Brazilian state in the new democracy, *Journal of Inter-American Studies and World Affairs*, 29, 63–94.

Weyland, K. (1998) The politics of corruption in Latin America, *Journal of Democracy*, 9 (2), 108–21.

Whitehead, L. (2001) The viability of democracy, in J. Crabtree and L. Whitehead (eds), *Towards Democratic Viability: the Bolivian Experience*. Basingstoke: Palgrave, 21–40.

Williams, M. (2001) *Market Reforms in Mexico: Coalitions, Institutions and the Politics of Policy Change*. Lanham, MD: Rowman & Littlefield.

Williamson, J. (ed.) (1990) *Latin American Adjustment: How Much Has Happened?*. Washington, DC: Institute for International Economics.

World Bank (1992) *Governance and Development*. Washington, DC: World Bank.

World Bank (1997) *World Development Report 1997: The State in a Changing World*. Washington, DC: Oxford University Press.

World Bank (1999) *Entering the 21st Century*. Washington, DC: Oxford University Press.

World Bank (2000a) Reforming public institutions and strengthening governance: a World Bank strategy. Washington, DC: unpubd paper.

World Bank (2000b) *Reforming Public Institutions and Strengthening Governance*. Washington, DC: World Bank, Oxford University Press.

World Bank (2000c) Bolivia: from patronage to a professional state. Washington, DC: unpubd paper, report 20115-BO.

World Bank (2002) *Building Institutions for Markets*. Washington, DC: Oxford University Press.

Zago, A. (1998) *La rebelión de los Ángeles: reportaje, los documentos del movimiento*. Caracas: Warp.

Zaid, G. (1987) *La economía presidencial*. Mexico City: Vuelta.

Zakaria, F. (1997) The rise of illiberal democracy, *Foreign Affairs*, 76 (6), 22–43.

Index